THE CULT OF MARGARET MILLAR

"When Margaret Millar decides to lead her readers up the garden path, even Agatha Christie has to walk behind."

— *Time and Tide*

"One of the most skillful writers of the suspense genre."

— *Library Journal*

"Among the crime writers who have come into prominence since the war she has few peers, and no superior, in the art of bamboozlement. She presents us with a plausible criminal situation, builds it up to a climax of excitement, and then in the last few pages shakes the kaleidoscope and shows us an entirely different pattern from the one we have been so busily interpreting. [Her] skill is shown at its finest in HOW LIKE AN ANGEL."

— Julian Symons
MORTAL CONSEQUENCES

"People have been telling me about Margaret Millar for years and now I am glad I didn't listen to them. Now that I have finally read one of her books [ASK FOR ME TOMORROW], I have 21 more to look forward to."

— Anatole Broyard
The New York Times

A burnt-out gambler plays private eye and finds murder in a Southern California religious cult. A major work by a great mystery writer is now back in print.

MARGARET MILLAR

HOW LIKE AN ANGEL

INTERNATIONAL POLYGONICS, LTD.
NEW YORK CITY

HOW LIKE AN ANGEL

Library of Congress Card Catalog
No. 82-82890
ISBN 0-930330-04-8

Printed and manufactured in the United States
of America.

This book is dedicated, with love, to
Betty Masterson Norton

INTRODUCTION

More than twenty years ago George Hammond, a young friend of mine who liked to explore the wild mountainous back country of Santa Barbara County, came across an area he wanted me to see.

We drove up a white-knuckle one-lane road, through streams and around precipitous curves to the top of a ridge of the Santa Ynez mountains. The view was incredible, the Pacific Ocean, the Santa Ynez valley, Lake Cachuma and the river and streams that fed it, and finally the San Rafael mountains where the last of the condors was fighting for survival. Here was Shangri-La, and it was not surprising to learn that a mystic had last occupied the place.

The buildings on the property had been ruined by vandals, the main lodge, the out-buildings, and finally the most unique, the tower. Picking our way through shattered glass and the other débris of sick minds we reached the top of the tower. It was here that my friend suggested I use the setting in a book about California cults.

"I know very little about such cults, " I told him.

"So start your own," George said.

I did. And here it is.

A nearby property on the same ridge is unlikely ever to be turned into a cult or vandalized. Heavily guarded by secret service men and Sheriff's officers, it is called not Shangri-La, but the Western White House.

M. Miller

Santa Barbara, Ca.
May 1982

What a piece of work is a man!
. . . in action, how like an angel! in
apprehension, how like a god! . . . And yet,
to me, what is this quintessence of dust?
man delights not me;
no, nor woman neither . . .

HAMLET

one

All night and most of the day they had been driving, through mountains, and desert, and now mountains again. The old car was beginning to act skittish, the driver was getting irritable, and Quinn, to escape both, had gone to sleep in the back seat. He was awakened by the sudden shriek of brakes and Newhouser's voice, hoarse from exhaustion and the heat and the knowledge that once more he'd made a fool of himself at the tables.

"This is it, Quinn. The end of the line."

Quinn stirred and turned his head, expecting to find himself on one of the tree-lined streets of San Felice, with the ocean glittering in the distance like a jewel not to be touched or sold. Even before he opened his eyes he knew something was wrong. No city street was so quiet, no sea air so dry.

"Hey, Quinn. You awake?"

"Yes."

"Well, flake off, will you? I'm in a hurry."

Quinn looked out of the window. The scenery hadn't changed since he'd gone to sleep. There were mountains and more mountains and still more, all covered with the same scrub oak and chaparral, manzanita and wild holly, and a few pines growing meagerly from the parched earth.

"This is nowhere," he said. "You told me you were going to San Felice."

"I said *near* San Felice."

"How far is near?"

"Forty-five miles."

"For the love of—"

"You must be from the East," Newhouser said. "In California forty-five miles is near."

"You might have told me that before I got in the car."

3

"I did. You weren't listening. You seemed pretty anxious to get out of Reno. So now you're out. Be grateful."

"Oh, I am," Quinn said dryly. "You've satisfied my curiosity. I've always wondered where nowhere was."

"Before you start beefing, listen. My turn-off to the ranch is half a mile down the road. I'm a day late getting back to work, my wife's a hothead, I lost seven hundred in Reno and I haven't slept for two days. Now, you want to be glad you got a ride this far or you want to put up a squawk?"

"You might have dropped me off at a truck stop where food was available."

"You said you had no money."

"I was figuring on a small loan, say five bucks."

"If I had five bucks I'd still be in Reno. You know that. You got the disease same as I have."

Quinn didn't deny it. "O.K., forget about money. I have another idea. Maybe that wife of yours isn't such a hothead after all. Maybe she wouldn't object to a temporary guest— all right, all right, it was just a suggestion. Do you have a better one?"

"Naturally, or I wouldn't have stopped here. See that dirt road down the line?"

When Quinn got out of the car he saw a narrow lane that meandered off into a grove of young eucalyptus trees. "It doesn't look like much of a road."

"It's not supposed to. The people who live at the end of it don't like to advertise the fact. Let's just say they're peculiar."

"Let's just ask how peculiar?"

"Oh, they're harmless, don't worry about that. And they're always good for a handout to the poor." Newhouser pushed his ten-gallon hat back, revealing a strip of pure white forehead that looked painted across the top of his brown leathery face. "Listen, Quinn, I hate like the devil to leave you here but I have no choice and I know you'll make out all right. You're young and healthy."

"Also hungry and thirsty."

"You can pick up something to eat and drink at the Tower and then hitch another ride right into San Felice."

"The Tower," Quinn repeated. "Is that what's at the end of the quote road unquote?"

"Yes."

"Is it a ranch?"

"They do some ranching," Newhouser said cautiously. "It's a—well, sort of a self-contained little community. So I've heard. I've never seen it personally."

"Why not?"

"They don't encourage visitors."

"Then how come you're so sure I'll get a big welcome?"

"You're a poor sinner."

"You mean it's a religious outfit?"

Newhouser moved his head but Quinn wasn't sure whether he was indicating affirmation or denial. "I tell you, I never saw the place, I just heard things about it. Some rich old dame who was afraid she was going to die built a five-story tower. Maybe she thought she'd have a shorter hitch to heaven when her time came, a head start, like. Well, I've got to be on my way now, Quinn."

"Wait," Quinn said urgently. "Be reasonable. I'm on my way to San Felice to collect three hundred bucks a friend of mine owes me. I promise to give you fifty if you'll drive me to—"

"I can't."

"That's more than a buck a mile."

"Sorry."

Quinn stood on the side of the road and watched Newhouser's car disappear around a curve. When the sound of its engine died out, there was absolute silence. Not a bird chirped, not a branch swished in the wind. It was an experience Quinn had never had before and he wondered for a minute if he'd suddenly gone deaf from hunger and lack of sleep and the heat of the sun.

He had never much liked the sound of his own voice but it

seemed very good to him then, he wanted to hear more, to spread it out and fill the silence.

"My name is Joe Quinn. Joseph Rudyard Quinn, but I don't tell anyone about the Rudyard. Yesterday I was in Reno. I had a job, a car, clothes, a girl friend. Today I'm in the middle of nowhere with nothing and nobody."

He'd been in jams before but they'd always involved people, friends to confide in, strangers to persuade. He prided himself on being a glib talker. Now it no longer mattered, there wasn't anyone around to listen. He could talk himself to death in that wilderness without causing a leaf to stir or an insect to scurry out of range.

He took out a handkerchief and dabbed at the sweat that was trickling down behind his ears. Although he'd often visited the city of San Felice, he knew nothing about this bleak mountainous back country, seared by the sun in summer, eroded by the winter rains. It was summer now. In the river beds dust lay, and the bones of small animals which had come to find water.

The silence, more than the heat and desolation, bothered Quinn. It seemed unnatural not even to hear a bird call, and he wondered whether all the birds had died in the long drought or whether they'd moved on to be nearer a water supply, to the ranch where Newhouser worked, or perhaps to the Tower. He glanced across the road at the narrow lane that seemed to end suddenly in the grove of eucalyptus.

"Hell, a little religion's not going to kill me," he said, and crossed the road, squinting against the sun.

Beyond the eucalyptus trees the path started to climb, and signs of life became evident as he followed it. He passed a small herd of cows grazing, some sheep enclosed in a pen made of logs, a couple of goats tethered in the shade of a wild holly tree, an irrigation ditch with a little sluggish water at the bottom. All the animals looked well-fed and well-tended.

The ascent became steeper as he walked, and the trees denser and taller, pines and live oaks, madrones and cotoneaster. He had almost reached the top of a knoll when he

6

came across the first building. It was so skillfully constructed that he was only fifteen or twenty yards away before he realized it was there, a long low structure made of logs and native stone. It bore no resemblance to a tower and he thought Newhouser might have made a mistake about the place, had been taken in by local rumors and exaggerations.

There was no one in sight, and no smoke coming out of the wide stone chimney. Crude half-log shutters were fastened over the windows on the outside as if the builder's idea had been to keep people in rather than to protect the place against intruders. With the huge sugar pines filtering the sunlight, the air seemed to Quinn suddenly cool and damp. Pine needles and orange-colored flakes of madrone bark muffled the sound of his footsteps as he approached.

Through a chink between the half-logs Brother Tongue of Prophets saw the stranger coming and began making small animal noises of distress.

"Now what are you making a fuss about?" Sister Blessing said briskly. "Here, let me see for myself." She took his place at the chink. "It's only a man. Don't get excited. His car probably broke down, Brother Crown of Thorns will help him fix it, and that will end the incident. Unless—"

It was part of Sister Blessing's nature to look for silver linings, find them, point them out to other people, and then ruin the whole effect by adding *unless*.

"—unless he's from the school board or one of the newspapers. In which case I shall deal firmly with him and send him on his way, wrapped in his original ignorance. It seems a bit early, though, for the school board to start harassing us about the fall term."

Brother Tongue nodded agreement and nervously stroked the neck of the parakeet perched on his forefinger.

"So he's probably a newspaperman. Unless he's another plain ordinary tramp. In which case I shall treat him with dispassionate kindness. There certainly isn't anything to get excited about, we've had tramps before, as you well know.

Stop making those noises. You can talk if you want to, if you have to. Suppose the building caught on fire, you could yell 'fire,' couldn't you?"

Brother Tongue shook his head.

"Nonsense, I know better. Fire. Say it. Go on. Fire."

Brother Tongue stared mutely down at the floor. If the place caught on fire he wouldn't give the alarm, he wouldn't say a word. He'd just stand and watch it burn, making sure first that the parakeet was safe.

Quinn knocked on the unpainted wooden door. "Hello. Is anyone here? I've lost my way, I'm hungry and thirsty."

The door opened slowly, with a squawk of unoiled hinges, and a woman stepped out on the threshold. She was about fifty, tall and strong-looking, with a round face and very shiny red cheeks. She was barefooted. The long loose robe she wore reminded Quinn of the muu-muus he'd seen on the women in Hawaii except that the muu-muus were bright with color and the woman's robe was made of coarse gray wool without ornament of any kind.

"Welcome, stranger," she said, and though the words were kind, her tone was wary.

"I'm sorry to bother you, madam."

"Sister, if you please. Sister Blessing of the Salvation. So you're hungry and thirsty and you've lost your way, is that it?"

"More or less. It's a long story."

"Such stories usually are," she said dryly. "Come inside. We never turn away the poor, being poor ourselves."

"Thank you."

"Just mind your manners, that's all we ask. How long since you've eaten?"

"I don't recall exactly."

"So you've been on a bender, eh?"

"Not the kind you mean. But I guess you'd have to call it a bender. It bent me."

She glanced sharply at the tweed jacket Quinn was carrying

8

over his arm. "I know a fine piece of wool when I see it, since we weave all our own cloth. Where'd you get this?"

"I bought it."

She seemed a little disappointed as if she had hoped he would say he had stolen it. "You don't look or act like a beggar to me."

"I haven't been one very long. I don't have the knack of it yet."

"Don't get sarcastic with me. I have to check up on our visitors, in self-protection. Every now and then some prying reporter comes along, or a member of the law bent on mischief."

"I'm bent only on food and water."

"Come in, then."

Quinn followed her inside. It was a single room with a stone floor that looked as if it had just been scrubbed. The biggest skylight Quinn had ever seen provided the place with light.

Sister Blessing saw him staring up at it and said, "If light is to come from heaven, according to the Master, let it come directly, not slanting in through windows."

A wooden table with benches along each side ran almost the entire length of the building. It was set with tin plates, stainless steel spoons, knives and forks, and several kerosene lamps, already cleaned and fueled for the night. At the far end of the room there was an old-fashioned icebox, a woodstove with a pile of neatly cut logs beside it, and a bird cage obviously made by an amateur. In front of the stove a man, middle-aged, thin and pale-faced, sat in a rocking chair with a bird on his shoulder. He wore the same kind of robe as Sister Blessing and he, too, was barefooted. His head was shaved and his scalp showed little nicks and scratches as if whoever had wielded the razor had bad eyes and a dull blade.

Sister Blessing closed the door. Her suspicions of Quinn seemed to be allayed for the time being and her manner now was more that of a hostess. "This is our communal eating room. And that is Brother Tongue of Prophets. The others are all at prayer in the Tower, but I'm the nurse, I must stay with Brother Tongue. He's been sickly, I keep him by the stove at night. How are you feeling now, Brother Tongue?"

The Brother nodded and smiled, while the little bird pecked gently at his ear.

"A most unfortunate choice of names," Sister Blessing added to Quinn in a whisper. "He seldom speaks. But then, perhaps prophets are better off not speaking too much. You may sit down, Mr.—?"

"Quinn."

"Quinn. Rhymes with sin. It could be a bad omen."

Quinn started to point out that it also rhymed with grin, spin, fin, but Sister Blessing replied brusquely that sin was by far the most obvious.

"I gather sin is what brought a young, able-bodied man like you to such a low estate?"

Quinn remembered what Newhouser had said about the people at the Tower, that they were especially hospitable to poor sinners. "I'm afraid so."

"Drinking?"

"Of course."

"Gambling?"

"Frequently."

"Womanizing?"

"On occasion."

"I thought so," Sister Blessing said with gloomy satisfaction. "Well, I'll make you a cheese sandwich."

"Thank you."

"With ham. There are rumors in town we don't eat meat. What nonsense. We work hard. We need meat to keep going. A ham and cheese sandwich for you, too, Brother Tongue? A drop of goat's milk?"

The Brother shook his head.

"Well, I can't force you to eat. But I can at least see that you get some fresh air. It's cool enough now to sit outside for a while. Put your little bird back in his cage and Mr. Quinn will help you with your chair."

Sister Blessing gave orders as if there was no doubt in her

mind that they would be carried out promptly and properly. Quinn took the rocking chair outside while Brother Tongue returned the parakeet to its cage and Sister Blessing started to prepare some sandwiches. In spite of her strange clothes and surroundings she gave the impression of an ordinary house-wife working in her own kitchen, pleased to be of service. Quinn didn't even try to guess what combination of circumstances had brought her to a place like the Tower.

She sat down on the bench opposite him and watched him eat. "Who told you about us, Mr. Quinn?"

"A man I hitched a ride with, he's a hand on a ranch near here."

"That sounds plausible."

"It should. It's true."

"Where do you come from?"

"First or last?" Quinn said.

"Either, perhaps both."

"I was born in Detroit and the last place I lived was Reno."

"A wicked place, Reno."

"At the moment I'm inclined to agree with you."

Sister Blessing gave a little grunt of disapproval. "I assume that you were, as they say in the vernacular, taken to the cleaners?"

"Thoroughly."

"Did you have a job in Reno?"

"I was a security officer at one of the clubs. Or a casino cop, however you want to put it. I still have a detective's license in Nevada but it probably won't be renewed."

"You were fired from your job?"

"Let's just say I was warned not to mix business with pleasure and I didn't get the message in time." Quinn started on the second sandwich. The bread was homemade and quite stale, but the cheese and ham were good and the butter sweet.

"How old are you, Mr. Quinn?"

"Thirty-five, thirty-six. Thirty-six, I guess."

"Most men your age are at home with their wives and families, not skittering about the mountainside looking for a hand-out. . . . So you're thirty-six. Now what? Are you going to start your life all over again, on a higher plane?"

Quinn stared at her across the table. "Look, Sister, I appreciate the food and hospitality, but I may as well make it clear that I'm not a candidate for conversion."

"Dear me, I wasn't thinking of that at all, Mr. Quinn. We don't go out seeking converts. No, they come to us. When they weary of the world they come to us."

"Then what happens?"

"We prepare them for their ascension of the Tower. There are five levels. The bottom one, where we all begin, is the earth level. The second is the level of the trees, the third mountains, the fourth sky, and fifth is the Tower of Heaven where the Master lives. I've never gotten beyond the third level myself. In fact"—she leaned confidentially toward Quinn, frowning—"I have some difficulty staying there, even."

"Now why is that?"

"It's because of the spiritual vibrations. I don't feel them properly. Or when I do feel them it turns out there's a jet plane overhead, or something's exploded, and the vibrations aren't spiritual at all. Once a tree fell, and I thought I was having the best vibrations ever. I was bitterly disappointed."

Quinn attempted to look sympathetic. "That's too bad."

"Oh, you don't really think so."

"But I do."

"No. I can tell. Skeptics always get a certain twist to their mouths."

"I have a piece of ham caught in my front tooth."

Before she covered her mouth with her hand, a little giggle escaped. She seemed flustered by the sound of it, as if it were a frivolous memento of the past she thought she'd left behind.

She got up and walked over to the icebox. "Shall I pour you some goat's milk? It's very nourishing."

"No, thank you. A cup of coffee would be—"

"We never use stimulants."

"Maybe you should try. Your vibrations might improve."

"I must ask you to be more respectful, Mr. Quinn."

"Sorry. The good food has made me a little light-headed."

"Oh, it wasn't that good."

"I insist it was."

"Well, I admit the cheese isn't so bad. Brother Behold the Vision makes it from a secret recipe."

"Please congratulate him for me." Quinn rose, stretched, and concealed a yawn. "Now I'd better be on my way."

"Where?"

"San Felice."

"It's almost fifty miles. How will you get there?"

"Walk back to the road and hitch another ride."

"You won't find many cars. Most people going to San Felice prefer to take the long way around, by the main highway. And once the sun goes down, cars aren't so likely to stop for a hitchhiker, especially in the mountains. Also, the nights are very cold."

Quinn studied her for a minute. "What's on your mind, Sister?"

"Why, nothing. I mean, I'm concerned with your welfare. Alone in the mountains on a cold night, with no shelter, and wild animals roaming about—"

"What are you leading up to?"

"Well, it occurred to me," she said carefully, "that we might find a simpler solution. Tomorrow morning Brother Crown of Thorns will probably be driving the truck to San Felice. Something's gone wrong with our tractor and Brother Crown has to buy some new parts. I'm sure he wouldn't mind if you rode along with him."

"You're very kind."

"Nonsense," she said with a frown. "It's pure selfishness on my part. I don't want to lie awake worrying about a tenderfoot wandering loose around the mountains. . . . We have a storage shed you can sleep in. There's a cot in it, and a couple of blankets."

"Are you always this hospitable to strangers, Sister?"

"No, we're not," she said sharply. "We get thieves, vandals, drunkards. We handle them as they deserve."

"How is it I get the royal treatment?"

"Oh, it's not very royal, as you will find out when you try sleeping on that cot. But it's the best we can offer."

From somewhere nearby a gong began to ring.

"Prayers are over," Sister Blessing said. For a few seconds she stood absolutely still, her right hand touching her forehead. "There. Well, we'd better get out of the kitchen now. Sister Contrition will be coming to start the fire for supper and it makes her nervous to have a stranger around."

"What about the others?"

"Each Brother and Sister has a special task until sundown."

"What I meant was, how do the others feel about having a stranger around?"

"You will be treated with courtesy, Mr. Quinn, to the extent that you display it yourself. Poor Sister Contrition has many problems, it might be wise to avoid her. It's the schools. She has three children and the authorities keep insisting she send them to school. And what would they learn in school, I ask you, that the Master can't teach them here if it's fit to learn?"

"It's a subject I'm not prepared to take sides on, Sister."

"You know, for a minute when I first saw you, I thought you might be one of the school authorities."

"I'm flattered."

"You needn't be," Sister Blessing said brusquely. "They're an officious, thick-headed lot. And the trouble they've caused poor Sister Contrition you wouldn't believe. It's no wonder she has as much difficulty with spiritual vibrations as I have."

Quinn followed her outside. Brother Tongue of Prophets was dozing in his rocking chair under a madrone tree, little patches of sunlight glistening on his shaved head.

A short broad-shouldered woman came around the side of the building followed by a boy about eight, a girl a year or so older, and a young woman of sixteen or seventeen. They wore identical gray wool robes except that those of the two younger children reached just below the knees.

They went silently into the communal eating room, with only the young woman giving Quinn a brief questioning glance. Quinn returned the glance. The girl was pretty, with brilliant brown eyes and black wavy hair, but her skin was blotched with pimples.

"Sister Karma," Sister Blessing said. "The poor girl has acne, no amount of prayer seems to help. Come along, and I'll show you where you're to sleep. You won't be comfortable but then neither are we. Indulge the flesh, weaken the spirit. That's what you've always done, no doubt?"

"No doubt at all."

"Doesn't it worry you? Aren't you afraid of what's coming?"

Quinn was more afraid of what might not be coming, money and a job. But all he said was, "I try not to worry about it."

"You *must* worry, Mr. Quinn."

"Very well, Sister, I will begin now."

"You're joking again, aren't you? You're a very peculiar young man." She looked down at her gray robe and at her bare feet, wide and flat and calloused. "I suppose I must seem peculiar to you, too. Be that as it may. I would rather seem peculiar in this world than in the next." She added, "Amen," as if to close the subject.

From the outside the storage room appeared to be a small replica of the other building. But inside, it was divided into compartments, each of them padlocked. One of the compartments had a small window and was furnished with a narrow iron cot with a thin gray mattress and a couple of blankets partially eaten by moths. Quinn felt the mattress with both hands. It was soft but without resilience.

"Hair," Sister Blessing said. "The Brothers' hair. It was an experiment on the part of Sister Glory of the Ascension, she's very thrifty. Unfortunately, it attracts fleas. Are you susceptible to fleas?"

"I'm susceptible to a lot of things, fleas are probably included."

"Then I'll have Brother Light of the Infinite dose the mattress with sheep dip. First, you'd better test your susceptibility, though."

"How do I do that?"

"Sit down and stay still for a few minutes."

Quinn sat down on the cot and waited.

"Are you being bitten?" Sister Blessing said, after a time.

"I don't think so."

"Well, do you feel anything?"

"Not even a vibration."

"Perhaps we won't bother with the sheep dip, then. You might not like the smell, and poor Brother Light of the Infinite has enough to do."

"As a matter of curiosity," Quinn said, "how many people live here at the Tower?"

"Twenty-seven, right now. At one time there were nearly eighty, but some have strayed, some have died, some have lost faith. Now and then a new convert comes to us, perhaps just casually appears on the doorstep as you did. . . . Has it occurred to you that the Lord might have guided your footsteps here?"

"No."

"Think about it."

"I don't have to. I *know* how I got here. This man, Newhouser, picked me up in Reno, said he was going to San Felice. That's what I understood anyway, but it turned out he meant —oh well, it doesn't matter."

"It matters to me," Sister Blessing said.

"How?"

"It's a very odd thing that you should turn out to have a detective's license. I can't believe it's a coincidence. I have a feeling in my bones that it was the will of Lord."

"Your vibrations must be improving, Sister."

"Yes, I think so," she said earnestly. "I think they are."

"Now if you don't mind telling me what my being a detective has to do with—"

"I haven't time right now. I must go and inform the Master that you're here. He doesn't like surprises, especially at mealtimes. He has a weak stomach."

"Let me go with you," Quinn said, getting up from the cot.

"Oh no, I couldn't. Strangers aren't allowed in the Tower."

"Well, would any of the Brothers and Sisters object if I wandered around a little?"

"Some will, some won't. Although all of us here are dedicated to a common cause, we have as many personality differences as you find in other places."

"In brief, I'm to stay here. Is that it?"

"You look tired, a little rest will do you good." Sister Blessing went out and closed the door firmly behind her.

Quinn lay down on the cot, rubbing his chin. He needed a shave, a shower, a drink. Or a drink, a shower, a shave. He dozed off trying to make up his mind about the exact order and dreamed he was back in his hotel room in Reno. He'd won ten thousand dollars and he didn't notice until he spread it out on the bed to count that the bills were all fives and all bore a picture of Sister Blessing instead of Lincoln.

It was still daylight when he awoke, sweating and confused. It took him a minute to remember where he was, the little room looked like a prison.

Someone pounded on the door and Quinn sat up. "Who is it?"

"Brother Light of the Infinite. I've come about the mattress."

"Mattress?"

The door opened and Brother Light of the Infinite entered the room, carrying a gallon tin can. He was a big man with a face crisscrossed with lines like an old paper bag. His robe was dirty and smelled, not unpleasantly, of livestock.

Quinn said, "This is very kind of you, Brother."

"Ain't kindness. Orders. Me with a hundred things to do and that woman can think of a hundred more. Go fix the mattress, she says. Can't let the stranger get all bit up, says she, so here I am wasting my time on fleas. You all bit up?"

"I don't think so."

Brother Light put the can of sheep dip on the floor. "Take off your shirt and look at your belly. They like bellies, the skin's softer, easier to get their teeth into."

"While I'm undressing, is there any chance of a shower around here?"

"There's water in the washroom, can't call it a shower exactly. . . . Why, you ain't even bit. Must have a hide like an elephant. No use wasting this stuff on you." He picked the can up again and started toward the door.

"Wait a minute," Quinn said. "Where's the washroom?"

"Off to the left a piece."

"I don't suppose you have a razor?"

Brother Light fingered his shaved scalp which bore numerous nicks and scratches like Brother Tongue's. "We got razors, you think I was *born* this way? Only today's not shaving day."

"It is for me."

"You take it up with Brother of the Steady Heart, he's the barber. Don't come bothering me, with all the things I got to do, cows to be milked, goats to be watered, chickens to be fed."

"Sorry to have put you to any trouble."

As he left, Brother Light banged the can of sheep dip against the door frame to indicate his low opinion of apologies.

Quinn, too, went outside, carrying his shirt and tie. He guessed, from the position of the sun, that it was between six and seven o'clock and that he'd slept for a couple of hours.

From the chimney of the communal dining room smoke billowed and the smell of it mingled with the smell of meat cooking and pine needles. The air was crisp and cool. It seemed to Quinn very healthful air and he wondered whether it had cured the rich old lady who'd built the Tower or whether she had died here, a step closer to heaven. As for the Tower itself, he still hadn't seen it and the only indication he'd had that it actually existed had been the gong sounding the termination of prayers. He would have liked to wander around the place and find the Tower for himself but Brother Light's attitude made him doubt the wisdom of this. The others might be even less friendly.

In the washroom he pumped water into a pail by hand. It was cold and murky, and the gray gritty bar of homemade soap resisted Quinn's attempt to work up a lather. He looked around for a razor. Even if he had found one it wouldn't have done much good, since the washroom contained no mirror. Perhaps the sect had a religious taboo against mirrors. That would account for the necessity of having Brother of the Steady Heart act as barber.

While he was washing and dressing, he considered Sister Blessing's remarks about the Lord guiding his footsteps to the Tower. *She's got bats in the belfry*, he thought. *Which is fine with me unless one of them flies out and bites me.*

When he went back outside, the sun was setting and the mountains had turned from dark green to violet. Two Brothers passed him on their way to the washroom, bowed their heads briefly and silently, and went on. Quinn heard the clinking of metal dishes and the sounds of voices coming from the dining room and he started toward it. He was halfway there when he heard Sister Blessing calling his name.

She came hurrying toward him, her robe flapping in the wind. *Like a bat's wings*, he thought, without amusement.

She was carrying a couple of candles and a package of wooden matches. "Mr. Quinn? Yoohoo, Mr. Quinn."

"Hello, Sister. I was just going to look for you."

She was flushed and out of breath. "I've made a terrible mistake. I forgot this was the Day of Renunciation, I was so busy getting Brother Tongue settled back in his own quarters in the Tower. He's well enough now not to need the heat of the stove at night."

"Take a minute to catch your breath, Sister."

"Yes, I must. I'm so flustered, the Master's stomach is bothering him again."

"And?"

"This being the Day of Renunciation, we can't eat with a stranger among us because of—dear me, I've forgotten the reason, but anyhow it's a rule."

"I'm not very hungry anyway," Quinn lied politely.

"Oh, you'll be *fed*, have no doubt of that. It's just that you'll have to wait until the others are through. It will take an hour, perhaps longer, depending on poor Brother Behold the Vision's teeth. They don't fit very well and he gets behind the others. It taxes Brother Light's patience since he works in the fields all day and has a manly appetite. You don't mind waiting?"

"Not at all."

"I've brought you candles and matches. And look what else." From the folds of her robe she produced a dog-eared book. "Something to *read*," she said with an air of triumph. "We're not allowed books except about the Faith but this is from one year when Sister Karma had to go to school. It's about dinosaurs. Do you think that will interest you?"

"Oh yes. Highly."

"I've read it myself dozens of times. I'm practically an expert on dinosaurs by this time. Promise you won't tell anyone I gave it to you?"

"I promise."

"I'll let you know when the others have finished eating."

"Thank you, Sister."

Quinn could tell from the way she handled the book that it was something very precious to her and that it was a sacrifice on her part to lend it to him. He was touched by her gesture but also a little suspicious of it: *Why me? Why do I get the special treatment? What does she want from me?*

Back in the storage shed he lit the two candles, sat down on the cot and tried to make some plans for the future. First he would hitch a ride in the truck with Brother Crown as far as San Felice. Then he would drop in on Tom Jurgensen and collect his three-hundred dollars. After that—

After that no plans were necessary. He knew all too well

what would happen. If he scraped together enough money he'd go back to Reno. If he couldn't make Reno, Las Vegas. If he couldn't get to Las Vegas, one of the poker parlors outside Los Angeles. A job, money; a game, no money. Every time he ran around the circle, the grooves got deeper. He knew he'd have to break out of it some time. Maybe this was it.

All right, he told himself, he'd get a job in San Felice where the only gambling was bingo at the country club once a week. He'd save some money, mail a check for his back rent to the hotel in Reno and have the clerk send on his clothes and the rest of the things he'd left as security. He might even, if everything turned out well, ask Doris to join him. . . . No, Doris was part of the circle. Like most of the other people who worked at the clubs, she spent her off-hours at the tables. Some of them had their whole lives under one roof; they slept, ate, worked and played there, with as much single-minded dedication as the Brothers and Sisters of the Tower.

Doris. It was only twenty-four hours since he'd said good-bye to her. She'd offered to lend him money but for reasons he wasn't sure of, either then or now, he'd refused. Maybe he turned it down because he knew money had strings attached, no matter how carefully they were camouflaged. He looked down at the book Sister Blessing had given to him and he wondered what strings were attached to it.

"Mr. Quinn?"

He got up and opened the door. "Come in, Sister. Did you have a good Renunciation Day dinner?"

Sister Blessing glanced at him suspiciously. "Good enough, considering the troubled state of Sister Contrition's mind."

"Just what is one supposed to renounce? Not food, I gather."

"None of your business. Come along now and no smart talking. The dining room's empty and I have your lamb stew heated up and a nice cup of cocoa."

"I thought you didn't believe in stimulants."

"Cocoa is not a *true* stimulant. We had a meeting of the

Council about that last year, and it was decided by a large majority that cocoa, because it contained other important nourishment, is quite permissible. Only Sister Glory of the Ascension voted no because she's so stin—thrifty. I told you about the hair in the mattress?"

"Yes," said Quinn, who preferred to forget it.

"You'd better hide the book. Not that anyone would spy on you, but why take a chance?"

"Why, indeed." He covered the book with a blanket.

"Have you read it?"

"Some."

"Don't you think it's very interesting?"

Quinn thought the strings attached to it might be more interesting but he didn't say so.

They went outside. An almost full moon hung low in the redwood trees. Stars studded the sky, hundreds more than Quinn had even seen, and even while he stood and watched, still more appeared.

"Haven't you ever seen a *sky* before?" Sister Blessing said with a touch of impatience.

"Not this one."

"It's the same as always."

"It looks different to me."

Sister Blessing peered anxiously up into his face. "Do you suppose you're having a religious experience?"

"I am admiring the universe," Quinn said. "If you want to put a tag on it, go ahead."

"You don't understand, Mr. Quinn. I prefer that you *not* have a religious experience right at the moment."

"Why?"

"It would be very inconvenient. I have something I want you to do for me and a conversion at this time would interfere."

"You can stop worrying, Sister. Now, about this something you want me to do—"

"I'll tell you later, when you've eaten."

The dining room was empty, and Brother Tongue's rocking

22

chair was gone and so was the bird cage. One place was set at the end of the table nearest the stove.

Quinn sat down and Sister Blessing filled a tin plate with lamb stew and another with thick slices of bread. As she had in the afternoon, she watched Quinn eat with a kind of maternal interest.

"Your color's not very good," she said, after a time. "But you have a hearty appetite and you seem healthy enough. What I mean is, if you were frail, I naturally couldn't ask you to do me any favors."

"Contrary to appearances, I am extremely frail. I have a bad liver, weak chest, poor circulation—"

"Nonsense."

"All right, what's the favor?"

"I want you to find somebody for me. Not find him in person, exactly, but find out what happened to him. You understand?"

"Not yet."

"Before I go on, I'd like to make one thing clear: I can pay you, I have money. Nobody around here knows about it because we all renounce our worldly possessions when we come to the Tower. Our money, our very clothes on our backs, everything goes into the common fund."

"But you kept something of your own in case of emergency?"

"Nothing of the kind," she said sharply. "My son in Chicago sends me a twenty-dollar bill every Christmas with the understanding that I hold on to it for myself and not give it to the Master. My son doesn't approve of all this." She gestured vaguely around the room. "He doesn't understand the satisfactions of a life of service to the Lord and His True Believers. He thinks I went a little crazy when my husband died, and maybe I did. But I've found my real place in the world now, I will never leave. How can I? I am needed. Brother Tongue with his pleurisy attacks, the Master's weak stomach, Mother Pureza's heart—she is the Master's wife and very old."

Sister Blessing got up and stood in front of the stove, rubbing her hands together as if she'd felt the sudden chill of death in the air.

"I'm getting old myself," she said. "Some of the days are hard to face. My soul is at peace but my body rebels. It longs for some softness, some warmth, some sweetness. Mornings when I get out of bed my spirit feels a touch of heaven, but my feet—oh, the coldness of them, and the aches in my legs. Once in a Sears catalogue I saw a picture of a pair of slippers. I often think of them, though I shouldn't. They were pink and furry and soft and warm, they were the most beautiful slippers I ever did see, but of course an indulgence of the flesh."

"A very small one, surely?"

"They're the ones you have to watch out for. They grow, grow like weeds. You get warm slippers and pretty soon you're wanting other things."

"Such as?"

"A hot bath in a real bathtub, with two towels. There, you see?" she said, turning to Quinn. "It's happening already. *Two* towels I asked for, when one would be plenty. It proves my point about human nature—nothing is ever enough. If I had a hot bath, I would want another, and then one a week or even one every day. And if everyone at the Tower did the same we'd all be lolling around in hot baths while the cattle starved and the garden went to weeds. No, Mr. Quinn, if you offered me a hot bath right this minute I'd have to refuse it."

Quinn wanted to point out that he wasn't in the habit of offering hot baths to strange women but he was afraid of hurting the Sister's feelings. She was as earnest and intense about the subject as if she were arguing with the devil himself.

After a time she said, "Have you heard of a place called Chicote? It's a small city in the Central Valley, a hundred miles or so from here."

"I know where it is, Sister."

"I would like you to go there and find a man named Patrick O'Gorman."

"An old friend of yours? A relative?"

She didn't seem to hear the question. "I have a hundred and twenty dollars."

"That's a lot of fuzzy pink slippers, Sister."

Again she made no response. "It may be quite a simple job, I don't know."

"Suppose I find O'Gorman, what then? Do I give him a message? Wish him a happy Fourth of July?"

"You do nothing at all, except come back here and tell me about it, me and only me."

"What if he's no longer living in Chicote?"

"Find out where he went. But please don't try to contact him, no purpose would be served and mischief could be done. Will you accept the job?"

"I'm in no position to pick and choose at the moment, Sister. I must remind you, though, that you're taking quite a risk sending me away from here with a hundred and twenty dollars. I might not come back."

"You might not," she said calmly. "In which case I will have learned another lesson. But then again you might come back, so I have nothing to lose but money I can't spend anyway and can't give to the Master because of my promise to my son."

"You have a trick of making everything seem very reasonable on first examination."

"And on second?"

"I wonder why you're interested in O'Gorman."

"Wonder a little. It won't do you any harm. I will tell you only that what I've asked you to do is highly important to me."

"All right. Where's the money?"

"In a good safe place," Sister Blessing said blandly, "until tomorrow morning."

"Meaning you don't trust me? Or you don't trust the Brothers and Sisters?"

"Meaning I'm no fool, Mr. Quinn. You'll get the money when you're sitting in that truck beside Brother Crown of Thorns at dawn tomorrow."

"Dawn?"

"Early to bed and early to rise puts color in the cheeks and sparkle in the eyes."

"That isn't how I heard it."

"The Master has made certain changes in the proverbs to make them suitable for our children to learn."

"I'm curious about the Master," Quinn said. "I'd like to meet him."

"He's indisposed tonight. Perhaps when you come to visit us again—"

"You seem pretty sure I'll be coming back, Sister. Maybe you don't know about gamblers."

"I knew about gamblers," Sister Blessing said, "long before you saw your first ace of spades."

two

Quinn was awakened, while it was still dark, by someone shaking him vigorously by the shoulder. He opened his eyes.

A short fat man, carrying a lantern, was peering down at him through thick-lensed spectacles. "My goodness gracious, I was beginning to think you were dead. You must get up now, immediately."

"Why? What's the matter?"

"Nothing's the matter. It's time to arise and greet the new day. I am Brother of the Steady Heart. Sister Blessing told me to give you a shave and some breakfast before the others get up."

"What time is it?"

"We have no clocks at the Tower. I'll be waiting for you in the washroom."

Quinn soon found out how some of the Brothers had acquired the scars on their chins and scalps. The razor was dull, the light from the lantern feeble, and Brother of the Steady Heart near-sighted.

"My, you are a jumpy one," Brother Heart said with amiable interest. "I guess you suffer from bad nerves, eh?"

"At times."

"While I'm at it I could give your hair a bit of a trim."

"No thanks. The shave's plenty. I wouldn't want to impose."

"Sister Blessing said I was to make you look as much like a gentleman as possible. She's taken quite a fancy to you, seems to me. It kind of rouses my curiosity."

"It kind of rouses mine, too, Brother."

Brother Heart looked as though he wanted to pursue the subject but didn't dare pry into Sister Blessing's affairs or state of mind. "Well, I'll go now and make breakfast. I have the fire lit, won't take a minute to boil some eggs for the two of us."

"Why will there just be two of us?"

Brother Heart's pudgy face turned pink. "It will be more peaceful without Sister Contrition around, she's the regular cook. Oh, but that woman's a devil in the morning. Sour, there's nothing worse than a woman gone sour."

By the time Quinn finished dressing and went over to the dining room, Brother of the Steady Heart had breakfast waiting on the table, boiled eggs and bread and jam. He continued the conversation as if it hadn't been interrupted: "In my day, the ladies didn't own such sharp tongues. They were quiet-spoken and fragile, and had small, delicate feet. Have you noticed what big feet the women have around here?"

"Not particularly."

"Alas, they have. Very large, flat feet."

For all his barber-shop chattiness, Brother Heart seemed nervous. He barely touched his food and he kept glancing over his shoulder as if he expected someone to sneak up on him.

27

Quinn said, "Why the big hurry to get rid of me before the others are up?"

"Well, now. Well, I wouldn't exactly put it that way."

"I would."

"It has nothing to do with you personally, Mr. Quinn. It's just, well, you might call it a precautionary measure."

"I might, if I knew what you were talking about."

Brother Heart hesitated for a moment, biting his underlip as though it itched to talk. "I suppose there's no harm in telling you. It concerns Sister Contrition's oldest child, Karma. Last time the truck was going to the city the girl hid in the back, under some burlap sacks. Brother Crown of Thorns drove halfway to San Felice before he discovered her. The burlap made her sneeze. Karma went to school for a while, it filled her head with bad ideas. She wants to leave here and find work in the city."

"And that's not possible?"

"Oh no, no. The child would be lost in the city. Here at least she is poor among poor."

The sun was beginning to rise and a faint rosy glow filled the skylight. From the invisible Tower came the sound of the gong, and almost immediately Sister Blessing hurried in the door. "The truck is ready, Mr. Quinn. You mustn't keep Brother Crown of Thorns waiting. Here, let me have your coat and I'll give it a good brushing."

Quinn had already brushed it but he gave it to her anyway. She took it outside and made a few swipes at it with her hand.

"Come along, Mr. Quinn. Brother Crown has a long day ahead of him."

He put his coat back on and followed her down the path to the dirt road. She said nothing about either the money or O'Gorman. Quinn had an uneasy feeling that she'd forgotten what happened the previous night and that she was a little crazier than he'd thought at first.

An old Chevrolet truck, lights on and engine chugging, was parked in the middle of the road. Behind the wheel, wearing a straw hat over his shaved head, sat a man younger than the

Brothers Quinn had met so far. Quinn guessed his age to be about forty. Brother Crown of Thorns acknowledged Sister Blessing's introduction with a brief smile that revealed a front tooth missing.

"At San Felice, Brother Crown will let you off wherever you wish, Mr. Quinn."

"Thanks," Quinn said, getting into the truck. "But about O'Gor—"

Sister Blessing looked blank. "Have a good trip. And drive carefully, Brother Crown. And don't forget, if there are temptations in the city, turn your back. If people stare, lower your eyes. If they make remarks, be deaf."

"Amen, Sister."

"As for you, Mr. Quinn, the most I can ask is that you behave with discretion."

"Sister, listen—about the money—"

"*Au revoir*, Mr. Quinn."

The truck started rolling down the road. Quinn turned to look back at Sister Blessing but she had already disappeared among the trees.

He thought, *Maybe the whole thing never happened and I'm crazier than the bunch of them put together. Which is quite a bit crazy.*

He said, shouting over the noise of the engine, "A fine woman, Sister Blessing."

"What's that? Can't hear you."

"Sister Blessing is a fine woman but she's getting old. Maybe she forgets things now and then?"

"I wish she would."

"Perhaps just little things, occasionally?"

"Not her," Brother Crown of Thorns said, shaking his head in reluctant admiration. "Memory like an elephant. Turn down your window, will you? God's air is fresh."

It was also cold, but Quinn turned the window down and his collar up and put his hands in his pockets. His fingers touched the cool smoothness of money.

He looked back in the direction of the Tower and said silently, *"Au revoir,* Sister. I think."

Because of the twisting roads and the age and temperament of the truck's engine, it took more than two hours to reach San Felice, a narrow strip of land wedged between the mountains and the sea. It was an old, rich, and very conservative city which held itself aloof from the rest of Southern California. Its streets were filled with spry elderly ladies and tanned elderly men and athletic young people who looked as if they'd been born on tennis courts and beaches and golf courses. Seeing the city again Quinn realized that Doris, with her platinum hair and heavy make-up, would feel conspicuous in it, and feeling that way she would make it a point to look even more conspicuous and end up beaten. No, Doris would never fit in. She was a night person and San Felice was a city of day people. For them dawn was the beginning of a day, not the tail-end of a night, and Sister Blessing and Brother Crown, for all their strange attire, would look more at home among them than Doris. *Or me,* Quinn thought, and he felt his plans and resolutions dissolving inside himself. *I don't belong here. I'm too old for tennis and skin-diving, and too young for checkers and canasta.*

His fingers curled around the money in his pocket. A hundred and twenty dollars plus the three hundred Tom Jurgensen owed him made four hundred and twenty. If he went back to Reno and played carefully, if his luck was good—

"Where do you want to get off at?" Brother Crown said. "I'm going to Sears myself."

"Sears will be fine."

"You got a friend in town?"

"I had one. Maybe I've still got him."

Brother Crown pulled into the parking lot behind Sears and braked the truck to a noisy stop. "Here you are, safe and sound, like I promised Sister Blessing. You and the Sister ever meet before?"

"No."

"She don't always make such a how-de-do over strangers."

"Maybe I remind her of somebody."

"You don't remind me of nobody." Brother Crown climbed down from the truck and started shuffling across the parking lot toward the back door of Sears.

"Thanks for the ride, Brother," Quinn called out after him.

"Amen."

It was nine o'clock, eighteen hours since Sister Blessing had welcomed him to the Tower as a stranger and treated him like a friend. He touched the money in his pocket again. He could feel its strings pulling at him and he wished he hadn't taken it. He thought of running after Brother Crown and giving it to him to return to Sister Blessing. Then he remembered that the possession of private money was not allowed at the Tower and handing it over now to Brother Crown would get Sister Blessing into trouble, perhaps of a very serious kind.

He turned and began walking quickly toward State Street.

Tom Jurgensen sold boats and marine insurance down at the foot of the breakwater. He had a tiny office whose windows were plastered with For Sale signs and pictures of yawls and sloops and ketches and cutters and schooners, most of them under sail.

When Quinn entered, Jurgensen was smoking a cigar and talking into the telephone which perched affectionately on his shoulder the way Brother Tongue's little bird had perched on his. "Sails by Rattsey, so what. The thing's a tub. I'm not bidding."

He put the phone down and leaned over the desk to shake Quinn's hand. "Well, Joe Quinn himself in person. How's the old boy?"

"Older. Also broke."

"I was hoping you wouldn't say that, Joe. Business has been lousy. This isn't a rich man's town any more. The penny-pinching middle class has moved in and they don't care about teakwood or mahogany, all they want—" Jurgensen broke off with a sigh. "You're absolutely flat?"

"Except for a little money that belongs to someone else."

"Since when did you ever let that worry you, Joe? I'm being funny, of course, ha ha."

"Ha ha, sure you are," Quinn said. "I've got your I.O.U. for three hundred dollars. I want the money now."

"I don't have it. This is damned embarrassing, old boy, but I just don't have it. If you'd settle for a boat, I've got a nice little sea mew, 300-pound keel, Watts sails, gaff rig—"

"Just what I need to get around Venice. Only I'm not going to Venice."

"Keep your shirt on, it was just a suggestion. I suppose you already have a car?"

"Bad supposing, Tom."

"Well, there's this crate—this dandy little '54 Ford Victoria my wife's been driving. She'll put up a terrible squawk if I take it away from her but what can I do? It's worth at least three hundred. Two-tone blue and cream, white-walls, heater, radio."

"I could do better than that on a '54 Ford in Reno."

"You're not in Reno like you're not in Venice," Jurgensen said. "It's the best I can do for you right now. Either take the car in full payment or use it until I can scrape up your money. It will suit me better if you just borrow it. That way Helen will be a little easier to handle."

"It's a deal. Where's the car?"

"Parked in the garage behind my house, 631 Gaviota Road. It hasn't been used for a week—Helen's visiting her mother in Denver—so you might have a little trouble starting it. Here are the keys. You going to be in town for a while, Joe?"

"In and out, I expect."

"Call me in a couple of weeks. I may have your money then. And take care of the crate or Helen will accuse me of losing it in a poker game. She may anyway, but—" Jurgensen spread his hands and shrugged. "You're looking pretty good, Joe."

"Early to bed and early to rise puts color in the cheeks and sparkle in the eyes. Like they say."

"Like who says?"

"The Brothers and Sisters of the Tower of Heaven."

Jurgensen raised his eyebrows. "You taken up religion or something?"

"Something," Quinn said. "Thanks for the car and I'll see you later."

Quinn had no trouble starting the car. He drove to a gas station, filled up the tank, added a quart of oil and parted with the first of Sister Blessing's twenty-dollar bills.

He asked the attendant the best way to get to Chicote.

"If it was me now, I'd follow 101 to Ventura, then cut over to 99. It's longer that way but you don't get stuck on 150, which hasn't half a mile of straightaway from one end to the other. You save trading stamps, sir?"

"I guess I could start."

As soon as he turned inland, at Ventura, he began to regret not waiting until night to make the trip. The bare hills, alternating with lemon and walnut groves, shimmered in the relentless sun, and the air was so dry that the cigarettes he'd bought in San Felice snapped in two in his fingers. He tried to cool off by thinking of San Felice, the breeze from the ocean and the harbor dotted with sails, but the contrast only made him more uncomfortable and he stopped thinking entirely for a while, surrendering himself to the heat.

He reached Chicote at noon. Since his last visit the small city had changed, grown bigger but not up and certainly not better. Fringed by oil wells and inhabited by the people who lived off them, it lay flat and brown and hard like something a cook had forgotten to take out of the oven. Underprivileged trees grew stunted along streets dividing new housing tracts from old slums. Small children played in the dust and weeds of vacant lots, looking just as contented as the children playing in the clean white sand of the San Felice beaches. It was in the teen-agers that Quinn saw the uneasiness caused by a too quick and easy prosperity. They cruised aimlessly up and down the streets in brand new convertibles and ranch wagons. They stopped only at drive-in movies and drive-in malt shops and restaurants, keeping to their cars the way soldiers in enemy territory kept to their tanks.

Quinn bought what he needed at a drugstore and checked in at a motel near the center of town. Then he ate lunch in an air-conditioned café that was so cold he had to turn up the collar of his tweed jacket while he ate.

When he had finished he went to the phone booth at the rear of the café. Patrick O'Gorman was listed in the directory as living at 702 Olive Street.

So that's all there is to it, Quinn thought with a mixture of pleasure and disappointment. O'Gorman's still in Chicote and I've made a quick hundred and twenty dollars. I'll drive back to the Tower in the morning, give Sister Blessing the information, and then head for Reno.

It seemed very simple, and yet the simplicity of it worried Quinn. If this was all there was to it, why had Sister Blessing played it so close to the chest? Why hadn't she just asked Brother Crown to call O'Gorman from San Felice or look up his address in the out-of-town phone books stocked both by the public library and the main telephone office? Quinn couldn't believe that she hadn't thought of both these possibilities. She was, in her own words and by Quinn's own observation, no fool. Yet she had paid a hundred and twenty dollars for information she could have got from a two-dollar phone call.

He put a dime in the slot and dialed O'Gorman's number.

A girl answered, breathlessly, as if she had raced somebody else to the phone. "This is the O'Gorman residence."

"Is Mr. O'Gorman there, please?"

"Richard's not a mister," the girl said with a giggle. "He's only twelve."

"I meant your father."

"My fath—? Just a minute."

There was a scurry at the other end of the line, then a woman's voice, stilted and self-conscious: "To whom did you wish to speak?"

"Mr. Patrick O'Gorman."

"I'm sorry, he's not—not here."

"When do you expect him back?"

"I don't expect him back at all."

"Perhaps you could tell me where I can reach him?"

"Mr. O'Gorman died five years ago," the woman said and hung up.

three

Olive Street was in a section of town that was beginning to show its age but still trying to preserve appearances. Seven-o-two was flanked by patches of well-kept lawn. In the middle of one a white oleander bloomed, and in the middle of the other stood an orange tree bearing both fruit and blossoms at the same time. A boy's bicycle leaned carelessly against the tree as if its owner had suddenly found something more interesting to do. The windows of the small stucco house were closed and the blinds drawn. Someone had recently hosed off the sidewalk and the porch. Little puddles steamed in the sun and disappeared even as Quinn watched.

The front door had an old-fashioned lion's-head knocker made of brass, newly polished. Reflected in it Quinn could see a tiny crooked reflection of himself. In a way it matched his own self-image.

The woman who answered the door was, like the house, small and neat and no longer young. Although her features were pretty and her figure still good, her face lacked any spark of interest or animation. It was as if, at some time during her life, she had stepped outside and had never been able to find her way back in.

Quinn said, "Mrs. O'Gorman?"

"Yes. But I'm not buying anything."

She's not selling either, Quinn thought. "I'm Joe Quinn. I used to know your husband."

She didn't exactly unbend but she seemed faintly interested. "That was you on the telephone?"

"Yes. It was kind of a shock to me, suddenly hearing that he was dead. I came by to offer my condolences and apologize if my call upset you in any way."

"Thank you. I'm sorry I hung up so abruptly. I wasn't sure whether it was a joke or not, or a piece of malice, having someone ask for Patrick after all these years. Everyone in Chicote knows that Patrick's gone."

Gone. Quinn registered the word and her hesitation before saying it.

"Where did you know my husband, Mr. Quinn?"

There was no safe reply to this but Quinn picked one he considered fairly safe. "Pat and I were in the service together."

"Oh. Well, come inside. I was just making some lemonade to have ready for the children when they get home."

The front room was small and seemed smaller because of the wallpaper and carpeting. Mrs. O'Gorman's taste—or perhaps O'Gorman's—ran to roses, large red ones in the carpet, pink and white ones in the wallpaper. An air-conditioner, fitted into the side window, was whirring noisily but without much effect. The room was still hot.

"Please sit down, Mr. Quinn."

"Thank you."

"Now tell me about my husband."

"I was hoping you'd tell me."

"But that isn't how it's done, is it?" Mrs. O'Gorman said. "When a man comes to offer condolences to the widow of his old war buddy, reminiscences are usually called for, aren't they? So please start reminiscing. You have my undivided attention."

Quinn sat in an uneasy silence.

"Perhaps you're the shy kind, Mr. Quinn, who needs a

little help getting started. How about, 'I'll never forget the time that—'? Or you might prefer a more dramatic approach. For instance, the Germans were coming over the hill in swarms and you lay trapped inside your wrecked tank, injured, with only your good buddy Pat O'Gorman to look after you. You like that?"

Quinn shook his head. "Sorry, I never saw any Germans. Koreans, yes."

"All right, switch locales. The scene changes to Korea. There's not much sense in wasting that hill and the wrecked tank—"

"What's on your mind, Mrs. O'Gorman?"

"What's on yours?" she said with a small steely smile. "My husband was not in the service, and he never allowed anyone to call him Pat. So suppose you start all over, taking somewhat less liberty with the truth."

"There isn't any truth in this case, or very little. I never met your husband. I didn't know he was dead. In fact, all I knew was his name and the fact that he lived here in Chicote at one time."

"Then why are you here?"

"That's a good question," Quinn said. "I wish I could think of an equally good answer. The truth just isn't plausible."

"The listener is supposed to be the judge of plausibility. I'm listening."

Quinn did some fast thinking. He had already disobeyed Sister Blessing's orders not to try and contact O'Gorman. To bring her name into it now would serve no purpose. And ten chances to one Mrs. O'Gorman wouldn't believe a word of it anyway, since the Brothers and Sisters of the Tower of Heaven didn't make for a very convincing story. There was one possible way out: if O'Gorman's death had taken place under peculiar circumstances (and Quinn remembered the way Mrs. O'Gorman had hesitated over the word "gone") she might want to talk about it. And if she did the talking, he wouldn't have to.

He said, "The fact is, I'm a detective, Mrs. O'Gorman."

Her reaction was quicker and more intense than he had anticipated. "So they're going to start in all over again, are they? I get a year or two of peace, I reach the point where I can walk down the street without people staring at me, feeling sorry for me, whispering about me. Now things will be right back where they were in the first place, newspaper headlines, silly men asking silly questions. My husband died by accident, can't they get that through their thick skulls? He was *not* murdered, he did *not* commit suicide, he did *not* run away to begin a new life with a new identity. He was a devout and devoted man and I will not have his memory tarnished any further. As for you, I suggest you stick to tagging parked cars and picking up kids with expired bicycle licenses. There's a bicycle in the front yard you can start with, it hasn't had a license for two years. Now get out of here and don't come back."

Mrs. O'Gorman wasn't a woman either to argue with or to try and charm. She was intelligent, forceful and embittered, and the combination was too much for Quinn. He left quickly and quietly.

Driving back to Main Street, he attempted to convince himself that his job was done except for the final step of reporting to Sister Blessing. O'Gorman had died by accident, his wife claimed. But what kind of accident? If the police had once suspected voluntary disappearance, it meant the body had never been found.

"My work is over," he said aloud. "The whys and wheres and hows of O'Gorman's death are none of my business. After five years the trail's cold anyway. On to Reno."

Thinking of Reno didn't help erase O'Gorman from his mind. Part of Quinn's job at the club, often a large part, was to be on the alert for men and women wanted by the police in other states and countries. Photographs, descriptions and Wanted circulars arrived daily and were posted for the security officers to study. A great many arrests were made quietly and quickly without interfering with a single spin of the roulette wheels. Quinn had once been told that more people wanted by the police were picked up in Reno and Las Vegas than in any other places in the country. The two cities were magnets for bank robbers and embezzlers, conmen and gangsters, any crook with a bank roll and a double-or-nothing urge.

Quinn parked his car in front of a cigar store and went in to buy a newspaper. The rack contained a variety, three from Los Angeles, two from San Francisco, a San Felice *Daily Press,* a *Wall Street Journal,* and a local weekly, *The Chicote Beacon.* Quinn bought a *Beacon* and turned to the editorial page. The paper was published on Eighth Avenue, and the publisher and editor was a man named John Harrison Ronda.

Ronda's office was a cubicle surrounded by six-foot walls, the bottom-half wood paneling, the top-half plate glass. Standing, Ronda could see his whole staff, seated at his desk he could blot them all out. It was a convenient arrangement.

He was a tall, pleasant-faced, unhurried man in his fifties, with a deep resonant voice. "What can I do for you, Quinn?"

"I've just been talking to Patrick O'Gorman's wife. Or shall we say, widow?"

"Widow."

"Were you in Chicote when O'Gorman died?"

"Yes. Matter of fact I'd just used my last dime to buy this paper. It was in the red at the time and might still be there if the O'Gorman business hadn't occurred. I had two big breaks within a month. First O'Gorman, and then three or four weeks later one of the local bank tellers, a nice little lady—why are some of the worst embezzlers such nice little ladies?—was caught with her fingers in the till. All ten of them. The *Beacon's* circulation doubled within a year. Yes, I owe a lot to O'Gorman and I don't mind admitting it. He was the ill wind that blew the wolf away from my door. So you're a friend of his widow's, are you?"

"No," Quinn said cautiously. "Not exactly."

"You're sure?"

"I'm sure. She's surer."

Ronda seemed disappointed. "I've always kept hoping Martha O'Gorman would suddenly come up with a secret boy friend. It would be a great thing if she married again, some nice man her own age."

"Sorry, I don't fit the picture. I'm older than I look and I have a vile temper."

"All right, all right, I get the message. What I said still goes, though. Martha should remarry, stop living in the past. Every year O'Gorman seems to become more perfect in her eyes. I admit he was a good guy—a devoted husband, a loving father —but dead good guys are about the same as dead bad ones where the survivors are concerned. In fact, Martha would be better off now if she found out O'Gorman had been a first-class villain."

"Perhaps that's still possible."

"Not on your life," Ronda said, shaking his head vigorously. "He was a gentle, timid man, the exact opposite of the fighting Irishman you hear about and maybe meet, though I never have myself. One of the things that drove the police crazy when they were on the murder kick was the fact that they couldn't find a single soul in Chicote who had a bad word to say about O'Gorman. No grudges, no peeves, no quarrels. If O'Gorman was done in—and there's no doubt of it, in my mind—it must have been by a stranger, probably a hitch-hiker he picked up."

"Timid men don't usually go in for picking up hitch-hikers."

"Well, he did. It was one of the few things he disagreed with Martha about. She thought it was a dangerous practice but that didn't stop him. Sympathy for the underdog was what motivated him. I guess he felt like an underdog himself."

"Why?"

"Oh, he was never much of a success, financially or any other way. Martha had the guts and force in the family, which is a good thing because in the following years she really needed them. The insurance company held off settling O'Gorman's policy for almost a year because his body wasn't found.

Meanwhile Martha and the two children were penniless. She went back to work as a lab technician in the local hospital. She's still there."

"You seem to know her well."

"My wife's one of her close friends, they attended the same high school in Bakersfield. For a time there, when I had to print a lot of stuff about O'Gorman, things were cool between Martha and me. But she came to understanding that I was only doing my job. What's your interest in the case, Quinn?"

Quinn said something vague about his work in Reno involving missing persons. Ronda seemed satisfied. Or, if he wasn't, he pretended to be. He was a man who obviously enjoyed talking and welcomed an occasion for it.

"So he was murdered by a hitchhiker," Quinn said. "Under what circumstances?"

"I can't remember every detail after such a time lapse but I can give you a general picture if you like."

"I would."

"It was the middle of February, nearly five and a half years ago. It had been a winter of big rains—most of the news I printed was rainfall statistics and stories on whose basement was flooded and whose backyard had been washed out. That year the Rattlesnake River, about three miles east of town, was running high. Now, and every summer, it's nothing but a dry ravine, so it's kind of hard to imagine what a torrent it was then. To make a long story short, O'Gorman's car crashed through the guardrail of the bridge and into the river. It was found a couple of days later when the flood subsided. A piece of cloth snagged on the door hinge had bloodstains on it, barely visible to the naked eye but quite clearly identified in the police lab. The blood was O'Gorman's type and the cloth was a piece of the shirt he'd been wearing when he left the house that night after dinner."

"And the body?"

"A few miles farther on, the Rattlesnake River joins the Torcido, which is fed by mountain snow and lives up to its name. Torcido means angry, twisted, resentful, and that about describes it, especially that year. O'Gorman wasn't a big man. He could easily have been carried down the Rattlesnake River into the Torcido and never found again. That's what the police believed then and still believe. There's another possibility, that he was murdered in the car after a struggle which tore his shirt, and then buried some place. I myself go along with the river theory. O'Gorman picked up a hitchhiker—don't forget it was a stormy night and a soft-hearted man like O'Gorman wouldn't pass up anyone on the road—and the hitchhiker tried to rob him and O'Gorman put up a fight. I myself believe the man must have been a stranger in these parts and didn't realize the river was only temporary. He may have thought the car would never be found."

"And then what happened to the stranger?" Quinn said.

Ronda lit a cigarette and scowled at the burning match. "Well, there's the weak point of the story, of course. He disappeared as completely as O'Gorman. For a while there the sheriff was picking up damn near everyone who wasn't actually born in Chicote, but nothing was proved. I'm an amateur student of crime in a way, and it seems to me a crime of impulse like this one, even though it's often bungled by lack of planning, may remain unsolved because of the very lack of planning."

"Who decided that it was a crime of impulse?"

"The sheriff, the coroner, the coroner's jury. Why? Don't you agree?"

"All I know is what you've told me," Quinn said. "And that hitchhiking stranger seems a little vague."

"I admit that."

"If he had a bloody struggle with O'Gorman, we'll have to assume the stranger got some blood on his own clothes. Were there any shacks or cottages in the vicinity where he could have broken in to change his clothes, steal some food and so on?"

"A few. But they weren't broken into, the sheriff's men checked every one of them."

"So we're left with a very wet stranger, probably with blood on him."

"The rain could have washed it away."

"It's not that easy," Quinn said. "Put yourself in the stranger's place. What would you have done?"

"Walked into town, bought some dry clothes."

"It was night, the stores were closed."

"Then I'd have checked into a motel, I guess."

"You'd be pretty conspicuous, the clerk would certainly remember and probably report you."

"Well, dammit, he must have done something," Ronda said. "Maybe he got a ride with somebody else. All I know is, he disappeared."

"Or she. Or they."

"All right, she, it, him or her, they disappeared."

"If they ever existed."

Ronda leaned across the desk. "What are you getting at?"

"Suppose the person in the car wasn't a stranger. Let's say it was a friend, a close friend, even a relative."

"I told you before, the sheriff couldn't find a single person who'd say a word against O'Gorman."

"The kind of person I'm thinking of wouldn't be likely to come forward and admit he had a grudge if he'd just murdered O'Gorman. Or she."

"You keep repeating *or she*. Why?"

"Why not? We're only dealing in possibilities anyway."

"I think you mean Martha O'Gorman."

"Wives," Quinn said dryly, "have been known to harbor grudges against husbands."

"Not Martha. Besides, she was at home that night, with the children."

"Who were in bed, sleeping?"

"Naturally they were in bed, sleeping," Ronda said irritably. "It was about 10:30. What do you think they were doing, playing poker and having a few beers? Richard was only seven then, and Sally five."

"How old was O'Gorman at the time?"

"Around your age, say forty."

Quinn didn't correct him. He felt forty, it seemed only fair that he should look it. "What about O'Gorman's description?"

"Blue eyes, fair skin, black curly hair. Medium build, about five foot nine or ten. There was nothing particularly arresting about his appearance but he was nice-looking."

"Have you a picture of him?"

"Five or six blown-up snapshots. Martha let me have them while she was still hoping O'Gorman would be found alive, maybe suffering from amnesia. Her hopes died hard but once they died, that was it. She's utterly convinced O'Gorman's car hit the bridge accidentally and O'Gorman was swept away by the river."

"And the piece of shirt with the bloodstains?"

"She thinks he was cut by the impact of the car against the guardrail. The windshield was broken and two of the windows, so it's possible. There's one argument against it, though: O'Gorman had the reputation of being a very cautious driver."

"What about suicide?"

"Again, it's possible," Ronda said, "and again there are elements that refute it. First, he was a healthy man, with no real financial worries or emotional problems, none that came to light anyway. Second, he was a strict Catholic, as Martha is. And I mean the kind that practices religion and believes every last word and comma of it. Third, he was in love with his wife and crazy about his children."

"A lot of what you've just told me doesn't come under the heading of fact. Think about it, Ronda."

"You think about it," Ronda said, grimacing. "After five years of veering this way and veering that way, maybe I need a fresh approach. Go on."

"All right. Let's say a fact is what can be proved. Fact one, he was healthy. Fact two, he was a practicing Catholic for whom suicide would constitute a deadly sin. The other things you mentioned are not facts but inferences. He may have had financial and emotional problems he didn't talk about.

44

He may not have been as crazy about his wife and children as he pretended to be."

"Then he put up quite a front. And, frankly, I don't believe O'Gorman had the brains to put up any kind of front. I'd never say anything like this to Martha, but to me O'Gorman seemed almost dull-witted, in fact, stupid."

"What did he do, for a living?"

"He was a pay-roll clerk for one of the oil companies. I'm pretty sure Martha helped him at night with his job though she'd die before admitting it. Martha's loyalties are strong, even to her own mistakes."

"Of which O'Gorman was one?"

"I think he'd have been a mistake for any really intelligent woman to marry. O'Gorman just didn't have it. The two of them were more like mother and son than husband and wife, though Martha was actually a few years younger. I suppose the truth is that the pickings in Chicote, for a woman as bright as Martha, weren't very good and she did the best she could. O'Gorman was, as I said, nice-looking with a lot of curly black hair and so on. When holes in the head are hidden by big blue eyes, even a woman like Martha can be susceptible. Fortunately, the kids take after her, they're both sharp as tacks."

"Mrs. O'Gorman," Quinn said, "appears to have quite an aversion to the police."

"It's justified. She went through a very rough experience, and this isn't a very civilized town. The sheriff's an eager beaver who couldn't build a dam if his life depended on it. His attitude throughout the whole affair seemed to be that Martha should have kept O'Gorman from going out in the rain that night, then nothing would have happened."

"Just why did he go out?"

"According to Martha, he thought he'd made an error in one of the books that day and wanted to return to the field office to check."

"Did anyone take the trouble to examine the books?"

"Oh yes. O'Gorman was right. A mistake had been made. The bookkeeper found it easily, a simple error in addition."

"What do you think that proves?"

"Proves?" Ronda repeated, frowning. "That O'Gorman was dull-witted but conscientious, just as I said he was."

"It could prove something else, though."

"Such as?"

"That O'Gorman made that mistake deliberately."

"Why would he do a thing like that?"

"So he'd have a legitimate excuse to go back to the field office that night. Did he often do work in the evenings?"

"I told you, I think Martha often helped him but she'd never admit it," Ronda said. "Anyway, you're out in left field as far as the facts are concerned. O'Gorman didn't have the brains or the character for intrigue of any kind. Granted, a man can put on an act of being stupider than he is. But he can't give a perfect performance twenty-four hours a day, 365 days a year, the way O'Gorman did. No, Quinn. There could only be one reason why he went back to the office that night, during the worst rainstorm of the year—he was scared stiff of being caught in an error and losing his job."

"You seem sure."

"Positive. You can sit there and dream up intrigues, secret meetings, conspiracies and whatever. I can't. I knew O'Gorman. He couldn't think his way out of a wet paper bag."

"As you pointed out yourself, however, he had Mrs. O'Gorman to assist him in his work. Maybe she helped him in other things, too."

"Look, Quinn," Ronda said, slapping the desk with the flat of his hand. "We're talking about two very nice people."

"As nice as the little lady you mentioned who was caught with her fingers in the till? I'm not trying to give you a bad time, Ronda, I'm just puzzling a few possibilities."

"The possibilities in this case are almost endless. Ask the sheriff, if you don't believe me. Practically every crime in the book, except arson and infanticide, was suggested and investigated. Maybe you'd be interested in seeing my file on the case?"

"Very much," Quinn said.

"I kept a personal file, in addition to what we printed in the *Beacon*, because of Martha being an old friend. Also because —well, frankly, I've always had the feeling that the case would be reopened some day, that maybe some burglar in Kansas City, or some guy up on another murder charge in New Orleans or Seattle, would confess to killing O'Gorman and settle everything once and for all."

"Didn't you ever think, or hope, that O'Gorman himself might turn up?"

"I hoped. I didn't think, though. When O'Gorman left the house that night he had two one-dollar bills in his wallet, his car, and the clothes on his back, and that's all. Martha handled the money for the family, she knew to a cent how much O'Gorman was carrying."

"No clothes were missing from his closet?"

"None," Ronda said.

"Did he have a bank account?"

"A joint one with Martha. He could easily have cashed a check that afternoon without Martha finding out about it until later, but he didn't. He also didn't borrow any money."

"Did he have anything valuable he might have taken along to pawn?"

"He owned a wrist watch worth about a hundred dollars, a present from Martha. It was found in his bureau drawer." Ronda lit another cigarette, leaned back in the swivel chair and studied the ceiling. "Aside from all the physical evidence which would rule out a voluntary disappearance, there is the emotional evidence: O'Gorman had become, over the years, completely dependent on Martha, he couldn't have lasted a week without her, he was like a little boy."

"Little boys his age can become a nuisance," Quinn said dryly. "Maybe the police were wrong to rule out infanticide."

"If that's a joke, it's a bad one."

"Most of mine are."

"I'll get that file for you," Ronda said, rising. "I don't know why I'm doing all this, except I guess I'd like to see the case closed once and for all so Martha could start seriously considering remarriage. She'd make a fine wife. You probably haven't seen her at her best."

"No, and I doubt that I will."

"She's lively, full of fun—"

"The pitch doesn't fit the product," Quinn said, "and I'm not in the market."

"You're very suspicious."

"By nature, training, experience and observation, yes."

Ronda went out and Quinn sat back in the chair, frowning. Through the glass paneling he could see the tops of three heads, Ronda's bushy gray one, a man's crew cut, and a woman's elaborate bee-hive-style coiffure, the color of persimmons.

The shirt, he thought. *That's it, it's the shirt that bothers me, the piece of cloth snagged on the hinge of the car door. On the stormiest night of the year why wasn't O'Gorman wearing a jacket or a raincoat?*

Ronda came back, carrying two cardboard boxes labeled simply Patrick O'Gorman. The boxes contained newspaper clippings, photographs, snapshots, copies of telegrams and letters to and from various police officials. Though most of them originated in California, Nevada and Arizona, others came from remote parts of the country and Mexico and Canada. The material was arranged in chronological order, but to go through it all would require considerable time and patience.

Quinn said, "May I borrow the file overnight?"

"What do you intend to do with it?"

"Take it to my motel and examine it. There are one or two points I'd like to go into more fully—the condition of the car, for instance. Was there a heater in it and was it switched on?"

"What's that got to do with anything?"

"If the accident happened the way Mrs. O'Gorman believes it did, O'Gorman was driving around on the stormiest night of the year in his shirt sleeves."

Ronda looked puzzled for a minute. "I don't think anything was ever brought up concerning a heater in the car."

"It should have been."

"All right, take the stuff with you for tonight. Maybe you'll come across some other little thing the rest of us missed."

He sounded as if he felt the project was hopeless, and by eight o'clock that night Quinn was beginning to share the feeling. The facts in the case were meager, and the possibilities seemed endless.

Including infanticide, Quinn thought. *Maybe Martha O'Gorman was getting pretty tired of her little boy, Patrick.*

One item that especially interested Quinn was from a transcript of Martha O'Gorman's testimony before the coroner's jury: "It was about 8:30. The children were in bed sleeping and I was reading the newspaper. Patrick acted restless and worried, he couldn't seem to settle down. Finally I asked him what was the matter and he told me he'd made a mistake that afternoon and wanted to go back to the field office to correct it before anyone discovered it. Patrick was so terribly conscientious about his work—please, I can't go on. Please. Oh Lord, help me—"

Very touching, Quinn thought. *But the fact remains, the children were asleep, and Martha and Patrick O'Gorman could have left the house together.*

No evidence was brought out about a heater in the car, although the piece of wool flannel with the bloodstains on it was discussed at length. The blood type was the same as O'Gorman's, and the flannel was part of a shirt O'Gorman frequently wore. Both Martha and two of O'Gorman's fellow clerks identified it. It was a bright yellow and black plaid, of the Macleod tartan, and his co-workers had kidded O'Gorman about an Irishman wearing a Scotch tartan.

"All right," Quinn said, addressing the blank wall. "Suppose I'm O'Gorman. I'm sick of being a little boy. I want to run away and see the world. But I can't face up to Martha so I have to disappear. I arrange to be in an accident while I'm wearing a shirt that will be identified as mine by a lot of people. I choose the time carefully, when the river is high and it's still raining. O.K., I rig the accident and the piece of

flannel with my own blood on it. Then what? I'm left standing in my underwear in a heavy rainstorm three miles from
town with only two bucks to my name. Great planning,
O'Gorman, really great."

By nine o'clock he was more than willing to believe in
Ronda's hitchhiking stranger.

four

Quinn ate a late dinner at El Bocado, a bar and grill across
the street from his motel. Entertainment facilities in Chicote
were limited and the place was crowded to the doors with
ranchers in ten-gallon Stetsons and oil workers in their field
clothes. There weren't many women: a few wives already
worried at nine about driving home at twelve; a quartet of
self-conscious girls celebrating a birthday and acting a good
deal noisier than the two prostitutes at the bar; a prim-faced
woman about thirty standing near the door. She wore a blue
turban, horn-rimmed spectacles and no make-up. She looked
as if she had entered the place thinking it was the YWCA,
and was now trying to muster the courage to walk out.

She spoke briefly to one of the waitresses. The waitress
glanced around the room, her eyes finally settling on Quinn.

She approached him without hesitation. "Would you mind
sharing your table, mister? There's a lady that has to eat
before she catches the bus to L.A. Those bus stops serve lousy
food."

So did El Bocado, but Quinn said politely, "I don't mind."
Then, to the woman in the turban, "Please sit down."

"Thank you very much."

She sat down opposite him as if she expected to find a bomb under the seat.

"This is very kind of you, sir."

"Not at all."

"It is, though." She added, with an air of disdain, "In *this* town a lady never knows what to expect."

"You don't like Chicote?"

"Does anyone? I mean, it's terribly uncouth. That's why I'm leaving."

She herself looked a bit too couth, Quinn decided. Some lipstick and a less severe hat that showed a little of her hair would have improved her. Even without them she was pretty, with the kind of earnest anemic prettiness Quinn associated with church choirs and amateur string quartets.

Over fish and chips and cole slaw, she told Quinn her name, Wilhelmina de Vries, her occupation, typist, her ambition, to be a private secretary to an important executive. Quinn told her his name, his occupation, security officer, and his ambition, to retire.

"A security officer," she repeated. "You mean a policeman?"

"More or less."

"Isn't that simply fascinating? My goodness, are you here working on a case?"

"Let's just say I'm having a little holiday."

"No one comes to Chicote for a holiday. It's the kind of place people are always trying to get out of, like me."

"I'm interested in California history," Quinn said. "Where towns like this got their names, for instance."

She looked disappointed. "Oh, that's easy. Some man came out here from Kentucky for his health in the late 1890's. He was going to grow tobacco, fields and fields of the world's finest tobacco for the world's finest cigars. That's what Chicote means, cigar. Only the tobacco didn't grow, and the ranchers switched to cotton, which did. Then oil was discovered and that was the end of Chicote as an agricultural center. But here I am, doing all the talking, and you just sit there." Her smile revealed a dimple in her left cheek. "Now it's your turn. Where do you come from?"

"Reno."

"What are you doing here?"

"Learning some California history," Quinn said with considerable truth.

"That's a funny way for a policeman to be spending his time."

"*Chacun à son gout,* as they say in Hoboken."

"How true," she murmured. "Just as true here, I suppose, as it is in Hoboken."

Although her face didn't change expression, Quinn had a feeling that he was being kidded, and that, if Miss Wilhelmina de Vries sang in a church choir or played in a string quartet, some of the notes she produced would be intentionally off-key just for the hell of it.

"Please tell me really and truly and honestly," she said, "why you're visiting Chicote."

"I like the climate."

"It's miserable."

"The people."

"Uncouth."

"The cuisine."

"A starving dog would turn up his nose at this awful stuff. You know something? I'll bet a dollar to a doughnut you're working on a case."

"I'm a betting man but I'm fresh out of doughnuts."

"No, seriously, you really *are* here on a case, aren't you?" Her blue-green eyes glistened behind the thick lenses of her spectacles. "There hasn't been anything interesting happening lately so it has to be an old case. . . . Does it involve money, a lot of money?"

It was one question Quinn could answer without hesitation. "Nothing I do involves a lot of money, Miss de Vries. What did you have in mind?"

"Nothing."

"So you're going down to Los Angeles to find a job?"

"Yes."

"Where's your suitcase?"

"Suit—oh, I checked it. At the bus depot. So I wouldn't have to carry it around. It's heavy, since all my clothes are in it and everything. And it's a terribly big suitcase in the first place."

If she'd simply claimed to have checked the suitcase, he might have believed her, having no reason not to. But she'd elaborated too much, as though she'd been trying to make the suitcase real to herself as well as Quinn.

The waitress brought Quinn's check.

"I must be going," he said, rising. "Nice to have met you, Miss de Vries. And good luck in the big city."

He paid the cashier and walked across the street to his motel. The garage belonging to the first unit was open. He stepped inside, watching the door of El Bocado café.

He didn't have long to wait. Miss Wilhelmina de Vries came out, stood hesitantly on the curb, and looked up and down the street. A wind had started blowing, brisk but very warm, and she was attempting to hold down her skirt and her turban at the same time. Modesty finally won out. She unwound the turban, which turned out to be a long blue scarf, and stuffed it into her purse. Under the street lamp her hair, released from its confinement, sprung up in all directions and shone in the light, the color of persimmons. She walked half a block down the street, climbed into a small dark sedan, and drove off.

Quinn had no chance to follow her. By the time he could get his own car out of the garage and on the road, she would be home, or at the bus depot or wherever else young ladies like Miss de Vries went after an unsuccessful attempt to pump information out of a stranger. She was, obviously, an amateur at the game, and the turban, and probably the spectacles, too, were a crude disguise. Quinn wondered why she'd bothered with a disguise when he didn't even know her. Then he remembered sitting in John Ronda's office at the *Beacon* and seeing through the glass partition the tops of three heads. One of them had had hair the color of persimmons.

All right, assume she was there, Quinn thought. Ronda had a loud, distinct voice, and the walls of his office were only six feet high. Miss de Vries could have overheard something of sufficient interest to her to make her assume a disguise and arrange a pick-up in the El Bocado café, maybe with the collaboration of the waitress. But exactly what had she heard? The only subject he and Ronda had discussed was the O'Gorman case, the details of which were common knowledge in Chicote, the evidence a matter of public record available to anyone.

Miss de Vries had made what could be construed as a reference to O'Gorman—"it has to be an old case"—and then practically nullified it by adding, "Does it involve a lot of money?" There was no money connected with the O'Gorman business except the two one-dollar bills O'Gorman was carrying when he left the house for the last time.

Ronda's only mention of a subject unconnected with O'Gorman was his brief remark about a nice little lady embezzler caught with her fingers in the till. Quinn wondered what had happened to the nice little lady, and the money, and who else had been involved.

He crossed the driveway and went into the motel office to pick up his key. The night clerk, an old man with arthritis-swollen hands, looked up from the movie magazine he was reading. "Yes, sir?"

"The key to number seventeen, please."

"Seventeen, yes, sir. Just a minute." He shuffled over to the key rack. "Ingrid's not about to make a go of it with Lars any more than Debbie will with Harry. And you can quote me."

"Oh, I will," Quinn said. "Daily."

"What's that number again?"

"Seventeen."

"It's not here." The old man peered at Quinn over the top of his bifocals. "Why, I gave you number seventeen not more than an hour ago. You told me your name and gave me the license number of your car like it's written right here in the book."

"I wasn't here an hour ago."

"You must of been. I gave you the key. Only you had a hat on, a gray fedora, and you were wearing a topcoat. Maybe you been drinking and don't remember? Liquor befogs the memory something fierce. They say Dean has trouble with his lines on account of belting too many."

"At nine o'clock," Quinn said wearily, "I turned my key in to the girl who was here in the office."

"My granddaughter."

"All right, your granddaughter. I haven't been back since. Now, if you don't mind, I want into my room, I'm tired."

"Been carousing around, eh?"

"That's right. Carousing around trying to forget Ingrid and Debbie. Now find your passkeys and let's get going."

Grumbling, the old man led the way outside and down the driveway. The air was still hot and dry, and not even the brisk wind could dispel the faint odor of oil that hung over the city.

Quinn said, "Pretty warm night for a hat and topcoat, isn't it?"

"I ain't wearing a hat and a topcoat."

"The man you gave my key to was."

"All that carousing's befogged your memory." They had reached the door of Quinn's room and the old man let out a sudden cry of triumph. "Lookie here, will you? See, the key's right in the lock where you left it. I told you. I gave it to you and you forgot about it. Now what do you think of that, eh?"

"Very little."

"You traveling fellows get careless, belting the booze and all."

There didn't seem to be any way of convincing the old man he was wrong, so Quinn said good night and locked himself in the room.

It looked, at first glance, exactly the way he'd left it, the bed rumpled, the pillows propped against the headboard, the goosenecked lamp switched on. The two cardboard boxes containing Ronda's file on O'Gorman were still on the desk. It was impossible for Quinn to tell whether anything had been removed from them. Even Ronda, who had collected the material, might find it difficult, since he probably hadn't looked through it for years.

Quinn removed the lid from the first box. In a large manila envelope were the pictures of O'Gorman which Martha had given to Ronda: one formal photograph, obviously very old, since O'Gorman looked about twenty at the time; the rest snapshots, O'Gorman with the children, with a dog and cat, with Martha; O'Gorman changing a tire, standing beside a bicycle. In every case O'Gorman looked like a part of the background, and it was the dog and cat, the children, Martha, the bicycle, which seemed the real subjects of the pictures. Only the formal photograph showed O'Gorman's face clearly. He'd been a handsome young man with curly black hair and large gentle eyes with a faint expression of bafflement in them, as though he found life puzzling and not quite what he'd been led to expect. It was the kind of face that would appeal to a lot of women, especially the ones who might think they could solve life's puzzles for him and, motherlike, kiss away the hurts and bruises it inflicted.

Quinn returned the pictures to the envelope, his movements slowed by a sudden feeling of depression. Until he studied the portrait, O'Gorman had seemed unreal to him. Now O'Gorman had become a human being, a man who loved his wife and children and house and dog, who worked hard at his job, a man too soft-hearted to leave a hitchhiker standing on the road on a stormy night yet brave enough to resist a robber.

He had two bucks in his pocket, Quinn thought as he took off his clothes and got into bed. *Why did he put up a fight for a lousy two bucks? It doesn't make sense. There must have been something else, something no one has men-*

tioned. . . . I must talk to Martha O'Gorman again tomorrow.
Maybe Ronda can arrange it for me.

He didn't remember, until just before he fell asleep, that he
had planned on driving back to the Tower in the morning,
and from there to Reno. Both places were beginning to seem
remote to him, dream stuff compared to the blunt and solid
reality of Chicote. He couldn't even conjure up a clear picture of Doris, and Sister Blessing was no more than a bulky
gray robe with a faceless head sticking out of one end and two
large bare feet out of the other.

five

Early the next morning Quinn returned to the motel office. A
middle-aged man, with a bald, sunburned pate, was untying a
bundle of Los Angeles papers.

"What can I do for you, Mr.—ah—Quinn, isn't it? Seventeen?"

"Yes."

"I'm Paul Frisby, owner and manager, with the aid of my
family. Is anything the matter?"

"Someone got into my room last night when I went across
the road to have dinner."

"I did," Frisby said coldly.

"Any particular reason why?"

"Two of them. It's our policy that when a guest checks in
without any luggage, we give his room the once-over when
he goes out to eat. In your case there was an additional
reason: the name on your car registration isn't Quinn."

"The car was lent to me by a friend."

57

"Oh, I believe you. But in this business it pays to be careful."

"Granted," Quinn said. "Only why the cloak-and-dagger routine?"

"Pardon?"

"The business of disguising yourself with a hat and topcoat and getting the key from the old man."

"I don't know what you're talking about," Frisby said, narrowing his eyes. "I have my own set of keys. Now what's this about grandpa?"

Quinn explained briefly.

"Grandpa has trouble with his eyes," Frisby said. "Glaucoma. You mustn't blame—"

"I'm not blaming anybody. I'd just like to know how someone else could walk in here, ask for my key and get it."

"We try to prevent things like that happening. But in the motel business they happen occasionally, especially if the impostor knows the name and car license number of the guest. Was anything taken?"

"I'm not sure. There were two boxes on the desk containing documents lent to me to examine. You must have seen the boxes when you were in the room, Frisby."

"Well. Well, as a matter of fact, yes."

"Did you open either of them?"

Frisby's face turned as red as the sunburn on his pate. "No. No, I didn't have to. I saw the label, O'Gorman. Everybody in Chicote knows all about that case. Oh certainly, I was curious about why a stranger should suddenly appear in town with a lot of stuff about O'Gorman."

There was a long uneasy silence.

"Just how curious were you?" Quinn said finally. "Did you tell your wife, for instance?"

"Well, I sort of mentioned it to her, yes."

"Anyone else?"

"Mister. Put yourself in my place for a minute—"

"Who else?"

After another silence Frisby said nervously, "I phoned the

58

sheriff. I thought there might be some hanky-panky going on that he ought to know about, maybe something real serious. I can see now I was wrong."

"Can you?"

"I'm a pretty good judge of character and you don't act like a man who's got anything much to hide. But yesterday it was different. You check in with no luggage, driving a car with someone else's name and address on it and you're toting around a lot of stuff about O'Gorman. You can't blame me for being suspicious."

"So you called the sheriff."

"I just talked to him. He promised he'd keep his eye out for you."

"Would keeping his eye out extend to tricking an old man into giving him the key to number seventeen?"

"Great Scott, no," Frisby said vigorously. "Besides, Grandpa's known the sheriff since he was a little boy."

"Everybody in Chicote seems to know everybody else."

"It's a fact. There's no metropolis anywhere near, we're not on a main highway and it's rugged country. Here we all are, dependent on each other for survival, so naturally we get to know each other."

"And naturally you're suspicious of strangers."

"It's a close community, Mr. Quinn. When something like the O'Gorman affair happens, it affects every one of us. Most of us knew him, went to school with him or worked with him or met him at church and civic gatherings and the P.T.A. Not that O'Gorman was much for getting involved with community business, but Mrs. O'Gorman was, and he tagged along." A small grim smile moved across Frisby's face. "You might say that's a fitting epitaph for O'Gorman: 'He tagged along.' What's your interest in the case, Mr. Quinn? You going to write it up, maybe, for one of those true-crime magazines?"

"Maybe."

"Be sure to let me know when it's published."

"I'll do that," Quinn said.

He ate breakfast in a coffee shop, sitting at a front table

so he could watch his car parked across the road with the O'Gorman file locked in the trunk. Although Frisby had given him no lead about the intruder of the previous night, he'd given him something else for which Quinn was grateful: an excuse to go around asking questions. He was, hereafter, an amateur writer looking for a new angle on the disappearance of O'Gorman.

He bought a pocket-sized notebook and a couple of ball point pens at a drug store before he drove to the *Beacon* office on Eighth Avenue. As soon as he opened the door he could hear John Ronda's voice distinctly above the clatter of typewriters and the ringing of a telephone. The red-haired Miss de Vries would have had no trouble at all eavesdropping even if she'd worn earmuffs.

Ronda said, "Good morning, Quinn. I see you've brought my file back safely."

"I'm not sure how safely." Quinn told him about the man with the topcoat and fedora.

Ronda listened, frowning and drumming his fingers on the desk. "Maybe he was just a petty thief after something else in the room."

"There wasn't anything else. I left my stuff in Reno, I intended to be back there by now."

"Why aren't you?"

"I got interested in O'Gorman," Quinn said easily. "I thought it might make an interesting article for one of the true-crime magazines."

"It already has, about a dozen times in the past five and a half years."

"Maybe I'll find a new angle. I started off on the wrong foot with Mrs. O'Gorman yesterday but I thought you might be able to fix that for me."

"How?"

"Call her, give me a little build-up."

Ronda looked pensively up at the ceiling. "I guess I could try it, but I'm not sure I want to. I know nothing about you."

"Ask questions, we'll get acquainted."

"All right. First, I'd better warn you, however, that I talked to Martha O'Gorman last night and she told me about your phone call and subsequent visit to her house. What interested me is that when you telephoned Martha at noon you apparently weren't aware that O'Gorman was dead."

"That's right, I wasn't."

"Why did you want to see him?"

"Professional ethics—"

"Which," Ronda interrupted, "obviously doesn't include telling whoppers to widows."

"—forbids me to name names, so I'll call my client Mrs. X. Mrs. X paid me to find out if a man named Patrick O'Gorman lived in Chicote."

"And?"

"That's all. I was merely to find out if he was still here, not talk to him or give him any message or contact him."

"Oh, come off it, Quinn," Ronda said brusquely. "All Mrs. X had to do was write a letter to the city authorities, the mayor, the sheriff, even the Chamber of Commerce. Why should she hire you to drive all the way up here?"

"She did."

"How much did she pay you?"

"A hundred and twenty dollars."

"For the love of heaven, she must be off her rocker."

"That's a good way of putting it," Quinn said. "For the love of heaven, she is."

"A nut, eh?"

"A lot of people would say so. By the way, all this is in confidence."

"Certainly. What's Mrs. X's connection with O'Gorman?"

"She didn't tell me, if there is one."

"It seems," Ronda said, "a funny job for a man like you to take."

"When I'm broke I take funny jobs."

"What broke you?"

"Roulette, dice, blackjack, casino."

"You're a professional gambler?"

Quinn's smile was humorless. "Amateur. The professionals win. I lose. This time I lost everything. Mrs. X's money looked nice and green and crisp."

"Telling whoppers to widows," Ronda said, "and taking money from nutty old women doesn't make you exactly a hero, Quinn."

"Not exactly. Mrs. X isn't old, by the way, and except for some rather obvious eccentricities, she's an intelligent woman."

"Then why didn't she simply write a letter, or make a phone call?"

"Neither is allowed where she lives. She's a member of an obscure religious cult which forbids unnecessary contact with the outside world."

"Then how," Ronda said dryly, "did she come across you?"

"She didn't. I came across her."

"How?"

"You probably won't believe me."

"I haven't so far. Keep trying, though."

Quinn kept trying and Ronda listened, shaking his head now and then in incredulity.

"It's crazy," he said when Quinn had finished. "The whole thing's crazy. Maybe you are, too."

"I'm not ruling out the possibility."

"Where is this place, anyway, and what's it called?"

"I can't tell you that. It's one of a number of cults, not uncommon in Southern California, made up of misfits, neurotics, the world's rejects. For the most part they mind their own business and stay out of trouble except for some brushes with the local authorities about schooling for the children."

"All right," Ronda said with a vague gesture. "Suppose I believe the whole implausible story, what do you want me to do?"

"Try and square me with Martha O'Gorman, for one thing."

"That may not be easy."

"And for another, tell me the name of the red-haired woman

who was in your outer office yesterday afternoon when you went to get the file on O'Gorman."

"Why do you want to know that?"

"She picked me up in the El Bocado café last night," Quinn said, "at the same time that the man in the fedora was searching my room."

"You think there's a connection?"

"I'd be a fool not to. She was making sure I didn't leave the place before the man had a chance to finish his job."

"You must be mistaken, Quinn. The young woman in question wouldn't dream of picking up a strange man in a place like El Bocado, let alone cover for a sneak thief. She's a respectable woman."

"That hardly surprises me," Quinn said dryly. "Everyone involved is, or was, the soul of respectability. It's what makes the case unique—no villains, no crooks, no shady ladies. O'Gorman was a good guy, Martha O'Gorman is a pillar of the community, Mrs. X is a dedicated cultist and the red-haired woman probably teaches Sunday School."

"Matter of fact, she does."

"Who is she, Ronda?"

"Dammit, Quinn, I'm not sure I ought to tell you. She's a very nice girl, and besides, maybe you made a mistake. Did you actually see her face when she was in here yesterday afternoon?"

"No. Just the top of her head."

"That's not enough evidence to prove she's the same woman who picked you up in the café. Besides, Willie's too smart an operator to pull a dumb trick like that."

"Willie," Quinn repeated. "Short for Wilhelmina?"

"Yes."

"Wilhelmina de Vries?"

"Why—why, yes," Ronda said, looking startled. "How did you know her name?"

"She told me last night at dinner."

"Actually she's Willie King now, she went through a quick marriage and divorce. . . . She *told* you her name?"

"Yes."

"Surely that in itself proves she wasn't up to any skulduggery."

"Call it what you like," Quinn said. "She was up to it and enjoying it."

"What else did she tell you?"

"A number of lies not worth repeating. By the way, does she happen to have a boy friend?"

The question seemed to annoy Ronda. He leaned forward, giving Quinn a long hard stare. "Now listen, Quinn. You can't come into a town like this and start making insinuations about some of our best citizens."

"So Willie King is going around with one of Chicote's best citizens."

"I didn't say that. I only—"

"Tell me, does Chicote have any bad citizens? All the ones I've met, or been told about, so far are truly sterling characters —no, I'm wrong. There was one exception, the nice little lady who embezzled from the local bank."

"What made you suddenly think of her?"

"She's been on my mind," Quinn said.

"Why?"

"In my profession, as well as yours, the sinners come in for more attention than the saints. Chicote's apparently teeming with saints but—"

"Lay off the town, will you? It's an average town, there are average people in it, average things happen."

"Tell me about the lady embezzler, Ronda."

"I repeat, why?"

"When Willie King was big-earing in this office yesterday, you were talking about the O'Gorman case mainly, but you mentioned the lady embezzler, too. I'm curious about which one Willie King—and perhaps her boy friend—is interested in."

"Everyone in Chicote," Ronda said with an evasive shrug, "is interested in both cases."

"To the extent of breaking into my motel room?"

"No, of course not."

"All right, then. Who's Willie's boy friend, Ronda?"

"I can't swear to anything but I've heard rumors. In a town this size, when a young attractive woman works for and with an eligible widower, it's always assumed she's also working on him."

"His name?"

"George Haywood. He's in real estate. Willie used to be his secretary but she's had a promotion. The ads Haywood puts in the *Beacon* list Willie as an associate. How close an associate is anybody's guess and nobody's business."

"It may be mine," Quinn said. "Willie didn't accidentally wander into the El Bocado café last night, accidentally wearing a disguise."

"It seems unlikely."

"Did Willie have any connection with the O'Gorman case?"

"Not that I know of."

"What about the embezzlement?"

"Well, connection is too strong a word."

"Pick a weaker one."

Ronda leaned back in the chair and folded his arms across his chest. "Willie herself had nothing to do with the embezzlements—there wasn't just one, it was a whole series, covering a period of ten or eleven years—except to the extent that she worked for George Haywood."

"And George Haywood was involved in the embezzlements?"

"Not voluntarily," Ronda said sharply. "His integrity has never been questioned. He couldn't help being involved, though. The embezzler was his younger sister, Alberta Haywood." Ronda paused, frowning up at the ceiling. "Her case was, in its way, just as tragic as O'Gorman's. They were both quiet, self-effacing people."

"Were? You mean she's dead, too?"

"More or less. She's been in Tecolote women's prison for

over five years and the chances are she'll be there for another five or even ten."

"What about a parole?"

"She has a hearing coming up soon but I don't think it will change anything for her."

"Why not?"

"Well, when a parole board meets to consider a case involving stolen money, the members want to be sure of two things, what happened to the money and whether the thief is sorry for taking it. Alberta Haywood may not be able to satisfy them. From what I've heard of her conduct at Tecolote prison she's docile but not penitent. And as for the money, it's a question of whether they'll believe her story or not. Some people do, some don't."

"What about you."

"Oh, I believe it," Ronda said. "She spent the money as she embezzled it, over a period of ten years or more. She gave some to charity, lent some to friends and relatives, speculated on the stock market and blew in the rest of it betting on the horses. This all fits the picture of the average embezzler. I made a study of the subject after Alberta Haywood was caught and I learned some pretty surprising facts. For instance, the amount of money embezzled in a year is a great deal more than that stolen by every burglar, bank robber, pickpocket and auto thief in the entire country."

"That's hard to believe."

"Check it yourself. It happens to be true. Another point interested me. Alberta Haywood seemed such an unlikely person to commit a crime, yet I found out that this very unlikeliness was what she had in common with the rest of them. The average embezzler has no previous record of dishonesty, he doesn't act like a criminal or consider himself one. Very often the community doesn't consider him one either, usually because he's given some of the money back to the very people he's defrauded. The City of Chicote stood solidly behind Alberta Haywood. She may have stolen a hundred thousand dollars of their money but the Boy Scouts had new furniture for their club house and the Crippled Children's Society a new station wagon. It's irrational thinking, of course, like suffering a stab in the back and then being grateful for a lollipop to ease the pain."

"Did you know Miss Haywood well?"

"As well as anyone outside her family, I suppose. She had a nodding acquaintance with nearly every person in town, but no close friends. At Tecolote she's been a model prisoner, obedient, quiet, causing no trouble. Naturally this will be in her favor at her parole hearing, but there's still the question of whether they'll believe her story of how she spent the money, although to me it's quite obvious she's telling the truth."

"Was an attempt ever made to connect the two crimes, Miss Haywood's embezzlements and O'Gorman's murder?"

"Oh yes. At one time the police toyed with the idea that Alberta actually murdered O'Gorman."

"For what reason?"

"When Alberta was arrested, the police were still looking under rocks in an attempt to find a motive for O'Gorman's murder. Someone turned over a big rock and came up with this: at one time O'Gorman, like Alberta, was a bookkeeper, so perhaps he had somehow found out in advance about Alberta's embezzlements, threatened to expose her, and been murdered to ensure his silence. There were quite a number of things wrong with the theory. First, Alberta was at a movie on the night of O'Gorman's death. Second, O'Gorman had no access to the bank's books except through Alberta herself. And it's a safe bet that when she had her fingers in the till she wouldn't invite a stranger in to show him her nail polish."

"He was a stranger to her?"

"For all practical purposes, yes. She may have seen him a couple of times while O'Gorman was working brieflly for her brother, George, as a real estate salesman. I say briefly because he lasted no longer than a month. Poor O'Gorman couldn't have sold sarongs in Tahiti. His personality was too low pressure, and more than that, he didn't care much for money, not enough to go after it tooth and claw the way salesmen have to. O'Gorman was content just to get by and so was Martha, although she worried about being able to send the two children to college."

"Did she ever get O'Gorman's insurance?"

"Oh yes, the company eventually paid up. But it wasn't much. Five thousand dollars, I think."

"Five thousand dollars," Quinn said, "makes a better motive than two dollars."

"What's that supposed to mean?"

"Your alleged hitchhiker got two dollars, Martha O'Gorman five thousand."

Ronda's face reddened as though in anger, but he spoke calmly. "There was some suspicion, naturally, directed against Martha. Nothing came of it. It's odd, people were a lot kinder to Alberta Haywood, who committed a crime, than they were to Martha, who was the innocent victim of one. But there again we run into the business of the new furniture for the Boy Scouts and the crippled children's station wagon. The good dumb people of Chicote didn't seem able or willing to figure out that they'd been taken for a hundred thousand dollars and got about five percent of it back. The rest of it went to bookies and so on."

"Did she give names and dates?"

"No. She refused, didn't want to get anyone else in trouble. However, a cigar-store owner told the police she'd been buying the racing form every day for six or seven months previous to the time she was caught."

"Just how was she caught?"

"The president of the bank became suspicious at the rate deposits had fallen off while other banks in the area were increasing their deposits. He called in the bank inspectors. For obvious reasons, the staff of the bank is never told in advance about the arrival of the inspectors. Anyway, one of them called Alberta Haywood in to explain a small error in a ledger he'd selected at random. She knew right away the jig was up. She confessed everything, and after a brief trial she was sent to Tecolote prison."

"Does she have any close relatives besides her brother George?"

"A sister, Ruth, who'd left town a year previously, after a family fight concerning the man she married. And a mother who's one of the town characters. Mrs. Haywood refused to attend Alberta's trial or have anything further to do with her, and I think she used her influence on George. He'd always been fond of his sister but he only visited her once, in the county jail before she was transferred to Tecolote. As far as her family is concerned, Alberta Haywood died the day the bank inspectors arrived. At least this goes for Mrs. Haywood and George. I don't know about the younger sister, Ruth. She's just sort of dropped out of the family picture."

"What's Mrs. Haywood like?"

"A holy terror," Ronda said with a grimace. "George deserves a medal for putting up with her. Or a kick in the pants."

"Does he live with her?"

"Yes. He's been a widower for seven or eight years. Real estate doesn't exactly sell like hot cakes around here any more but he does fairly well. After Alberta was sent up we all thought George should leave Chicote and settle in a larger city where the name Haywood wouldn't be something to live down. But George is a fighter. He stayed. . . . Well, there you have it, Quinn, the story of Alberta Haywood. And the moral is, if you embezzle a lot of money, don't give it away, don't gamble it away. Put it in some safe place to impress the parole board."

"When is her hearing coming up?"

"Next month," Ronda said. "I reminded George of it when he came in with his usual ad a couple of weeks ago. He wasn't interested enough even to discuss it."

"You seem very interested."

"It's news. Where the news is, the *Beacon* shines. That's what it says on the masthead. One of these days I'll think of something better, or at least more accurate. Now, if you don't mind, Quinn, I'll have to let you go. I have work to do."

"What about squaring me with Martha O'Gorman?"

"That won't be easy. You didn't exactly impress her."

"I'll do better if I have a second chance."

"All right," Ronda said. "I'll get in touch with her at the hospital lab. Call me around eleven."

six

Quinn called George Haywood's office from a pay phone in a drug store. A man who identified himself as Earl Perkins said Mr. Haywood was at home with a cold.

"Is Mrs. King there?" Quinn said.

"No, she won't be back until after lunch. She's out of town showing a piece of property Mr. Haywood was supposed to handle. If it's anything urgent, you can call Mr. Haywood's home, 5-0936."

"Thanks."

Quinn dialed 5-0936 and asked for George Haywood.

"He's sick." The woman's voice was cracked with age but it was still forceful. "He's in bed with a cold."

"I wonder if I may talk to him for a minute."

"You may not."

"Is that Mrs. Haywood?"

"Yes."

"I'm not going to be in the city very long and I'd like to see Mr. Haywood about an urgent matter. My name is Joe Quinn. If you'll tell him I called—"

"I'll tell him at the proper time." She hung up, leaving

Quinn wondering whether the proper time might be noon or next Christmas.

He bought a copy of the Chicote *Beacon* and ordered a cup of coffee at the lunch counter. The *Beacon* printed a minimum of world news interspersed with long dull accounts of local doings and long dull lists of names of the people who did them. It was no wonder that John Ronda had expressed gratitude to O'Gorman and Alberta Haywood: at least they'd given him something interesting to write about. Ronda would undoubtedly welcome a chance to reopen either case. *Maybe that's why he's putting himself out for me*, Quinn thought. *The* Beacon *needs another boost and a new clue to O'Gorman's murderer would knock the Women's Club canasta parties and the YMCA wienie roasts right off the front page.*

At eleven o'clock he called Ronda at his office.

"Well, I did it," Ronda said, sounding pleased with himself. "Martha was reluctant, naturally, but I talked her around. She'll meet you at noon in the cafeteria at the hospital. It's on C Street near Third Avenue. The cafeteria's in the basement."

"Thanks very much."

"Did you get in touch with Haywood?"

"No. He's in bed with a cold and his mother refused to let me talk to him."

Ronda laughed as if at some private joke he didn't want to explain. "What about Willie King?"

"She's out of town."

"Bad timing all around, eh?"

"For me," Quinn said. "For Willie and George Haywood it's very convenient timing."

"You have a suspicious mind, Quinn. If the incident in the café last night happened as you said it did, Willie will certainly have some legitimate explanation for her actions. She's a respectable businesswoman."

"Everyone in Chicote seems respectable," Quinn said. "Maybe if I hang around long enough some of the respectability will rub off on me."

The hospital was new and the cafeteria in the basement was light and airy with wide windows looking out on a plaza with a fountain. Beside one of the windows Martha O'Gorman was waiting at a small table. She looked neat and attractive in her white uniform. Her face, which Quinn had last seen twisted with anger, was now composed.

She spoke first. "Sit down, Mr. Quinn."

"Thank you."

"What's your pitch this time?"

"No pitch," Quinn said. "The umpire hasn't thrown the ball in yet."

She raised her eyebrows. "So you expect umpires in this dirty game? You *are* naïve. Umpires are to make sure of fair play, to protect both sides equally. That isn't how it's worked out for me and my children, let alone for my husband."

"I'm sorry, Mrs. O'Gorman. I wish I could—well, help."

"I've suffered more at the hands of people who tried to help me than I have at those of indifferent strangers."

"Then allow me to be an indifferent stranger."

She sat stiff and uncompromising, her hands folded on the table. "Let's not beat around the bush, Mr. Quinn. Why did some woman hire you to locate my husband?"

"That information was given to John Ronda in strict confidence," Quinn said, flushing. "I didn't expect him to repeat it."

"Then you're a poor judge of people. He's the town blabbermouth."

"Oh."

"Not that he intends any harm—blabbermouths never do, do they?—but he dearly loves to talk. And print. What about the woman, Mr. Quinn? What's her motive?"

"I really don't know. Ronda probably told you that, too, didn't he?"

"Oh, yes."

"I took the job because I needed it," Quinn said. "She didn't ask me for references, I didn't ask her. I assumed that Mr. O'Gorman was a relative or an old friend with whom she'd lost contact. Naturally, if I had known I was going to run into this kind of situation I'd have asked her more questions."

"How long has she been living with this cult, or whatever it is?"

"She claims that her son sends her a twenty-dollar bill every Christmas. She gave me a hundred and twenty dollars."

"Six years then," Martha O'Gorman said thoughtfully. "If she's been living apart from the world that long, it's possible she never found out Patrick is dead."

"Quite possible."

"What does she look like?"

Quinn described Sister Blessing as well as he could.

"I don't remember Patrick knowing anyone like that," Mrs. O'Gorman said. "We were married sixteen years ago, and his friends were my friends."

"My description of her isn't very good, I'm afraid. When a group of people all wear the same shapeless gray robes it's hard to differentiate them. That's probably the purpose of the robes, to suppress style and individuality. It works, anyway."

He realized, even as he spoke, that it was an exaggeration. Sister Blessing had managed to retain her individuality, and so, to a certain extent, had the others: Brother Light of the Infinite with his anxious concern for the livestock that were his responsibility, Sister Contrition trying to save her children from the evil ways of the world they would learn in school, Brother Tongue, mute, with only a little bird for his voice, Sister Glory of the Ascension thriftily constructing a mattress from the Brothers' hair, Brother of the Steady Heart wielding his razor with myopic zeal—they were, and always would be, individuals, not ants in an ant hill or bees in a beehive.

"She was once a nurse?" Martha O'Gorman said.

"So she told me."

"I know a lot of nurses now, of course, but I didn't in those days before I started to work here. Besides, most of the people Patrick and I considered our friends are still living in Chicote."

"Like John Ronda and his wife?"

"His wife, certainly. John, perhaps."

"And George Haywood?"

She hesitated, looking out at the fountain as if the moving water had half hypnotized her. "I've met Mr. Haywood, though not socially. A long time ago Patrick worked for him for a few weeks. It wasn't a satisfactory arrangement. Patrick was much too honest for that kind of job."

Her version, Quinn noted, was a lot different from Ronda's. "Are you acquainted with a Mrs. King, one of Haywood's associates?"

"No."

"What about Alberta Haywood?"

"The one who stole the money? I was never introduced to her but I used to see her occasionally in the bank when I cashed Patrick's paycheck. Why on earth are you asking me about all these people? They have nothing to do with Patrick or me. It's been seven years or more since Patrick worked for Mr. Haywood, and, I repeat, I never met him socially and I don't know either his associate or his sister."

"Your husband was a bookkeeper, Mrs. O'Gorman?"

She looked suddenly cautious. "Well, yes. He took a correspondence course. He didn't have a natural talent for figures, but—"

"But you helped him?"

"Sometimes. You got that from Ronda, I suppose. Well, it's no secret. It's a wife's job to help her husband when he needs it. I'm not ashamed either of helping him or of his needing help. I'm a realistic woman, Mr. Quinn, I don't fight facts. If Patrick was not overly endowed with brains, he could lean a little on mine, as I leaned, more than a little, on the fine qualities he possessed which I didn't, sweetness, generosity, tolerance. Those aren't my good points. They were Patrick's. We borrowed from each other, and we leaned on each other, and we had a full, happy life together."

Tears glistened in her eyes, and Quinn wondered whether they were caused by regrets for the once full and happy life or by a realization that it had not been as full or happy as she liked to pretend. Had the O'Gormans been an ideal couple,

74

or a couple whose ideals prevented any admission of failure? Had O'Gorman accepted the fact of his own inferiority with the same equanimity as his wife did?

"For a long time after Patrick's accident," she said, dabbing at her eyes with a handkerchief, "there were rumors, whispers, insinuations. People would stare at me and I could see them thinking, is that the Martha O'Gorman we know or is it some monster who would kill her husband for his insurance money? No, I wasn't imagining things, Mr. Quinn. My own friends were suspicious. Ask John Ronda, he was one of them. For me it was a double tragedy: I not only lost my husband, I was suspected of causing his death, either by murdering him or giving him reasons to end his own life."

"What reasons?"

"The obvious. He was henpecked, I was too bossy, I wore the pants for the family, that sort of thing. A few people, like Ronda and his wife, knew the truth, that there wouldn't have been any pants in the family to wear if I hadn't assumed responsibility. Patrick was kind, gentle, loving, but money meant nothing to him. Unpaid bills were no more than pieces of paper. I would have liked nothing better than to go out and take a job myself, but it would have destroyed Patrick's confidence in himself, which was never very high. I walked a tightrope between Patrick's weaknesses and his needs."

"Not many women could make a situation like that into a full and happy life."

"No?" she said. "You don't seem to know much about women."

"Granted."

"Or about love."

"Perhaps not. I'm trying to learn, though."

"I'm afraid you're too old to learn now," she said quietly. "Love happens while you're still young enough to endure the hardships it inflicts and while you're still able to roll with the punches or stagger to your feet after an eight-count. My son Richard," she added with a proud little smile, "is a fight fan, he's teaching me the jargon."

"Ronda tells me he's very bright."

"I think so, though I may be prejudiced."

"Tell me about your husband's accident, Mrs. O'Gorman."

Her gaze was steady and direct. "There's nothing to tell that wasn't in the file John Ronda lent to you yesterday afternoon."

"One thing wasn't mentioned. Did your husband's car have a heater in it?"

"No. We never spent money on luxuries."

"What was he wearing when he left the house?"

"You know what he was wearing, if you read my testimony at the inquest—a plaid flannel shirt, yellow and black."

"Was it raining that night?"

"Yes. It had been for several days."

"But Mr. O'Gorman didn't wear a raincoat or any kind of jacket?"

"I know what you're getting at," she said. "But it won't work. Patrick didn't need a raincoat because our garage is attached to the house, and at the oil field he parked in what used to be a plane hangar right next to his office. He didn't have to go out in the rain."

"It was cold as well as rainy, I understand."

"Patrick never minded the cold. He didn't even own a topcoat."

"According to a newspaper clipping from Ronda's file, the temperature that night was thirty-nine degrees, which is pretty cold."

"The shirt was wool," she said. "A heavy wool flannel. Besides, when he left the house he was in a big hurry. He was almost frantic to get to the office and correct the mistake he'd made before anyone found out about it."

"Frantic," Quinn repeated. It seemed a strong word to use, one that didn't fit the picture he had of O'Gorman as a quiet, low-pressure, unambitious man. "The accident occurred while he was on his way to the oil field?"

"Yes."

"If he was frantic and in a big hurry, it seems unlikely he'd have stopped to pick up a hitchhiker, doesn't it?"

"There was no hitchhiker," she said bluntly, "except in the busy little brains of Ronda and the sheriff. In addition to your argument, that Patrick was in too much of a rush, there's another: only a week before, a Chicote couple had been robbed by a hitchhiker and Patrick had given me his solemn promise that he would never again stop to pick up a strange man on the road."

"What about a woman? Or a man he knew?"

"What man? What woman? No one had a grudge against Patrick. And if anyone had asked him to hand over the money he had, Patrick would have done it quite willingly. No violence would have been necessary." She spread her hands in a gesture of resignation. "You see now why I know it was an accident. There's nothing to back up any other theory. Patrick was in a hurry, he drove faster than usual and visibility was poor on account of the heavy rain."

"You loved your husband very much, didn't you, Mrs. O'Gorman?"

"I would have done anything for him. Anything in the world. And I still—" She turned away, biting her underlip.

"You still would, Mrs. O'Gorman?"

"I meant, suppose something terrible happened inside Patrick that might—suppose he went suddenly and completely out of his mind—well, then if he ever comes back, or is ever found, I will stick by him."

"People don't go suddenly and completely out of their minds. There are always previous signs of disturbance. Did your husband show any such signs?"

"No."

"No fits of moodiness, temper tantrums, prolonged bouts of drinking, changes in such habits as sleeping, eating, dressing?"

"None," she said. "Perhaps he was quieter than he used to be, more thoughtful."

"By thoughtful, do you mean considerate or pensive?"

"Pensive. Once I jokingly accused him of having a daydream and he said it wasn't a daydream, it was a daymare. I remember it because it was such a funny word, one I'd never heard before. Have you?"

"Yes," Quinn said. "It's something you don't wake up from."

seven

The Haywood Realty Company occupied an air-conditioned office on the ground floor of a small hotel. Its walls were covered with maps of the city and county, an aerial photograph of Chicote, an engraving of Washington crossing the Delaware and another of Lincoln in his youth.

A sallow-faced young man in shirt sleeves identified himself as Earl Perkins. Although there were a number of desks with nameplates on them, Perkins was the only occupant of the office, and Quinn wondered whether business was so bad the others hadn't bothered to appear, or whether it was so good they were all out, like Willie King, showing property.

"When do you expect Mrs. King to be back?" Quinn said.

"Any time. And I mean just that, any time. People get away with murder in a place like this. There are no *rules*. Are you a business man, Mr.—?"

"Quinn. I'm in business, yes."

"Then you know that a business can't operate properly without hard and fast rules strictly adhered to by its employees. Without rules, what have we? Chaos."

Quinn glanced around the almost empty office. "Nice quiet kind of chaos."

"Chaos doesn't always show on the surface," Perkins said sourly. "For instance, my lunch hour is from twelve to one. It is now almost one, and I haven't eaten yet. A trivial example to you, perhaps, but not to me. *I* could have shown that property and been back here by eleven o'clock, because *I* don't fool around and then try to make up for it by buttering up the boss."

"How long has Mrs. King worked for Mr. Haywood?"

"I don't know. I was just hired last January."

"Is there a Mr. King?"

"Not in evidence," Perkins said with satisfaction. "She's a divorcée."

"Have you lived in Chicote very long?"

"All my life except for the two years I spent at San Jose State College. Can you beat that, two whole years of college and I end up—well. *Well*, it's about *time*."

The door opened with a blast of hot, dry air and Willie King came in, wearing a white sleeveless dress and a wide-brimmed straw hat. Because of the hat she didn't notice Quinn at first.

"I'm sorry I'm late, Earl."

"Well, I should *think* so," Perkins said. "My ulcer—"

"The place is as good as sold. I had to lie a little about the climate, though." She put her handbag on one of the desks, removed her hat, and saw Quinn. Except for a brief tightening of the mouth, her face didn't change expression. "I—I'm sorry, I didn't realize we had a client. Can I help you, sir?"

"Oh, I think so," Quinn said.

"I'll be with you in a minute. You'd better go and have your lunch now, Earl. And remember, no pepper, no ketchup."

"It's not pepper that's eating away my insides," Perkins said. "It's lack of *rules*."

"All right, you go and think up some good rules. Make a list."

"I already made a list."

"Make another one."

"By God, I will," Perkins said and slammed the door after him.

"He's only a boy," Willie King said in a maternal tone.

"Much too young to have ulcers. I don't suppose you have ulcers, Mr. Quinn?"

"I might acquire a few if I try to swallow some of the stories you tell, Mrs. King. With or without pepper and ketchup. Did you enjoy your trip to L.A.?"

"I changed my mind."

"You decided Chicote was couth enough for you after all?"

"What I said about Chicote still goes. It's a hole."

"Then crawl out of it."

"I might fall in a worse one," she said with a shrug of her bare shoulders. "Besides I have ties here. Connections."

"Such as Mr. Haywood."

"Mr. Haywood, naturally. He's my boss."

"Off the job as well as on?"

"I don't know what you're talking about," she said blandly. "Unless you could be referring to last night?"

"I could be, yes."

"As a matter of fact, that was entirely my own idea. I heard you talking to Mr. Ronda in his office when I went in with our ads for the next issue of the *Beacon*. You were discussing the O'Gorman case. Naturally my curiosity was aroused. To the people of Chicote the word O'Gorman is what the word *earthquake* is to San Franciscans. Everybody's got a story about it, or a theory. Everybody knew O'Gorman or claimed to have known him. So"—she paused and took a deep breath—"so I got this idea, that maybe you were working on the case and that you might have found a new lead, and that you and I—"

"You and I what?"

"We could solve the case together. Make a scoop. Become famous."

"That was your idea, eh? Dreams of glory?"

"Oh, it sounds kind of silly when I say it in cold blood like this, but that's the honest truth about why I picked you up and tried to pump you last night."

"And who," Quinn said, "was your friend?"

"What friend?"

"The man who searched my room."

"I know nothing about that," she said, frowning. "Maybe you're just making it up to confuse me."

"Where was George Haywood last night?"

"In bed with a cold, I guess. He's been away from the office all week, he has bronchitis. . . .Good heavens, you don't think for a minute that Mr. Haywood—"

"Yes, I think for a minute that Mr. Haywood got into my motel room while you were putting on your little act at El Bocado."

"Why, that's terrible," Willie King said vehemently. "That's just a terrible thing to think, it really is. Mr. Haywood is one of the most respected and well-liked businessmen in the whole community. He's a wonderful person."

"Chicote seems to have more wonderful people in it than heaven. But one of them got into my room by tricking an old man out of the key and I still think it was Haywood and that you helped him."

"That's libel. Or is it slander? I get them mixed up."

"You get a lot of things mixed up, Mrs. King. Now why don't you try telling the truth for a change? What's George Haywood's interest in me? What did he want from my room, and, more important, what did he get?"

"You'd realize how ridiculous all this is if you met Mr. Haywood."

"I'm trying to."

"Why?" Her face had turned almost as white as her dress.

"So I can ask him why he used you as a decoy to—"

"No. Please. You *can't* do that. He doesn't know anything about my picking you up in that awful place. He'd be mad if he found out about it, he might even fire me."

"Come off it, Mrs. King."

"No, I mean it. He's a stickler for conventions, especially since that business about his sister, Alberta. Because she did something wrong, he feels he's got to avoid the slightest hint of nonconformity or even bad taste. And that goes for his employees, too. Do you want to get me fired?"

"No."

"Then please don't tell him about last night. He'd never understand that I was just sort of playing a game—you know, Willie King, girl detective. Mr. Haywood isn't the type for games, he's too sober-minded. Promise you won't tell on me?"

"I might," Quinn said, "in return for a few favors."

Willie King studied him thoughtfully for a minute. "If you mean the kind I think you mean—"

"You read me wrong, Mrs. King. I only want to ask you a few questions."

"Ask ahead."

"Do you know Haywood's mother?"

"Do I not," Willie King said grimly. "What about her?"

"She had two daughters, didn't she?"

"Not to hear her tell it. George—Mr. Haywood isn't even allowed to mention their names, especially Alberta's."

"What happened to the other one?"

"Ruth? She ran away and got married to a man her mother didn't approve of, a fisherman from San Felice named Aguila. That was the end of her as far as the old girl was concerned."

"Where is Mrs. Aguila now?"

"In San Felice, I guess. Why?"

"Just checking."

"But why are you checking the Haywood family?" she said sharply. "Why aren't you talking to the people who knew O'Gorman?"

"Mr. Haywood knew him."

"Only very briefly, and in the line of business."

"So did Alberta Haywood."

"She may have met him, but I'm not even sure of that."

"George Haywood," Quinn said, "was very fond of his sister, is that right?"

"Yes, I suppose so."

"So fond, in fact, that after her embezzlement was discovered George himself had to answer a lot of questions from the police?"

It was only a guess on Quinn's part, and he was surprised

by the vehemence of her reaction. "They were more than questions, I can tell you. They were downright accusations with question marks. Where was the money? How much of it had Alberta lent or given to George? How could George have lived in the same house with her and not have guessed that she was up to something? Didn't he see the racing forms she brought home every day?"

"Well, didn't he?"

"No. She didn't take them home. Not a single copy was found in her room or anywhere else in the house."

"A careful lady, Alberta. Or else someone took the trouble to clean up after her. Did you know her, Mrs. King?"

"Not very well. Nobody did. I mean, she was one of those background people you see every day but you don't think of as a person until something happens."

" 'You don't think of as a person until something happens,' " Quinn repeated. "Perhaps that was her main motive, getting some attention."

"You're wrong," Willie King said with a brisk shake of her head. "She suffered horribly, incredibly. I went to the trial. It was terrible, it was like watching an animal that's been badly injured and can't tell you where it hurts so you can help."

"Yet George Haywood turned his back on her?"

"He had to. Oh, it must seem inhuman to you. You weren't there. I was. The old lady threw a fit every hour on the hour to prevent George from having anything to do with Alberta."

"Why all the vindictiveness on Mrs. Haywood's part?"

"It's in her nature, for one thing. For another, Alberta was always a disappointment to her mother. She was shy and plain, she didn't have boy friends, she didn't get married and produce children, she wasn't even interesting to live with. Years and years of disappointment to a woman like Mrs. Haywood —well, I got the impression she used the embezzlement as an excuse to do what she'd always wanted to do to Alberta, kick her out and have done with her, forget her." Willie King looked down at her hands, slim and pale, bare of rings. "Then there was George, of course, the apple of her eye. When his first wife died I think Mrs. Haywood would have danced in the streets if it hadn't been for the neighbors. It meant George belonged entirely to her again, head, heart and gall bladder. That woman is a monster. But don't let me go on about that. I could talk for weeks."

She didn't have to talk for weeks to make one point clear: the old lady and Willie King were fighting for the same man.

The telephone rang and Mrs. King answered it in a crisp, professional voice: "Haywood Realty Company. Yes . . . I'm sorry, the house across from Roosevelt Park didn't meet FHA specifications. We're going to work on another loan for you . . . Yes, as soon as possible." She put down the phone and made a little grimace in Quinn's direction. "Well, it's back to work for me. I hate to break this up, I've enjoyed talking to you, Mr. Quinn."

"Maybe you'd like to talk some more, say this evening?"

"I really couldn't."

"Why not? Taking a bus to L. A.?"

"Taking my kid sister to a movie."

"I'm sorry," Quinn said, rising. "Perhaps next time I come to town?"

"Are you leaving?"

"There's nothing to keep me here since you have a date with your kid sister."

"When are you coming back?"

"When do you want me to come back?"

Willie gave him a long, direct stare. "Stop kidding around. I know when a man's serious about wanting a date with me and when he's not. You're not. And I'm not."

"Then why are you interested in when I'm coming back?"

"I was merely being polite."

"Thanks," Quinn said. "And thanks for the information."

"You're welcome. Good-bye."

Quinn walked down the street to his car, drove a block west, made a u-turn and parked in the parking lot of a supermarket. From there he had a view of the Haywood Realty Company and the clock on top of the city hall.

At 1:30 Earl Perkins returned from lunch, looking as if it hadn't agreed with him. Two minutes later Willie King came out wearing the wide-brimmed straw hat and clutching her handbag. She looked flustered but determined as she climbed into her car and headed south.

Quinn followed her at a distance. Judging from the direct route she took to her destination, Quinn surmised that either she considered herself secure or she was in too much of a hurry to care.

She pulled into the driveway of an old frame house bearing a Haywood Realty "For Sale" sign on a porch pillar, unlocked the front door and went inside. For a minute Quinn thought he'd been mistaken about her after all—she was apparently doing just what she said she was going to do, get back to work. The house faced Roosevelt Park and was without doubt the one she had referred to on the telephone.

He was on the point of leaving when a green Pontiac station wagon stopped in front of the house and a man got out. In spite of the heat he wore a dark gray suit and a matching fedora. He was tall and thin and he walked with slow deliberation as if he'd been told not to hurry. Halfway up the porch steps he was seized by a fit of coughing. He leaned on the railing, holding one hand to his mouth and the other against his chest. When he had finished coughing he let himself into the house, using a key from a large key ring he pulled from his pocket.

Neat, safe and simple, Quinn thought. *When George and Willie want to get together without the old lady or anyone else knowing about it, they meet by prearrangement in one of Haywood Realty's vacant houses. Maybe a different house each time. And Willie's impassioned plea for me not to go to George and get her fired was just an attempt to prevent me from seeing him and asking questions. Well, it was a good performance, I almost fell for it. In fact, I almost fell for Willie.*

Quinn stared at the old frame house as if he were expecting one of the blinds to snap up and reveal some secrets. Nothing happened. It was a dead end and he knew it. Even if he waited and accosted George Haywood, he couldn't force any information out of him, he had no authority to ask him questions, and no proof that Haywood had been the man who had searched his motel room.

He turned on the ignition and pulled the car away from the curb. It was nearly two o'clock, checking-out time at the motel. By sticking to the mountain roads and by-passing San Felice, he figured he could reach the Tower by five.

Willie heard George's key in the lock and the front door open and close again. She wanted to run out into the hall and fling herself into his arms. Instead she waited, motionless, in the darkened living room, wondering whether the time would ever come when she would be able to act the way she felt in George's presence. Lately he seemed to discourage her enthusiasm as if he had too many serious problems on his mind to endure any extra demands on him.

"I'm in here, George." The empty room amplified her voice like an echo chamber. It sounded too hearty. She must remember to speak low.

George came in from the hall. He had taken off his hat and was holding it across his chest as if he were hearing the strains of "The Star-Spangled Banner." She felt a giggle tickling her throat and swallowed hard to suppress it.

"You were followed," he said.

"No. I swear I didn't see—"

"Quinn's car is parked across the street."

She raised a corner of one of the shades and looked out. "I don't see any car."

"It was there. I told you to be careful."

"I tried." The giggle in her throat had been replaced by a lump she couldn't do anything about except pretend it wasn't there. "Are you feeling better today, George?"

He shook his head impatiently as if there was no time to be bothered by such trivialities. "Quinn's on to something. He called the office and then the house. Mother brushed him off as I asked her to."

At the mere mention of Mrs. Haywood, Willie's body began to stiffen. "I could have done the same thing."

"I'm afraid you've lost his confidence."

"I don't think so. He asked me for a date tonight."

"Did you accept?"

"No."

"Why not?"

"I—didn't think you'd want me to."

"You might have gotten some useful information."

She stared at the old brick fireplace. She thought of all the fires that had been built there and left to die and she wondered if there'd ever be another one.

"If I've hurt your feelings," he said in a gentler voice, "I'm sorry, Willie."

"Don't be. Obviously you have more important matters on your mind than my feelings."

"I'm glad you see that."

"Oh, I do. You've made it quite clear."

He put his hands on her shoulders. "Willie, don't. Please. Be patient with me."

"If you'd only tell me what all this is about—"

"I can't. It's a serious business, though. A lot of people are involved, good people."

"Does it matter what kind of people they are? And how do you tell the difference between good people and bad people? Do you ask your mother?"

"Leave her out of it, please. She hasn't the faintest idea what's going on."

"I'll leave her out if she'll leave me out." She turned to face him, ready for a fight. But he looked too tired and pale to endure a fight. "Forget it, George. Let's go out and come in again, shall we?"

"All right."

"Hello, George."

He smiled. "Hello, Willie."

"How are you?"

"Fine. And you?"

"I'm fine, too." But she turned her face away from his kiss. "This isn't much better than the first time, is it? You're not really thinking of me, you're thinking of Quinn. Aren't you?"

"I'm forced to."

"Not for long."

"What do you mean, not for long?"

"He's leaving town."

George's hands dropped to his sides as if she'd slapped them down. "When?"

"This afternoon, I guess. Maybe right this minute."

"Why? Why is he leaving?"

"He said he had no reason to stay since I wouldn't go out with him tonight. Naturally he was joking."

She waited, hoping George would deny it: *Of course Quinn wasn't joking, my dear. You're a very attractive woman. He's probably leaving town to avoid a broken heart.*

"He was joking," she repeated.

But George didn't even hear her this time. He was crossing the room, putting on his hat as he moved.

"George?"

"I'll call you in the morning."

"Where are you going? We haven't even talked yet, George."

"I haven't time right now. I'm showing a client the Wilson house out in Greenacres."

She knew the Wilson property was being handled by Earl Perkins and that George wouldn't interfere, but she didn't argue.

At the archway that led into the hall he turned and looked back at her. "Do me a favor, will you, Willie?"

"Certainly. You're the boss."

"Tell my mother I won't be home for dinner and not to wait up for me."

"All right."

It was a big favor and they both knew it.

Willie stood, listening to the front door open and close, then the sound of the station wagon motor and the squeaking of tires as the car made too quick a start. Head bowed, she walked over to the old fireplace. The inside was charred by the heat of a thousand fires. She stretched her hands out in front of her as if one of the fires might have left a little warmth for her.

After a time she went outside, locking the house behind her, and drove to the post office. Here, from a pay phone, she called George's house.

"Mrs. Haywood?"

"Yes."

"This is Willie King."

"Mrs. King, yes, of course. My son is not at home."

Willie clenched her jaws. In all their conversations Mrs. Haywood never referred to George as anything but *my son*, with a distinct emphasis on the *my*. "Yes, I know that, Mrs. Haywood. He asked me to tell you he'll be away for the evening."

"Away where?"

"I don't know."

"Then he won't be with you?"

"No."

"He's been away a great many evenings lately, and days, too."

"He has a business to run," Willie said.

"And of course you're a big help to him?"

"I try to be."

"Oh, but you are. He tells me you're a most *aggressive* salesman—or is it saleswoman? One thing baffles me about my son's business. I find it quite extraordinary the number of real estate deals that are consummated at night—the word *is* consummated, isn't it?"

"The word is whatever you want to make it, Mrs. Haywood."

There was a brief silence during which Willie put her hand over the receiver so that Mrs. Haywood wouldn't hear her angry breathing.

"Mrs. King, you and I are both fond of George, aren't we?"

89

I am, Willie thought. *You're not fond of anything*. But she said, "Yes."

"Has it occurred to you to wonder, perhaps, exactly where he's going tonight?"

"That's his business."

"And not yours?"

"No." *Not yet*, she added silently.

"Dear me, I think it should be your business if you're as interested in my son as you appear to be. He is, of course, a man of fine character, but he's human and there are temptresses around."

"Are you urging me to spy on him, Mrs. Haywood?"

"Using one's eyes and ears is not spying, surely." There was another silence, as if Mrs. Haywood was taking time out to plan a more devastating attack. But when she spoke again her voice sounded curiously broken. "I have this feeling, this very terrible feeling, that George is in trouble. . . . Oh, you and I have never been friendly, Mrs. King, but I haven't considered you a real threat to George's welfare."

"Thank you," Willie said dryly. She was puzzled by Mrs. Haywood's sudden change of voice and attitude. "I have no reason to believe George is in trouble he can't handle."

"He is. I feel it, I know it. It involves a woman."

"A woman? I'm sure you're mistaken."

"I wish I were but I'm not. There have been too many things recently, too many unexplained out-of-town trips. Where does he go? What does he do? Whom does he see?"

"Have you asked him?"

"Yes. He told me nothing, but he couldn't hide his guilt. And what else besides a woman would he be feeling guilty about?"

"I'm quite sure you're mistaken," Willie said again. But this time she could hear the doubt in her own voice, and for a long time after she'd hung up she remained in the cramped, airless booth, her forehead resting against the telephone.

eight

Finding the dirt lane that led to the Tower was more difficult than Quinn thought it was going to be. He went two or three miles beyond it before he realized he had missed it. He made a precarious turn, and driving very slowly, in low gear, he tried to spot the only landmark he could recall, the grove of eucalyptus trees. The piercing sun, the strain of driving around endless blind curves, the utter desolation of the country, were beginning to fray his nerves and undermine his confidence. Ideas that had seemed good in Chicote, decisions that had seemed right, looked frail and foolish against the bleak, brown landscape; and the search for O'Gorman seemed unreal, absurd, a fox hunt without a fox.

A young doe bounded out from a clump of scrub oak and leaped gracefully across the road in front of him, avoiding the bumper of the car by inches. She looked healthy and well-nourished. Quinn thought, *She didn't get that way on the food supply she'd find around here at this time of year. I must be near irrigated land.*

He stopped the car at the top of the next hill and looked around. In the distance, to the east, he saw something glisten in the slanting rays of the sun. It was his first view of the Tower itself, a mere reflection of light from glass.

He released the brake and the car rolled silently down the hill. Half a mile farther on he spotted the grove of eucalyptus trees and the narrow dirt lane. Once he was on it he had a strange feeling of returning home. He was even a little excited at the prospect of being greeted, welcomed back. Then he saw one of the Brothers plodding along the road ahead of him. He honked the horn as he came alongside.

It was Brother Crown of Thorns, who had driven him to San Felice the previous morning.

"One good lift deserves another," Quinn said, leaning across the seat to open the door. "Get in, Brother."

Brother Crown stood rigid, his arms folded inside his robe. "We been expecting you, Mr. Quinn."

"Good."

"Not good, not good at all."

"What's the matter?"

"Pull your car off the road and leave it here," Brother Crown said shortly. "I got orders to take you to the Master."

"Good." Quinn parked the car and got out. "Or isn't that good, either?"

"A stranger snooping around inside the Tower is tempting the devil to destroy us all, but the Master says he wants to talk to you."

"Where is Sister Blessing?"

"In torment for her sins."

"Just what does that mean, Brother?"

"Money is the source of all evil." Brother Crown turned, spat on the ground, and wiped his mouth with the back of his hand before adding, "Amen."

"Amen. But we weren't talking about money."

"You were. Yesterday morning. I heard you say to her, 'About the money . . .' I heard it and I had to tell the Master. It is one of our rules, the Master's got to know everything so's he can protect us against ourselves."

"Where is Sister Blessing?" Quinn repeated.

Brother Crown merely shook his head and started walking up the dusty road. After a moment's hesitation Quinn followed him. They passed the communal dining hall, the storage shed where Quinn had spent the night, and a couple of small buildings which he hadn't seen before. Fifty yards beyond the path rose sharply, and the steepness of the ascent and the unaccustomed altitude made Quinn breathe heavily and rapidly.

Brother Crown paused for a minute and looked back at him with contempt. "Soft living. Weak constitution. Flabby muscles."

"My tongue's not flabby, though," Quinn said. "I don't tattle to the teacher."

"The Master's got to be told everything," Brother Crown said, flushing. "I acted for Sister Blessing's own good. We got to be saved from ourselves and the devil that's in us. We all carry a devil around inside us gnawing our innards."

"So that's it. I thought my liver was acting up again."

"Have your jokes. Laugh on earth, weep through eternity."

"I'll buy that."

"Buy," Brother Crown said. "Money. Hell words leading to everlasting damnation. Take off your shoes."

"Why?"

"This here's consecrated ground."

In a clearing, on top of the hill, the Tower rose five stories into the sky. It was made of glass and redwood in the shape of a pentagon surrounding an inner court.

Quinn left his shoes outside the entrance arch which bore an engraved inscription: THE KINGDOM OF HEAVEN IS WAITING FOR ALL TRUE BELIEVERS. REPENT AND REJOICE. From the inner court scrubbed wooden steps with a rope guardrail led up the five levels of the Tower.

"You're supposed to go up alone," Brother Crown said.

"Why?"

"When the Master gives an order or makes a suggestion, it don't pay to ask why."

Quinn started up the stairs. At each level heavy oak doors led into what he decided must be the living quarters of the cultists. There were no windows opening onto the court except at the fifth level. Here Quinn found the door open.

A deep, resonant voice said, "Come in. Please close the door behind you, I feel a draft."

Quinn went inside, and in that first instant he realized why the Tower had been built there in the wilderness and why the old lady whose money had built it felt that she was getting closer to heaven. The expanse of light and sky was almost too much for the eye to take in. Windows on all five sides revealed mountains beyond mountains, and three thousand feet below lay a blue lake in a green valley like a diamond on a leaf.

The scenery was so overpowering that the people in the room seemed of no importance. There were two of them, a man and a woman wearing identical white wool robes loosely belted with scarlet satin. The woman was very old. Her body had shriveled with the years until it was no larger than a little girl's, and her face was as creased and brown as a walnut. She sat on a bench looking up at the sky as if she expected it to open for her.

The man could have been anywhere from fifty to seventy years old. He had a gaunt, intelligent face, and eyes that burned like phosphorus at room temperature. Sitting cross-legged on the floor, he was working on a small hand loom.

"I am the Master," he said easily and without self-consciousness. "This is Mother Pureza. We bid you welcome and wish you well."

"*Buena acogida,*" the woman said as if she were translating the words to a fourth person present who couldn't understand English. "*Salud.*"

"We bear you no malice."

"*No estamos malicios.*"

"Mother Pureza, it is not necessary for you to translate for Mr. Quinn."

The woman turned and gave him a stubborn look. "I like to hear my native tongue."

"And so do I, at the proper time and place. Now if you will kindly excuse us, Mr. Quinn and I have some matters to discuss."

"I want to stay and listen," she said querulously. "It gets lonely waiting all by myself for the doors of the Kingdom to open and receive me."

"God is always with you, Mother Pureza."

"I wish He'd say something. I get so lonely, waiting, watching. . . . Who is that young man? Why is he here in my Tower?"

"Mr. Quinn has come to see Sister Blessing."

"Oh, oh, oh, he can't do that!"

"That is what I must explain to him, in private." The Master put a firm hand on her elbow and guided her to the steps. "Be careful going down, Pureza. It is a long fall to the inner court."

"Tell the young man that if he wants to visit my Tower he must wait for an engraved invitation from my secretary, Capirote. Send for Capirote immediately."

"Capirote isn't here, Pureza. That was a long time ago. Now take hold of the guardrail and walk slowly."

The Master closed the door quietly and returned to his position at the loom.

"Her Tower?" Quinn said.

"She commissioned it to be constructed. Now it belongs to us all. There is no private property in our community unless someone commits a material sin like our poor Sister Blessing." He held up one hand in a silencing gesture. "Please make no denials, Mr. Quinn. Sister Blessing has confessed in full and is repenting in full."

"I want to see her. Where is she?"

"What you want doesn't carry much weight with us. When you trespassed upon our property, you were, in a sense, entering another country with a different constitution, a different set of laws."

"I gather it's still part of the Union," Quinn said. "Or is it?"

"There has been no formal secession, that is true. But we do not accept as law what we do not believe to be right."

"By 'we' you mean 'I,' don't you?"

"I have been chosen to receive revelations and visions beyond the others. However, I am only an instrument of the divine will, a mere servant among its other servants. . . . I can see I am not convincing you."

"No." Quinn wondered what the man had been in real life besides a failure. "You wanted to talk to me. What about?"

"Money."

"I thought that was a dirty word around here."

"It is sometimes necessary to use dirty words to describe dirty transactions, such as accepting a large sum of money from a woman for performing a very small service." He touched his forehead with his right hand while his left pointed to the sky. "You see, I know everything."

"You didn't get it in a vision," Quinn said. "And accepting a large sum of money from a woman doesn't seem to have bothered you much. This place wasn't built with green stamps."

"Hold your vicious tongue, Mr. Quinn, and I shall hold my temper, which can be equally vicious, I assure you. Mother Pureza is my wife, dedicated to my work, sharing my visions of the glory that awaits us. Oh, the glory, oh, if you could see the glory, you would understand why we are all here." The Master's face underwent an abrupt, unexplained change. The visionary suddenly became the realist. "You wish to make your report to Sister Blessing about the man O'Gorman?"

"I not only wish to, I intend to."

"That will be impossible. She is in isolation, renewing her vows of renunciation, a trivial punishment considering the magnitude of her sins, concealing money, withholding it from the common fund, trying to reëstablish contact with the world she promised to leave behind her. These are grave infractions of our laws. She could have been banished from our midst entirely but the Lord told me in a vision to spare her."

The Lord, Quinn thought, *plus a little common sense. Sister Blessing's too useful to banish. There wouldn't be anybody left to keep the rest of them healthy while waiting to die.*

"You are to make your report to me," the Master said. "I will see that she gets it."

"Sorry, my instructions were specific. No Sister, no report."

"Very well. No report, no money. I demand an immediate return of what is left of the sum Sister Blessing gave you. That seems to me quite a fair and just idea."

"There's only one thing the matter with it," Quinn said. "The money's gone."

The Master pushed the loom aside with a sweep of his hand. "You spent a hundred and twenty dollars in a day and a half? You're lying."

"Living costs have gone up in my part of the Union."

"You gambled it away, is that it? Gambled and boozed and debauched—"

"Yes, I had a pretty busy time what with one thing and another. Now I'd like to do what I was paid to do and get out of here. The climate in your country doesn't agree with me, there's too much hot air."

A rush of blood stained the Master's face and neck but he said in a controlled voice, "I have long since been accustomed to the gibes of the ignorant and the unbelievers. I can only warn you that the Lord will smite you with the sword of His wrath."

"Consider me smote." Quinn's tone was considerably lighter than his feelings. The place was beginning to oppress him, the glorification of death hung over it as the smell of oil hung over Chicote. He thought, *Once you get the idea that dying is great, it's an easy step up to thinking you're doing someone a favor by helping him die. The old boy's been harmless so far but his next vision might have me in a featured role.*

"Let's quit playing games," Quinn said. "I came to see Sister Blessing. Aside from the fact that she paid me to do a job, I happen to like her, and I want to make sure she's all right. Now it's no secret that you've had some trouble with the law—the law of my part of the Union, of course—and you just might be asking for more."

"Is that a threat?"

"That's exactly what it is, Master. I'm not leaving here until I assure myself that Sister Blessing is alive and in good health, as she was yesterday morning when I left here."

"Why shouldn't she be alive? What kind of nonsense is this? You talk as if we were barbarians, savages, maniacs—"

"You're close."

The Master got clumsily to his feet, kicking aside the loom. It crashed against the wall. "Leave. Leave here immediately, or I will not be responsible for what happens to you. Get out of my sight."

Suddenly the door opened and Mother Pureza came in

97

making little clucking noises with her tongue. "Oh, that's not polite, Harry. It really isn't polite after I sent him an engraved invitation through Capirote."

"Oh God," the Master said and covered his face with his hands.

"And you needn't scold me for eavesdropping, either. I told you I was lonely, *triste, desamparada*—"

"You have not been abandoned, Pureza."

"Then where *is* everybody? Where is Mama, and Dolores who brought my breakfast, and Pedro who polished my riding boots, and Capirote? Where *is* everybody? Where have they all gone, Harry? Why didn't they take me with them? Oh Harry, why didn't they wait for me?"

"Hush now, Pureza. You must be patient." He crossed the room and took her in his arms and patted her thinning hair, her emaciated shoulders. "You must not lose courage, Pureza. Soon you will see them all again."

"Will Dolores bring me breakfast in bed?"

"Yes."

"And Pedro, may I hit him with my riding crop if he doesn't listen to me?"

"Yes." The Master's voice was an exhausted whisper. "Whatever you like."

"I might hit you too, Harry."

"All right."

"Not hard, though. Just a tap on the dome to sting a little and let you know I'm alive. . . . But I won't *be* alive then, Harry. I won't *be* alive. Oh, I'm so confused. How can I give you a little tap on the dome to let you know I'm alive when I won't *be* alive?"

"I don't know. Please stop it. Please be quiet and go to your room."

"You never help me think any more," she said, moving her head back and forth. "You used to help me think, you used to explain everything to me. Now you tell me to be quiet, to go to my room, to watch the sky and wait. Why did we come here, Harry? I know there was a reason."

"For eternal salvation."

"Is that all? . . . Oh, oh, oh, there's a strange young man standing over there, Harry. Tell Capirote to show him out, and in the future not to admit anyone without a proper calling card. And hurry up about it. My orders are to be obeyed immediately, I am Dona Isabella Constancia Querida Felicia de la Guerra."

"No, no, you are Mother Pureza," the Master said softly. "And you are going to your room to take a rest."

"But why?"

"Because you are tired."

"I am not tired. I am lonely. You're the one who's tired, aren't you, Harry?"

"Perhaps."

"So tired. Poor Harry, *muy amado mio.*"

"I'll help you, Pureza. Hang onto my arm."

Over the old woman's head he beckoned to Quinn to follow, and the three of them started off down the stairs. At the fourth level the Master opened the door and Mother Pureza went inside with just one small moan of protest. The Master leaned against the door and closed his eyes. A minute went by, two minutes. Quinn was beginning to think the man was in a trance or had gone to sleep standing up.

Suddenly his eyes opened. He touched his forehead. "I feel your pity, Mr. Quinn. I do not accept it, you are wasting your time and energy on pity as I wasted mine on anger. You observe I am no longer angry? Kicking a loom, how trivial it was, how small it will look in eternity. I am purified, I am cleansed."

"Good for you," Quinn said. "Now I'd like to see Sister Blessing."

"Very well, you'll see her. You'll regret your evil thoughts and dark suspicions. She is in spiritual isolation. Did I put her there? No, she went of her own accord. She is renewing her vows of renunciation. At my insistence? No, no, Mr. Quinn. At her own. Your simple mind cannot grasp the situation."

"It can try."

"In spiritual isolation, the senses do not exist. The eyes do not see, the ears do not hear, the flesh cannot feel. Perhaps, if the isolation is complete, she will not even know you are there."

"Then again perhaps she will. Especially if I can see her alone."

"Of course. I have total faith in the Sister's devotion to the spirit."

She was in a small square room on the ground floor. It contained no furniture but the wooden bench she sat on, facing the window, in a shaft of sunlight. Sweat, or tears, had streaked her forehead and cheeks, and there were moist patches on her robe. When Quinn spoke her name she didn't answer but her hunched shoulders twitched and her eyelids blinked.

"Sister Blessing, you asked me to come back and I did."

She turned and looked at him, mute and suffering. The fright in her eyes was so intense that Quinn felt like shouting at her: *Snap out of it, get away from this bughouse before you're as nutty as the old woman, recognize the Master for what he is, a schizo and a fear peddler. His racket's as old as the hills. It doesn't take the curse off it because he believes in it himself, it only makes it doubly dangerous.*

He said, in a conversational tone, "Remember those pink fuzzy slippers you told me you saw in a Sears catalogue? There was a pair just like that in a store window in Chicote."

For a moment something besides fear showed in her eyes, interest, curiosity. Then it was gone, and she was speaking in a listless monotone: "I have renounced the world and its evils. I have renounced the flesh and its weakness. I seek the solace of the spirit, the salvation of the soul."

"It's lucky you don't lisp," Quinn said, trying to coax a smile out of her. "I didn't find O'Gorman, by the way. He disappeared five and a half years ago. His wife thinks she's a widow, so do a lot of other people. What do you think?"

"Having done without comfort, I will be comforted by the Lord. Having hungered, I will feast."

"Did you know O'Gorman? Was he a friend of yours?"

"Having trod the rough earth, my feet uncovered, I will walk the smooth and golden streets of heaven."

"Maybe you'll meet O'Gorman," Quinn said. "He seems to have been a good man, no enemies, nice wife and kids. In fact, a very nice wife, it's too bad she's wasting her life in uncertainty. I think if she knew definitely that O'Gorman wasn't coming back, she could start living again. You're listening, Sister. You're hearing me. Answer just one question, will O'Gorman be coming back?"

"Having here forsaken the pride of ornament, I will be of infinite beauty. Having humbled myself in the fields, I will walk tall and straight in the hereafter, which does belong to the True Believers. Amen."

"I'm going back to Chicote, Sister. Have you any message for Martha O'Gorman? She deserves a break. Give it to her if you can, Sister. You're a generous woman."

"I have renounced the world and its evils. I have renounced the flesh and its weakness. Having done without comfort—"

"Sister, listen to me."

"—I will be comforted by the Lord. Having hungered, I will feast. Having trod the rough earth, my feet uncovered, I will walk the smooth and golden streets of heaven. Having here forsaken the pride of ornament, I will be of infinite beauty."

Quinn went out and closed the door quietly. Sister Blessing was as far beyond reach as O'Gorman.

nine

The inner court contained rows of crude wooden benches placed around a stone shrine that reminded Quinn of a barbecue pit. The Master was standing in front of the shrine, head bowed, arms folded across his chest.

He said, without turning, "Well, Mr. Quinn? You found Sister Blessing alive and in good health?"

"I found her alive."

"And you are still not satisfied?"

"No," Quinn said. "I'd like to know a lot more about this place and the people in it, their names, occupations, where they came from."

"And what, pray, would you do with such information?"

"Try to solve the O'Gorman case."

"You're a stranger to me, Mr. Quinn. I have no obligations to you, but purely out of generosity I'll tell you one thing. The name O'Gorman is unknown here."

"Sister Blessing just picked it out of a hat?"

"Out of a dream," the Master said quietly. "Or you would call it a dream. I do not. I think the spirit of Patrick O'Gorman is wandering in hell, seeking salvation. He spoke to Sister, he asked her help because that is her name, Sister Blessing of the Salvation. Otherwise he would have chosen me to help him since I am the Master."

Quinn stared at him. The man obviously believed what he was saying. It would be useless to argue with him, possibly dangerous. "Why is O'Gorman in hell, Master? All indications are that he led an exemplary life, according to his lights."

"He was not a True Believer. Now, of course, he repents, he pleads for a second chance. He calls out to the Sister while she is asleep and her mind is receptive to his vibrations. The good Sister was both curious and afraid. The combination dulled her wits and made her do a very foolish thing."

"Hiring me."

"Yes." There was a trace of pity in the Master's faint smile. "You see, Mr. Quinn, you were asked to find someone who is wandering through the eternal abysses of hell. A formidable task, even for a brash young man like you, don't you agree?"

"If I accepted your premise, I'd have to agree."

"But you don't."

"No."

"You have a better premise, Mr. Quinn?"

"I think Sister Blessing may have known O'Gorman years ago, before she came here."

"You are quite wrong," the Master said calmly. "The good Sister never even heard the name until O'Gorman communicated with her from the depths of hell, seeking salvation. My heart bleeds for that poor miserable wretch, but what can I do? His repentance came too late, he will suffer throughout eternity for his ignorance and self-indulgence. Beware, Mr. Quinn, beware. It will happen to you unless you change your ways and renounce the world and its evils, the flesh and its weakness."

"Thanks for the advice, Master."

"It is not advice. It is a warning. Renounce and be saved. Repent and rejoice. . . . You see Mother Pureza as an old woman, frail of body and sick of mind. I see her as a creature of God, one of the Chosen."

"Also one of the taken," Quinn said. "Just how much of her money was spent on this place?"

"You cannot make me angry again, Mr. Quinn. I regret that you are trying to. Have I not treated you with consideration? Answered your questions? Allowed you to see Sister Blessing? And still you are not satisfied? You are a greedy man."

"I want to find out what happened to O'Gorman so I can tell his wife the truth."

"Tell her Patrick O'Gorman is wandering in hell, suffering the torments of the forever damned. That is the truth."

Outside, Quinn put his shoes back on and straightened his tie while the Master watched from the arched doorway. The sun was beginning to set and smoke was rising from the chimney of the dining hall straight into the windless air. The only members of the cult in sight were Sister Contrition's two smaller children sliding on flattened cardboard boxes down an incline slippery with pine needles, and Brother Tongue of Prophets approaching the entrance of the Tower carrying his little bird in a cage. Behind him, puffing and red-faced, trotted Brother of the Steady Heart, who had shaved Quinn the previous morning.

The Brothers greeted the Master by touching their foreheads and bowing. Then they nodded politely in Quinn's direction.

"Peace be with you, Brothers," the Master said.

"Peace be with you," Brother Heart echoed.

"What brings you here?"

"Brother Tongue thinks his parakeet is sick. He wants Sister Blessing to look at it."

"Sister Blessing is in isolation."

"The parakeet is acting very funny," Brother Heart said apologetically. "Show the Master, Brother Tongue."

Brother Tongue put his head on his shoulder and pressed his hand against his mouth.

"The bird no longer speaks," Brother Heart translated, "and sits with his head hidden."

Brother Tongue pointed to his chest and moved his hand rapidly back and forth.

"The bird's pulse is very fast," Brother Heart said. "It has palpitations. Brother Tongue is very worried, he wants the Sister to—"

"Sister Blessing is in isolation," the Master repeated sharply. "The bird looks perfectly all right to me. Perhaps it's as tired of talking as I am of listening. Place a cover over its cage and let it rest. All birds have accelerated heartbeats, it's quite normal, nothing to worry about."

Brother Tongue's mouth quivered and Brother Heart

emitted a long deep sigh, but neither of them put up an argument. They disappeared around the corner of the building, their bare feet leaving little puffs of dust.

The brief encounter puzzled Quinn. The bird had looked to him, as well as to the Master, in good health, and he wondered if it had been used as an excuse to obtain permission to see Sister Blessing. *Or perhaps,* he thought, *to take another look at me. No, I'm getting too suspicious. Another couple of hours in this place and I'll be receiving O'Gorman's vibrations from hell. I'd better flake off.*

The Master had the same idea at the same time. "I can waste no more of my strength on you, Mr. Quinn. You must leave now."

"All right."

"Tell Mrs. O'Gorman my prayers are being offered to ease her husband's agony."

"I don't think that will be much of a consolation."

"It is not my fault he went to hell. If he had come to me I would have saved him. . . . Peace be with you, Mr. Quinn. I shall not expect you back, unless you come humbly and penitently as a convert."

"I'd prefer an engraved invitation from Capirote," Quinn said, but the Master had already closed the door.

Quinn walked back to the dirt lane. About a dozen Brothers and Sisters were standing in front of the dining hall when he passed but none of them greeted him. Only one glanced curiously in his direction, and Quinn recognized the leather-skinned face of Brother Light of the Infinite, the man who'd come to the storage shed to rid the mattress of fleas. It was as if the whole colony had been warned to ignore Quinn's presence because he was a threat to them. But as soon as he walked past he could feel a dozen pairs of eyes on the back of his neck.

The feeling persisted even after he'd reached his car and there was no one in sight. Each tree looked as if it had a Brother or Sister stationed behind it to watch him.

He released the brake and the car started coasting down the

dirt lane. His mind went back to his first departure from the Tower, with Brother Crown driving the dilapidated truck before the sun came up. There had been, he recalled, a reason for the timing: to get the truck away from the place before Sister Contrition's oldest daughter, Karma, tried to hitch a ride to the city.

Quinn broke out in a sweat. The eyes on the back of his neck felt like crawling insects. His hand reached up to rub them off and found nothing but his own cold damp skin.

He said aloud, "Karma?"

There was no answer.

He had reached the main road by this time. He stopped the car, turned off the ignition and got out. Then he opened the back door. "This is the end of the line, friend."

The gray bundle on the floor stirred and whimpered.

"Come on," Quinn said. "You can make it back to the Tower before it gets dark if you start now."

Karma's long black hair appeared, then her face, blotched with pimples, sullen with resentment. "I'm not going back."

"A little bird tells me you are."

"I hate little birds. I hate Brother Tongue. I hate the Master and Mother Pureza and Brother Crown and Sister Glory. Most of all I hate my own mother and those awful yapping children. Yes, and I even hate Sister Blessing."

"That's a heap of hate," Quinn said.

"There's more. I hate Brother Behold the Vision because his teeth click when he eats and I hate Brother Light because he called me lazy, and I hate—"

"All right, all right, I'm convinced you're a first-class hater. Now get out of there. Start moving."

"Please, please take me with you. I won't be a nuisance, I won't even speak. You can pretend I'm not here. When we reach the city I'll find a job. I'm not lazy the way Brother Light claims I am. . . . You're going to say no, aren't you?"

"Yes, I'm going to say no."

"Is it because you think I'm just a child?"

"There are other reasons, Karma. Now be a good girl, save us both a lot of trouble—"

"I'm already in trouble," she said calmly. "So are you. I hear things."

"What things?"

She sat up on the back seat, tucking her long hair behind her ears. "Oh, things. They talk in front of me as if I were too young to understand."

"Did Sister Blessing talk in front of you?"

"All of them."

"It's Sister Blessing in particular that I'm interested in," Quinn said.

"She talks plenty."

"About me?"

"Yes."

"What did she tell you?"

"Oh, things."

He gave her a hard look. "You're giving me the run-around, Karma, stalling for time. It won't do any good. Come out of there before I drag you out by the hair."

"I'll scream. I'm a good screamer and sounds carry in the mountains. They'll all hear me, they'll think you tried to kidnap me. The Master will be furious, he may even kill you. He has a terrible temper."

"He may also kill you."

"I don't care. I have nothing to live for."

"All right, you asked for it."

Quinn reached into the back seat to grab her. She took a long deep breath and opened her mouth to scream. He cut off the sound by pressing his hand against her mouth.

"Listen, you crazy kid. You'll get us both in a mess. I can't possibly take you with me to San Felice. You're going to need money, clothes, someone to look after you. You may not like it here but at least you're protected. Wait until you're older, then you can leave under your own power. Are you listening to me, Karma?"

She nodded.

"If I take my hand away, will you promise to be quiet and discuss this in a reasonable way?"

She nodded again.

"All right." He removed his hand from her mouth and leaned wearily against the back of the seat. "Did I hurt you?"

"No."

"How old are you, Karma?"

"Going on twenty-one."

"Sure, but how far have you got to go? Come on, the truth."

"I'm sixteen," she said, after a time. "But I could easily find a job in the city and earn money to buy some stuff for my face so I'll look like other girls."

"You have a very pretty face."

"No, it's terrible, all these terrible red things that they say I'll grow out of but I don't. I never will. I need money for the stuff to make them go away. One of my teachers told me about it last year when I went to school, acne ointment she called it. She was real nice, she said she used to have acne herself and she knew how I felt."

"And that's the reason you want to go to the city, to buy acne ointment?"

"Well, that's what I'd do first," she said, running her hands along her cheeks. "I need it very bad."

"Suppose I promise you that I'll buy some for you and see that you get it? Will you postpone your trip to the city until you're a little more capable of looking after yourself?"

She thought about it for a long time, twisting and untwisting a strand of her hair. "You're just trying to get rid of me."

"That's true. But I'd also like to help you."

"When could you get it for me?"

"As soon as possible."

"How would you know it's the right stuff?"

"I'll ask the pharmacist, the man who sells it."

She turned and looked up at him, very earnestly. "Do you think I will be pretty, as pretty as the girls at school?"

"Of course you will."

It was getting quite dark but she made no move to get out of the car and go back to the Tower. "Everyone here is so ugly," she said. "And dirty. The floors are cleaner than we are. At school there were showers with hot water and real soap, and each of us had a big white towel all to ourselves."

"How long have you been here at the Tower, Karma?"

"Four years, since it was built."

"And before then?"

"We were at some place in the mountains, the San Gabriel Mountains down south. It was just a lot of wooden shacks. Then Mother Pureza came along and we got the Tower."

"She was a convert?"

"Yes, a rich one. We don't get many rich ones. I guess the rich ones are too busy having fun spending their money to worry about the hereafter."

"Are you worried, Karma?"

"The Master scares me with his funny eyes," she said. "But with Sister Blessing I'm not scared. I don't really hate her the way I said I did. She prays every day for my acne."

"Do you know where she is now?"

"Everyone does. She's in isolation."

"For how long?"

"Five days. Punishment always last five days."

"Do you know the reason she's being punished?"

Karma shook her head. "There was a lot of whispering I couldn't hear, between her and the Master and Brother Crown. Then when my mother and I went to make dinner yesterday at noon, Sister Blessing was gone and Brother Tongue was crouched by the stove, crying. He just worships Sister Blessing because she babies him and makes a big fuss over him when he's sick. The only one that acted glad was Brother Crown and he's meaner than Satan."

"How long has Brother Crown been a convert?"

"He came about a year after the Tower was built. That would be three years ago."

"What about Sister Blessing?"

"She was with us in the San Gabriel Mountains. Nearly all the rest were, too, including a lot that have gone away since because they quarreled with the Master, like my father."

"Where's your father now, Karma?"

"I don't know," she said in a whisper. "And I can't ask. When someone is banished his name can never be mentioned again."

"Have you ever heard anyone here refer to a man called Patrick O'Gorman?"

"No."

"Can you remember that name, Patrick O'Gorman?"

"Yes. Why?"

"I'd appreciate it if you'd keep your ears open for it," Quinn said. "You needn't tell anyone I asked you to do this, it's strictly between you and me, like the ointment. Is it a bargain?"

"Yes." She touched her cheeks, her forehead, her chin. "Do you really and honestly think I will be pretty when my acne goes away?"

"I know it."

"How will you send me the ointment? The Master opens all the mail packages and he'd just throw something out if he thought it was drugs. He doesn't believe in drugs or doctors, only faith."

"I'll bring the stuff to you myself."

It was too dark now to see her face but Quinn felt her little movement of protest or dissent. "They don't want you to come here any more, Mr. Quinn. They think you're trying to make trouble for the colony."

"I'm not. The colony, as such, doesn't interest me."

"You keep on coming."

"My first visit was an accident, my second was to give Sister Blessing the information she asked for."

"Is that the honest truth?"

"Yes," Quinn said. "It's getting late, Karma. You'd better start back before they send out a lynching party for me."

"I won't be missed. I told mother I was going to bed because I had a sore throat. She'll be busy in the kitchen until late. By that time," she added bitterly, "I expected to be half-way to the city. Only I'm not. I'm right here. I'll be right here until I die. I'll be old and ugly, and dirty like the rest of them. Oh, I wish I could die this very minute and go to heaven before I commit all the sins I'll probably commit when I get the chance, like having beautiful dresses and shoes and talking back to the Master and washing my hair every day in perfume."

Quinn got out of the car and held the door open for her. She climbed out slowly and awkwardly.

"Can you find your way in the dark?" Quinn said.

"I've been up and down this road a million times."

"Good-bye for now, then."

"Are you really coming back?"

"Yes."

"And you won't forget the stuff for my acne?"

"No," Quinn said. "And you won't forget your part of the bargain?"

"I'm to keep my ears open if anyone mentions Patrick O'Gorman. I don't think they will, though."

"Why not?"

"We're not allowed to talk about the people we knew before we were converted, and there's no one in the colony called O'Gorman. When I'm looking after Mother Pureza I often read the book the Master keeps with our other-world names in it. There's no O'Gorman in it. I have a very good memory."

"Can you remember Sister Blessing's name?"

"Naturally. Mary Alice Featherstone and she lived in Chicago."

Quinn asked her about some of the others but none of the names she mentioned meant any more to him than Mary Alice Featherstone did.

In the light of the rising moon he watched Karma walk back toward the Tower. Her step was brisk and buoyant as if she had forgotten all about wanting to die and was concentrating instead on the sins she intended to commit when her chance came.

Quinn drove to San Felice, checked in at a motel on the waterfront and went to sleep to the intermittent croaking of a foghorn and the sound of surf crashing against the break-water.

ten

By nine o'clock in the morning the sun had burned off most of the fog. The sea, calm at low tide, was streaked with colors, sky-blue on the horizon, brown where the kelp beds lay, and a kind of gray-green in the harbor itself. The air was warm and windless. Two children, who looked barely old enough to walk, sat patiently in their tiny sailing pram waiting for a breeze.

Quinn crossed the sandy beach and headed for the break-water. Tom Jurgensen's office was padlocked but Jurgensen himself was sitting on the concrete wall talking to a gray-haired man wearing a yachting cap and topsiders and an im-maculate white duck suit. After a time the gray-haired man turned away with an angry gesture and walked down the ramp to the mooring slips.

Jurgensen approached Quinn, unsmiling. "Are you back, or haven't you left?"

"I'm back."

"You didn't give me much chance to raise the money. I said a week or two, not a day or two."

"This is a social call," Quinn said. "By the way, who's your friend in the sailor suit?"

"Some joker from Newport Beach. He wouldn't know a starboard tack from a carpet tack but he's got a seventy-five-foot yawl and he thinks he's Admiral of the fleet and Lord of the four winds. . . . How broke are you, Quinn?"

"I told you yesterday. Flat and stony."

"Want a job for a few days?"

"Such as?"

"The Admiral's looking for a bodyguard," Jurgensen said. "Or, more strictly, a boat guard. His wife's divorcing him and he got the bright idea of cleaning everything out of his safe deposit boxes and taking it aboard the *Briny Belle* before his wife could get a court order restraining him from disposing of community property. He's afraid she'll find out where he is and try to take possession of the *Briny* and everything on it."

"I don't know anything about boats."

"You don't have to. The *Briny's* not going anywhere until the next six-foot tide can ease her past the sand bar. That will be in four or five days. Your job would be to stay on board and keep predatory blondes off the gangplank."

"What's the pay?"

"The old boy's pretty desperate," Jurgensen said. "I think maybe you could nick him for seventy-five dollars a day, and that's not seaweed."

"What's the Admiral's name?"

"Alban Connelly. He married some Hollywood starlet, which doesn't mean much, since every female in Hollywood under thirty is a starlet." Jurgensen paused to light a cigarette. "Think of it, loafing all day in the sun, playing gin rummy over a few beers. Sound good?"

"Neat," Quinn said. "Especially if the Admiral's luck isn't too good."

"With ten million dollars, who needs luck? You want me to go and tell him about you, give you a little build-up?"

"I could use the money."

"Fine. I'll skip down to the *Briny* and talk to him. I suppose you can start work any time?"

"Why not?" Quinn said, thinking, *I have nothing else to do:*

O'Gorman's in hell, Sister Blessing's in isolation, Alberta Hay-wood's in jail. None of them is going to run away. "Do you know many of the commercial fishermen around here?"

"I know all of them by sight, most of them by name."

"What about a man called Aguila?"

"Frank Aguila, sure. He owns the *Ruthie K*. You can see her from here if you stand on the sea wall." Jurgensen pointed beyond the last row of mooring slips. "She's an old Monterey-type fishing boat, anchored just off the port bow of the black-masted sloop. See it?"

"I think so."

"Why the interest in Aguila?"

"He married Ruth Haywood six years ago. I just wondered how they were getting along."

"They're getting along fine," Jurgensen said. "She's a hard-working little woman, often comes down to the harbor to spruce up the boat and help Frank mend his nets. The Aguilas don't socialize much, but they're pleasant, unassuming people. . . . Come along, you can wait in my office while I go out to the *Briny Belle* to see Connelly."

Jurgensen unlocked his office and went inside. "There's the typewriter, you can write yourself a couple of references to make Connelly feel he's getting a bargain. And you don't have to bother with details. By ten o'clock Connelly will be too cockeyed to read anyway."

When Jurgensen had gone Quinn looked up Frank Aguila's number in the telephone directory and dialed. A woman who identified herself as the baby-sitter said that Mr. and Mrs. Aguila were down in San Pedro for a couple of days attending a union meeting.

When Quinn reached the *Briny Belle* a young man in over-alls was painting out the name on her bow while Connelly leaned over the rail urging him to hurry.

Quinn said, "Mr. Connelly?"

"Quinn?"

"Yes."

"You're late."

"I had to check out of my motel and make arrangements for my car."

"Well, don't just stand there," Connelly said. "You're not about to be piped aboard if that's what you're waiting for."

Quinn walked up the gangplank, already convinced that the job wasn't going to be as pleasant as Jurgensen had let on.

"Sit down, Quinn," Connelly said. "What's-his-name, that jackass who sell boats—did he tell you my predicament?"

"Yes."

"Women don't know anything more about a boat than its name, so I'm having the *Briny's* name changed. Pretty clever, no?"

"Fiendishly."

Connelly leaned back on his heels and scratched the side of his large red nose. "So you're one of those sarcastic bastards that likes to make funnies, eh?"

"I'm one of those."

"Well, *I* make the funnies around here, Quinn, and don't you forget it. I make a funny, everybody laughs, see?"

"You can buy it cheaper in a can."

"I don't think I'm going to like you," Connelly said thoughtfully. "But for four or five days I'll go through the motions if you will."

"That sounds fair."

"I'm a fair man, very fair. That's what that little blonde tramp, Elsie, doesn't understand. If she hadn't grabbed for it, I'd have thrown it to her. If she hadn't gone around bleating about her career, I'd have bought her a career like some other guy'd buy her a bag of peanuts. . . . What's-his-name said you play cards."

"Yes."

"For money?"

"I have been known to play for money," Quinn said carefully.

"O.K., let's go below and get started."

That first day established the pattern of the ones that followed. In the morning Connelly was relatively sober and he talked about what a good guy he was and how badly Elsie had treated him. In the afternoon the two men played gin rummy until Connelly passed out at the table; then Quinn would deposit him on a bunk and go up on deck with a pair of binoculars to see if there was any sign of activity on Aguila's fishing boat, the *Ruthie K*. In the evening Connelly started in drinking again and talking about Elsie, what a fine woman she was and how badly he had treated her. Quinn got the impression that there were two Elsies and two Connellys. The evening Elsie who was a fine woman should have married the morning Connelly who was a good guy, and everything would have turned out fine.

On the fourth afternoon Connelly was snoring on his bunk when Quinn went on deck with the binoculars. The Captain, a man named McBride, and two crewmen Quinn hadn't seen before had come aboard with their gear, and there was a great deal of quiet activity.

"We get under way at midnight tomorrow," McBride told Quinn. "There's a 6.1 tide. Where's Nimitz?"

"Asleep."

"Good. We can get some work done. You coming with us, Quinn?"

"Where are you going?"

"Nimitz is dodging the enemy," McBride said briskly. "My orders are top-secret. Also our friend has an engaging little habit of changing his mind in mid-channel."

"I like to know where I'm going."

"What does it matter? Come on along for the ride."

"Why the sudden burst of friendship, Captain?"

"Friendship, hell," McBride said. "I hate gin rummy. When you play with him, I don't have to."

Quinn focused the binoculars on the *Ruthie K*. He couldn't see anyone on board but a small skiff was tied up alongside that hadn't been there on the previous days. After about fifteen minutes a woman in jeans and a T-shirt appeared on the bridge and hung what looked like a blanket over the railing. Then she disappeared again.

Quinn approached Captain McBride. "If Connelly wakes up tell him I had to go ashore on an errand, will you?"

"I just took a look at him. He'd sleep through a typhoon."

"That's fine with me."

He went back to Jurgensen's office, borrowed a skiff and rowed out to the *Ruthie K*. The woman was on deck, and the railing by this time was lined with sheets and blankets airing in the sun.

Quinn said, "Mrs. Aguila?"

She stared down at him suspiciously like an ordinary housewife finding a salesman at her front door. Then she pushed back a strand of sun-bleached hair. "Yes. What do you want?"

"I'm Joe Quinn. May I talk to you for a few minutes?"

"What about?"

"Your sister."

An expression of surprise crossed her face and disappeared. "I think not," she said quietly. "I don't discuss my sister with representatives of the press."

"I'm not a reporter, Mrs. Aguila, or an official. I'm a private citizen interested in your sister's case. I know her parole hearing is coming up soon and the way things are she's pretty sure to be turned down."

"Why? She's paid her debt, she's behaved herself. Why shouldn't they give her another chance? And how did you find me? How did you know who I was?"

"I'll explain if you'll let me come aboard."

"I haven't much time," she said brusquely. "There's work to be done."

"I'll try to be brief."

Mrs. Aguila watched him while he tied the skiff to the buoy and climbed awkwardly up the ladder. The boat was a far cry from the spit and polish of the *Briny Belle* but Quinn felt more at home on it. It was a working boat, not a plaything, and the deck glistened with fish scales instead of varnish, and Elsie and the Admiral wouldn't have been caught dead in the cramped little galley.

Quinn said, "Mrs. King, an associate of your brother, told me your married name and where you lived. I was in Chicote the other day talking to her and a few other people like Martha O'Gorman. Do you remember Mrs. O'Gorman?

"I never actually *met* her."

"What about her husband?"

"What is this anyway?" Mrs. Aguila said sharply. "I thought you wanted to discuss my sister, Alberta. I'm not interested in the O'Gormans. If there's a way I can help Alberta I'm willing to do it, naturally, but I don't see how the O'Gormans come into it. All three of them lived in Chicote, that's the only connection."

"Alberta was a bookkeeper. So, in a sense, was O'Gorman."

"And a few hundred other people."

"The difference is that nothing spectacular happened to the few hundred other people," Quinn said. "And within a month both Alberta and O'Gorman met up with quite unusual fates."

"Within a month?" Mrs. Aguila repeated. "I'm afraid not, Mr. Quinn. Alberta met up with her fate years and years before that, when she first started tampering with the books. Not to mince words, she was stealing from the bank before Patrick O'Gorman even came to Chicote. God knows what made her do it. She didn't need anything, she didn't seem to want anything more than she had except possibly a husband and children, and she never mentioned even that. I often think back to the four of us, Alberta, George and Mother and I, eating our meals together, spending the evenings together, behaving like any ordinary family. And all that time, all those years, Alberta never gave the slightest hint that anything was wrong. When the crash came I was already married to Frank and living here in San Felice. One evening I went out to pick up the newspaper from the driveway and there it was on the front page, Alberta's picture, the whole story. . . ." She turned her head away as if the memory of that day was too painful to face again.

"Were you close to your sister, Mrs. Aguila?"

"In a way. Some people have described Alberta as cold but she was always affectionate towards George and me in the sense that she liked to buy us things, arrange surprises for us. Oh, I realize now the money she was spending didn't belong to her and that she was using it to try and purchase what she didn't have, love. Poor Alberta, she reached out for love with one hand and pushed it away with the other."

"She had no serious romance?" Quinn said.

"She had dates occasionally but men always seemed puzzled by Alberta. There were few repeats."

"How did she occupy her spare time?"

"She did volunteer work and went to movies, lectures, concerts."

"Alone?"

"Usually. She didn't seem to mind going places alone, although Mother always made a fuss about it. She considered it a reflection on her that Alberta didn't have lots of friends and a busy social life. The truth is, Alberta didn't want a social life."

"Didn't want one, or despaired of her ability to get one?"

"She showed no signs of despair. In fact, during my last year at home, she seemed quite contented. Not in the happy, fulfilled sense, but as if she'd resigned herself to her life and intended to make the best of it. She settled for spinsterhood is what it amounted to, I suppose."

"How old was she then?"

"Thirty-two."

"Isn't that a little early to settle for spinsterhood?" Quinn said.

"Not to a woman like Alberta. She was always very realistic about herself. She didn't dream, the way I did, of an ideal lover tooling up to the front door in a red convertible." She laughed self-consciously and put her hand on the rail of the boat in a gesture that was both proud and protective. "I never thought I'd be happy in an old tub that smells of fish scales and mildew."

She paused as if she expected Quinn to contradict her, and Quinn obliged by stating that the *Ruthie K* was not an old tub but a fine seaworthy craft. "But to return to Alberta, Mrs. Aguila. In view of her years of embezzling, I can't agree with your description of her as 'realistic.' She must have known that one day she'd be caught. Why didn't she stop? Or run away while she had the chance?"

"She may have wanted to be punished. This will sound funny to you, I guess, but Alberta had a very strict, stern conscience. She was highly moral in everything she did. If she made a promise she kept it, no matter how long it took or what lengths she had to go to. I remember when we got into trouble as children Alberta was the first to admit guilt and accept punishment. She had a lot more courage than I. She still has."

"Still has," Quinn repeated. "Does that mean you visit her in prison?"

"Whenever I can, which isn't often. Seven or eight times so far, I guess."

"Do you write to her?"

"Once a month."

"And she writes back?"

"Yes."

"Do you have any of her letters, Mrs. Aguila?"

"No," she said, flushing. "I don't keep them. None of my children can read yet, but they have older friends, and then there are baby-sitters and Frank's relatives. I'm not ashamed of Alberta but for the children's sake and Frank's I don't advertise the fact that she's my sister. It wouldn't do her any good."

"What kind of letters does she write?"

"Brief, pleasant, polite. Exactly the kind I'd expect from her. She doesn't seem unhappy. Her only complaint isn't about the prison at all, it's about George."

"Because she doesn't hear from him?"

Ruth Aguila stared up at Quinn, her mouth open a little in surprise. "What on earth gave you that idea?"

"I understood that George, at the insistence of his mother, cut off all relations with Alberta."

"Who told you?"

"John Ronda, the editor of the Chicote *Beacon*, and Mrs. King, who's an associate of George's."

"Well, I don't know them so I can't call them liars. But I never heard such nonsense in my life. George is utterly incapable of turning his back on a member of his family. He's absolutely devoted to Alberta. To him she's not a woman nearly forty who's been convicted of a major crime, she's still the little sister he has to protect, see to it that she gets a square deal. I'm his little sister, too, but George knows I'm married and being looked after so I'm not really important to him any more. It's Alberta he adores and worries about and fusses over. Why should those two people have told you such a lie?"

"I'm pretty sure," Quinn said, "that they both believed it themselves."

"Why should they? Where would they get a story like that?"

"Obviously from George, since they're friends of his, Mrs. King a particularly close one."

Ruth Aguila's protest was immediate and firm. "That's really absurd. George wouldn't deliberately make himself out to be a heel when the truth is he's done everything possible for Alberta, more than she wants him to. That's what she complains about in her letters. George's visits every month distress her because he's so emotional. He keeps trying to help her and she refuses. She says she's old enough to carry her own burden and the sight of George's suffering only aggravates hers. She's told him she doesn't want to see him, at least not so often, but he keeps right on going anyway."

"People in prison are usually very eager, pathetically eager, to have visitors."

"I repeat, Alberta is realistic. If seeing George's suffering only aggravates her own, then it makes sense that she shouldn't want him to visit her very often."

"It may make sense, in a way," Quinn said. "But to me it sounds like the kind of explanation she might use to cover up the real one."

"And just what might the real one be?"

"I don't know. Perhaps she's afraid George might break down the defenses she's constructed in order to adjust to and accept her present environment. You said she doesn't seem unhappy. Is that what you want to believe, Mrs. Aguila, or the truth?"

"It happens to be both."

"Yet she spoke of her suffering," Quinn said. "Is there such a thing as happy suffering?"

"Yes. If you want punishment and are getting it. Or if you have something good to look forward to at the end of a bad time."

"Say, for instance, a large sum of money?"

She looked down at the oil-stained water lapping at the *Ruthie K's* gray hull. "The money's all gone, Mr. Quinn. Some of it she gave away, most of it she gambled away. She told me in a letter that she used to spend week ends in Las Vegas when George and Mother thought she'd gone to Los Angeles or San Francisco to shop and see the shows. It's funny, isn't it?—Alberta is the last woman on earth I'd suspect of gambling."

"Las Vegas is full of the last women on earth anyone would suspect of gambling."

"It must be a very peculiar compulsion, especially when someone keeps losing week after week."

"When you keep losing," Quinn said, "is when you don't think of stopping."

Mrs. Aguila was shaking her head in sorrow. "To think of all the trouble she went to year after year to steal that money, and then all she did was throw it away—it doesn't make sense to me, Mr. Quinn. Alberta never acted on impulse like that. She was a planner, a methodical, minute-by-minute planner.

Everything she did was well thought out in advance, from her wardrobe budget to the route she drove to and from her office. Even a simple business like attending a movie, she conducted like a campaign. If the feature picture began at 7:30, dinner had to be served at exactly six, the dishes washed and put away by seven, and so on. It wasn't much fun going any place with her because all the time she was doing one thing you could practically feel her planning the next move."

Quinn thought, *She's doing one thing now, staying in jail, what next move has she planned? If Ronda is correct, she won't even be free for years.*

He said, "I understand that the mistake that tripped Alberta up at the bank was a very trivial one."

"Yes."

"I recall another trivial mistake that had consequences even more drastic than Alberta's did."

"What was it?"

"The night O'Gorman disappeared he was on his way back to his office to correct a mistake he'd made during the day. Two bookkeepers, two trivial errors, two disastrous fates within a month in one small city. Add these to the fact that O'Gorman worked for George Haywood at one time and that he probably knew Alberta, at least by sight. Add still another fact, that when I went to Chicote to ask questions about O'Gorman, George's curiosity was aroused to the extent that he broke into my motel room and searched it."

"You'd realize what a fantastic story that is if you knew George."

"I'm trying to know George," Quinn said. "So far I haven't had much of a chance."

"As for your other suspicions, and that's all they are, you seem to forget that the authorities went into every possible angle when O'Gorman disappeared. There was hardly a person in Chicote who wasn't questioned. George sent me every copy of the *Beacon*."

"Why?"

"He thought I'd be interested since I came from Chicote and knew O'Gorman slightly."

"How much is slightly?"

"I saw him in the office a couple of times. A good-looking man, though there was something effeminate about him that repelled me. Maybe that's too strong a word but it's how he affected me."

"That type can be very appealing to certain women," Quinn said. "You told me you haven't met Martha O'Gorman."

"She was pointed out to me on the street once."

"By whom?"

She hesitated for a moment. "George. He thought she was a very attractive woman and he wondered why she'd thrown herself away on a man like O'Gorman."

Quinn wondered, too, in spite of all the good things Martha O'Gorman had said about her marriage. "Was George interested in her?"

"I think he could have been if she hadn't already been married. It's a shame she was. George needed, and still needs, a wife. His own died when he was barely thirty. The longer he waits, the more he lives at home alone with Mother, the harder it will be for him to break away. I know how hard it is. I had to do it, break away or be broken."

It seemed to Quinn that whenever he turned another corner, he met up with George Haywood, and that the connection between the two cases, which he'd suspected from the beginning, was not Alberta Haywood as he'd once thought, but George. George and Martha O'Gorman, the respectable businessman and the grieving widow. And maybe the reason Martha hadn't remarried had nothing to do with her devotion to O'Gorman's memory; she was waiting for George to break away from his mother. *That would make two of them,* he thought. *Martha O'Gorman and Willie King, and I wouldn't bet a nickel on Willie's chances.*

He said, "You've spoken of George's loyalty to and fondness for his sister. Did it work both ways?"

"Yes. Too much so."

"Too much?"

Twin spots of color appeared on her cheeks and her hands gripped the railing tightly as if she were afraid of falling overboard. "I shouldn't have said that, I guess. I mean, I'm no psychologist, I have no right to go around analyzing people. Only—well, I can't help thinking George made a mistake going back home after his wife died. George used to be a warm, affectionate man who could give love and accept it—I mean real love, not the neurotic kind like my mother's and Alberta's. Perhaps it's uncharitable of me to talk this way about them, and I probably wouldn't do it if they'd acted decent about my marriage to Frank. That's a long answer to a short question, isn't it?

"More briefly, yes, Alberta was very fond of George. Without him around, her whole life might have been different, more satisfactory to her, so that she wouldn't have had to steal and gamble, she'd have gotten married like any ordinary woman. I think George understands this, in a way, and is ridden by guilt because of it. And so he goes to visit her, and they watch each other suffer, and—oh, it's such a rotten mess it makes me sick. I suppose what I'm trying to say is that I hate them. I hate all three of them. I don't want Frank or my children to be forced to have anything to do with any of them."

Quinn was surprised by the violence of her feelings, and he guessed that she was, too. She looked anxiously around at the boats moored nearby as if to make sure nobody had overheard her outburst. Then she turned back to Quinn with a sheepish little smile. "Frank says this always happens when I talk about my family. I start out by being very unemotional and detached, and end up in hysterics."

"I wish all the hysterics I had to deal with were as quiet."

"The fact is, the only thing I want from my family is to be let alone. When I watched you climbing up that ladder, knowing you were going to talk about Alberta, I felt like pushing you overboard."

"I'm glad you didn't," Quinn said. "This is my only suit."

When he returned to the *Briny Belle* it was five o'clock. The Admiral was pacing up and down the bull run, wearing a new white outfit and the same old dirty expression. "Where the hell you been, you lazy bum? You're supposed to stay on board twenty-four hours a day."

"I saw this fancy blonde on the breakwater. She looked like Elsie, so I thought I'd better check. It was Elsie all right—"

"Weeping Jesus! Let's get out of here. Call the Captain. Tell him we're leaving immediately."

"—Elsie Doolittle from Spokane. Nice girl."

"Why, you lousy bum," Connelly said. "You can't help making funnies, eh? At my expense, eh? I ought to kick your teeth in."

"You might mess up your sailor suit."

"By God, if I were twenty years younger—"

"If you were twenty years younger you'd be the same as you are now, a knuckle-headed lush who couldn't beat a cocker spaniel at gin rummy without cheating."

"I didn't cheat!" Connelly shouted. "I never cheated in my life. Apologize this instant or I'll sue you for libel."

Quinn looked amused. "I caught on to you halfway through the first game. Either stop cheating or take lessons."

"You won. How could I have been cheating if you won?"

"I took lessons."

Connelly's mouth hung open like a hooked halibut's. "Why, you double-crossed me. You're nothing but a thief."

He began screaming for Captain McBride, the crew, the police, the harbor patrol. About a dozen people had gathered around by this time. Quinn went quietly down the gangplank, without waiting for his salary. In his pocket he had about three hundred dollars of Connelly's money, the equivalent of four days' pay at seventy-five a day. He felt better about it than if he'd accepted it from Connelly's hand.

Take a long walk on a short deck, Admiral.

eleven

The Tecolote Prison for Women was a collection of concrete buildings built on a two-hundred-acre plateau above Deer Valley. Quinn guessed that the site had been chosen to discourage escapees, since there was no place to escape to. The countryside was more bleak than that which surrounded the Tower. There were no towns within fifty miles, and the stony soil and sparse rainfall had discouraged farmers and ranchers. The paved road that led to Tecolote stopped at the prison gates as if the engineers who built it had quit and gone home in despair.

At the administration building Quinn told the woman in charge that he wanted to see Alberta Haywood, and presented the private detective's license issued to him by the State of Nevada. After half an hour's questioning he was taken across a paved courtyard and left in one of the ground-floor rooms of a three-storied concrete building. The room looked as though someone had once started to decorate it. Half the windows were curtained and several oil paintings hung on the walls. There were two or three upholstered chairs, but most of the seating space was provided by wooden benches similar to the benches in the community dining hall at the Tower.

Other people were waiting: an elderly couple who stood close together beside the doorway exchanging anxious whispers; a young woman whose identity was hidden, or lost, under layers of make-up; a man Quinn's age, with dull eyes and sharp clothes; three blue-uniformed women with the artificial poise and nervous group-gaiety of volunteer social workers; a man and his teen-aged son who looked as though they'd had an argument about coming, not their first, not their last; a gray-haired woman carrying a paper bag with a split in it. Through the split Quinn could see the red sheen of an apple.

Names were called by a guard and people were led away until only Quinn and the father with the teen-aged boy were left in the room.

The man began to talk in a low intense voice. "You're to be more polite to your mother this time, you hear me? None of this sullen stuff. She's your own mother."

"Don't I know it? I get it rubbed in my face every day at school."

"None of that now. Put yourself in her shoes. She's lonely, she looks forward to seeing you. The least you can do is smile, be pleasant, tell her she's looking good and we miss her."

"I can't. I can't do it. None of it's true."

"Shut up and listen to me. You think I'm enjoying myself? You think everybody else is having fun? You think your mother likes being locked in a cage?"

"I don't think anything," the boy said listlessly. "I don't want to think anything."

"Don't make things any tougher for us than they are, Mike. There's a limit to what I can take."

The guard reappeared. "You can come along now, Mr. Williams. How are you doing, Mike? Still getting those fancy grades of yours in school?"

When the boy didn't answer, his father said, "He's doing great in school. Doesn't take after me, I can tell you. His mother's got the brains in the family. She passed them along to him. He ought to be grateful."

"I'm not. I don't want any brains from her, I don't want anything."

The three of them went out into the corridor.

Quinn waited another ten or fifteen minutes. He studied the

paintings on the walls, the upholstery on the chairs, and the view from the windows of a three-storied concrete structure identical to the one he was in. Quinn wondered how many of its occupants would be rehabilitated. The same people who were building spaceships to reach the moon were sending their fellow human beings to eighteenth-century penal colonies, and more money was spent on seven astronauts than on the quarter of a million people confined to prisons.

A heavy-set woman in a blue serge uniform appeared at the door. "Mr. Quinn?"

"Yes."

"Your name isn't on Miss Haywood's approved visiting list."

"I explained that to the people in the administration building."

"Yes. Well, it's entirely up to Miss Haywood whether she'll talk to you or not. Come this way, please."

The visiting room was buzzing with conversation and nearly every cubicle was filled. Alberta Haywood sat behind the wire screen with as much composure as if she were still at her desk in the bank. Her small hands were loosely clasped on the counter in front of her and her blue eyes had an alert, kindly expression. Quinn half expected her to say, *Why, of course, we'd be delighted to open an account for you. . . .*

Instead, "My goodness, you do stare. Is this your first visit to a prison?"

"No, it's not."

"The matron said your name is Quinn. Several of my old customers were named Quinn and I thought you might be one of them. I see now, of course, that you're not. We've never met before, have we?"

"No, Miss Haywood."

"Then why did you come here?"

"I'm a private detective," Quinn said.

"Really? That must be very interesting work. I don't recall ever having met a private detective before. What exactly do they do?"

"What they're paid to do."

"One naturally assumes that," she said with a hint of rebuff in her voice. "It fails to shed any light on why you should want to see me. My world has been rather limited these past few years."

"I was hired to find Patrick O'Gorman."

Quinn wasn't prepared for her reaction. A look of fury crossed her face, and her mouth opened as if she was struggling to catch her breath. "Then find him. Don't waste your time here, go and find him. And when you do, give him what's coming to him. Show him no mercy."

"You must have known him pretty well to feel so strongly about him, Miss Haywood."

"I don't feel strongly about *him*. I barely knew him. It's what he did to me."

"And what was that?"

"I wouldn't be here in this place if he hadn't disappeared like that. For a month the whole town did nothing else but talk about him, O'Gorman this, O'Gorman that, why, how, who, when, on and on and on. I would never have made that silly error in the books if my mind hadn't been distracted by all the shenanigans over O'Gorman. It made me so nervous I couldn't concentrate. Such incredible fussing over one ordinary little man, it was quite absurd. Naturally my work suffered. It required a great deal of concentration and careful planning."

"I'm sure it did," Quinn said.

"Some fool of a man decides to run away from home and *I* end up serving a prison term—I, a perfectly innocent bystander."

She sounded as if she really thought she was a perfectly innocent bystander and Quinn wondered whether she had always thought so or whether the years at Tecolote, the hours of boredom, of waiting, had made her slightly, perhaps more than slightly, paranoid. She was the martyr, O'Gorman the villain. The white and the black.

She was staring at Quinn through the wire mesh, her eyes

narrowed. "Give me your honest opinion, was that fair?"

"I'm not well enough acquainted with the details to form an opinion."

"No further details are necessary. O'Gorman put me behind these bars. It may even have been deliberate on his part."

"That hardly seems likely, Miss Haywood. He couldn't have anticipated the results of his disappearance on your powers of concentration. You were only slightly acquainted with him anyway, weren't you?"

"We nodded," she said, as if she regretted doing even that much for the man responsible for her predicament. "If our paths should cross in the future, of course, I intend to cut him dead, shun him like a rattlesnake."

"I don't think your paths will cross again, Miss Haywood."

"Why not? I'm not going to be stuck in this place forever."

"No, but O'Gorman may very well be stuck in his," Quinn said. "The majority of people believe he was murdered."

"Who'd go to the trouble of murdering O'Gorman? Unless, of course, he pulled the same kind of dirty trick on somebody else as he did on me."

"There was no evidence of anyone bearing a grudge against him."

"Anyway, he wasn't murdered. He's not dead. He *can't* be."

"Why not?"

She half rose as if she were going to run away from the question. Then she realized that the matron was watching her, and sat down again. "Because then I wouldn't have anyone to blame. Somebody's got to be blamed. Somebody's responsible. It must be O'Gorman. He did it to me deliberately. Perhaps he thought I acted too snobbish towards him? Or he was angry because George fired him?"

"What happened to O'Gorman wasn't intended to involve you at all, Miss Haywood."

"It *did* involve me."

"It wasn't planned that way, I'm sure," Quinn said.

"They keep telling me that, too, only they don't know everything."

She didn't explain who "they" were, but Quinn assumed she was referring to the prison psychologists and perhaps George as well.

"Your brother George comes to visit you quite frequently, Miss Haywood?"

"Every month." She pressed her finger tips hard against her temples as if she felt a sudden intense pain. "I wish he wouldn't. It's too sad. He talks of old friends, old places, that I can't afford to think about any more or I'd lose my—I would get overly emotional. Or else he talks of the future and that's even worse. In this place, though you realize there will be a future, you can't feel it inside you because every day is like a year. By my estimate," she added with a small bitter smile, "I'm now about 1875 years old and it's a little late to be thinking of futures. I don't say things like this to them, naturally. They'd call it depression, melancholia, they'd have some name for it, any name but the right one, prison. Prison. It's funny how they try to avoid that word around here and substitute 'Correctional Institution' or 'Branch of the Adult Authority.' Fancy terms that fool no one. I'm a prisoner in a prison, and listening to George prattle merrily on about a trip to Europe and a job in his office makes me sick. How can a trip to Europe seem real to someone who's locked in a cell and hasn't been further than the canteen for over five years? Why am I here? Why are we all here? There must be, there has to be, a better method. If society wants revenge for our crimes why don't they flog us in front of the city hall? Why don't they torture us and get it over with? Why do they leave us here to pass endless unproductive hours when we might be doing something useful? We're like vegetables, only vegetables grow and get eaten and we don't even have that much satisfaction. We're not wanted even for dog food." She held out her hands. "Put me in a meat grinder, chop me up, let me feed some hungry dog, some starved cat!"

Her voice had risen, and people in the adjoining cubicles were standing and peering over the partitions at her.

"Let me be useful! Grind me up! Listen to me, all of you!

132

Don't you want to be ground up to feed the starving animals?"

The matron hurried over, her keys jangling against her blue serge thighs. "Is anything the matter, Miss Haywood?"

"Prison. I'm in prison and the animals are starving."

"Hush, now. They're not starving."

"You don't care about them!"

"I care more about you," the matron said pleasantly. "Come along, I'll take you back to your room."

"Cell. I am a prisoner in a prison and I live in a cell, not a room."

"Whatever it is, you're going back to it and I don't want any fussing and carrying-on. Now be a good girl, eh?"

"I am not a good girl," Miss Haywood said distinctly. "I am a *bad woman* who lives in a *cell* in a *prison*."

"Good grief."

"And watch your language."

The matron put a firm hand on Alberta Haywood's elbow and guided her out. The conversations in the room began again but the voices were quieter, more guarded, and when Quinn got up to leave, the eyes that followed him seemed full of accusations: *You didn't answer her question, mister. Why are we all here?*

Quinn returned to the administration building, and after another series of delays was given permission to see the psychiatric social worker who counseled the inmates due for parole hearings.

Mrs. Browning was young, earnest, baffled. "This is a period of great strain for all of them, naturally. Still, the report of Miss Haywood's crack-up surprises me. I suppose it shouldn't. I've had very little actual contact with her." She adjusted her spectacles as if she hoped to bring Miss Haywood into clearer focus. "In an institution like this, where the psychology department is understaffed, it's the squeaky wheel that gets the grease, and heaven knows we have enough squeaky wheels without bothering about the quiet ones like Miss Haywood."

"She's never caused any trouble?"

"Oh no. She does her work well—in the prison library—and she teaches a couple of courses in bookkeeping." To Quinn it was a nice piece of irony, but Mrs. Browning seemed unaware of it as she continued, "She has a natural talent for figures."

"So I gathered."

"I've frequently noticed that among women there is a correlation between mathematical ability and a lack of warmth and emotion. Miss Haywood is respected by the other inmates but she's not well liked and she has no special friends or confidantes. This must have been true of her before she was sent here because only one person comes to visit her, a brother, and his visits are anything but satisfactory."

"In what sense?"

"Oh, she seems to look forward to them, yet she's upset for a long time afterwards. And by upset I don't mean the way she acted today. Miss Haywood withdraws, becomes completely silent. It's as if she has so very much to say, to get off her chest, that she can't allow herself to begin."

"She began today."

"Yes, perhaps it's a breakthrough." But Mrs. Browning's eyes were strained as if the silver lining they saw was very faint and far away. "There's another odd thing about Miss Haywood, at least it's odd to me when I consider her circumstances: she's nearly forty, she has a prison record, she's without a husband and family to return to, she can hardly get another job in the only field she's trained in; in other words, her future appears pretty black, and she herself claims she's only waiting to die. Yet she takes extraordinarily good care of herself. She diets, and to diet in a place like this which has to serve a lot of cheap starchy food requires a great deal of will power. She exercises in her cell, half an hour in the morning, half an hour at night, and the eighteen dollars she's permitted to spend in the canteen every month—supplied by her brother—goes for vitamin pills instead of cigarettes and chewing gum. I can only presume that if she's waiting to die she's determined to die healthy. . . ."

twelve

Quinn spent the night in San Felice, and by noon the following day he was back in Chicote. The weather had not improved during the week and neither had Chicote. It lay parched and prosperous under the relentless sun, a city of oil that needed water.

He checked in at the same motel downtown.

Mr. Frisby, on duty in the office, looked a little surprised. "My goodness, it's you again, Mr. Quinn."

"Yes."

"I'm glad you're not bearing a grudge about that little episode in your room a week ago. I've warned Grandpa to be more careful in the future, and it won't happen a second time, I can assure you."

"No, I don't think it will."

"Any luck yet with your story about O'Gorman?"

"Not much."

Frisby leaned across the counter. "I wouldn't want this to get around—the sheriff's a friend of mine, sometimes he appoints me special deputy—but in my opinion the case was bungled."

"Why?"

"Civic pride, that's why. None of the authorities would admit we've got juvenile delinquency around here same as the big cities got, maybe even worse. Now according to my way of thinking, here's what happened: O'Gorman was on his way back to his office at the oil field when a carful of young punks spotted him and decided to have a little fun and games.

They forced him right off the road. They did the same thing to me last year, I ended up in a ditch with two broken ribs and a concussion. Just kids they were, too, and with no motive at all except they wanted to raise hell. Some of the kids around here, especially on the ranches, learn to drive when they're ten, eleven years old. By the time they're sixteen they know everything about a car except how to behave in it. Well, I was luckier than O'Gorman. I ended up in a ditch, not a river."

"Was there any evidence that O'Gorman was forced off the road?"

"A big dent in the left side of the bumper."

"Surely the sheriff must have noticed it."

"You bet he did," Frisby said. "I pointed it out to him myself. I was there when they pulled the car out of the river and the first thing I looked for were marks like were found on my car last year. That dent was in the very same spot and there was a faint trace of dark green paint in it. Maybe not enough to take any scrapings for scientific tests, but enough so you could see if you looked real close and knew exactly what to look for."

Reliving the excitement had sent the blood rushing up into Frisby's face. It seemed to be increasing in size and getting ready to explode like a bright pink balloon. But even as Quinn watched, the balloon began diminishing and its color began fading.

"Everything was there to support my theory," Frisby said with a sudden deep sigh. "Except for one thing."

"And that was?"

"Martha O'Gorman."

The name struck Quinn's ears like a discord he'd been expecting to hear and was trying to avoid. "What about Mrs. O'Gorman?"

"Now I don't claim the lady was lying. What I've seen of her, she seems a nice, quiet-spoken young woman, not like some of these overpainted floozies you meet on the street."

"What did Martha O'Gorman say about the dent in the bumper?"

"Said she'd put it there herself a week beforehand. She claimed she backed into a lamppost while she was trying to park on the left side of a one-way street. What street and what lamppost she couldn't remember, but everybody believed her."

"Except you."

"It seemed a peculiar thing to forget, to my mind." Frisby glanced uneasily out of the window as if he half expected the sheriff to be lurking outside. "Let's suppose for a minute that I was right in thinking O'Gorman was forced off the road by another car, only this car contained not a bunch of juveniles but somebody who had reason to hate O'Gorman and want him dead. In that case Mrs. O'Gorman's story would make a pretty good cover-up, wouldn't it?"

"For herself?"

"Or a—well, a friend, say."

"You mean a boy friend?"

"Well, it happens every day," Frisby said defensively. "Heck, I don't want to cast aspersions on an innocent woman, but what if she's not innocent? Think about that dent, Mr. Quinn. Why didn't she remember where she got it so her story could be checked?"

"There's a point in her favor you seem to have overlooked. The lampposts in Chicote are all dark green."

"So were about fifteen percent of the cars that year."

"How do you know that?"

"I did my own checking," Frisby said. "For a whole month I kept track of the cars that came here. Out of nearly five hundred, over seventy of them were dark green."

"You went to a lot of trouble to try and prove Mrs. O'Gorman was lying."

Frisby's soft round face was swelling and getting pink again. "I *wasn't* trying to prove she was lying. I wanted to find out the truth, that's all. Why, I even went around examining lampposts on one-way streets to see if I could locate the one she hit, or said she hit."

"Any luck?"

"They were all pretty beat-up, as a matter of fact. They were put in too close to the curbs. That was a long time ago, before somebody dreamed up those crazy tailfins."

"So you proved nothing."

"I proved," Frisby said brusquely, "that fifteen percent of the cars on the road that year were dark green."

From a drug store Quinn telephoned the hospital where Martha O'Gorman worked and was told that she had taken the day off because of illness. When he called her at home the O'Gorman boy said his mother was in bed with a migraine and couldn't come to the phone.

"Give her a message, will you please?"

"Sure thing."

"Tell her Joe Quinn is staying at Frisby's Motel on Main Street. She can get in touch with me there if she wants to."

She won't want to, he thought, hanging up the phone. *O'Gorman's more real to her than I am. She's still waiting for him to walk in the door—or is she?*

Or is she? The little question with the big answer echoed and reëchoed in his mind.

Martha O'Gorman called out from the bedroom, "Who was that on the phone, Richard? And don't yell, the windows are open. Come right in here and tell me."

Richard came in and stood at the foot of the bed. The shades were drawn and the room was so dark his mother was merely a white shapeless lump. "He said his name was Joe Quinn and I was to tell you he was staying at Frisby's Motel on Main Street."

"Are you—are you sure?"

"Yes."

There was a long silence, and the lump on the bed remained motionless, but the boy could sense the tension in the air. "What's the matter, Mom?"

"Nothing."

"You've been acting kind of funny lately. Are you worrying about money again?"

"No, we're doing fine." Martha sat up suddenly and swung her legs over the side of the bed in an attempt at vivacity. The movement brought a spasm of pain to the entire left side of her head. Pressing her hand tight against her neck to lessen the pain, she said in a falsely cheerful voice, "As a matter of fact, my headache's much better. Perhaps we should do something to celebrate."

"That'd be great."

"It's too late for me to go to work now and tomorrow's my day off and the next day's Sunday. We'd have time to take a little camping trip. Would you and Sally like that?"

"Gosh, yes. It'd be super."

"All right, you get the sleeping bags out of the storeroom and tell Sally to start fixing some sandwiches. I'll pack the canned goods."

The mere act of standing up was agonizing to her but she knew it had to be done. She had to get out of town. It was easier to face physical pain than it would be to face Quinn.

After lunch Quinn drove over to the office of the Haywood Realty Company. Earl Perkins, the young man he'd met before, was talking on the telephone at the rear of the room. His facial contortions indicated that either his stomach was bothering him again or he was having trouble with a client.

Willie King sat behind her desk, elegant and cool in a silk sundress the same green as her eyes. She didn't seem overjoyed at Quinn's return. "Well, what are you doing back here?"

"I've grown very fond of Chicote."

"Baloney. Nobody's fond of this place. We're just stuck here."

"What's sticking you? George Haywood?"

She looked as if she wanted to get angry and couldn't quite make it. "Don't be silly. Haven't you heard about me and Earl Perkins? I'm madly in love with him. We're going to get married and live happily ever after, all three of us, Earl and I and his ulcer."

"Sounds like a great future," Quinn said. "For the ulcer."

She flushed slightly and stared down at her hands. They were large and strong, and, except for the orange polish on the fingernails, they reminded Quinn of Sister Blessing's. "Go away and leave me alone, will you please? I have a headache."

"This seems to be headache day for the ladies of Chicote."

"I mean it. Just go away. I can't answer any of your questions. I don't really know how I got into all this—this mess."

"What mess, Willie?"

"Oh, everything." She watched her hands wrestle each other as if they were separate entities over which she had no control. "Have you heard about Jenkinson's law? It says, everybody's crazy. Well, you can add Willie King's law, everything's a mess."

"No exceptions?"

"I don't see any from where I sit."

"Change seats," Quinn said.

"I can't. It's too late."

"What brought on all the gloom, Willie?"

"I don't know. The heat, maybe. Or the town."

"It's the same heat you've had all summer in the same town."

"I need a vacation, I guess. I'd like to take a trip some place where it's cold and foggy and rains every day. A couple of years ago I drove up to Seattle thinking that would be the right place. And you know what happened? When I got there Seattle was having the worst heat wave and the worst drought in its history."

"Which goes to prove Willie King's law all over again?"

She stirred restlessly in her chair as if she was having a delayed reaction to Quinn's suggestion about changing seats. "You never give a straight or serious answer to anything, do you?"

"Not if I can help it. That's Quinn's law."

"Break it for once and tell me why you've come back here?"

"To talk to George Haywood."

"About what?"

"His visits to his sister Alberta in Tecolote prison."

"Where on earth did you get a crazy idea like that?" she said impatiently. "You know perfectly well George broke off all connections with Alberta years ago. I told you."

"What you tell me isn't necessarily the truth."

"All right, so I've lied a little here and there, off and on, but not about that."

"Maybe you didn't lie about it, Willie," Quinn said. "But you were certainly misinformed. George goes to see his sister once a month."

"I don't believe it. What reason would he have for pretending?"

"That's one of the questions I intend to ask him, right this afternoon if I can arrange it."

"You can't."

"Why not?"

She bent forward in the chair, her hands clasped tight against her stomach as if to ease the sharp pain of a cramp. "He's not here. He left the day before yesterday."

"For where?"

"Hawaii. He's been having a bad time with bronchial asthma for the past couple of months and the doctor thought a change of climate would help."

"How long will he be away?"

"I don't know. Everything happened so suddenly. He came into the office three days ago and out of the blue he announced he was flying to Hawaii the next morning for a vacation."

"Did he ask you to make a reservation for him?"

"No. He said he'd made it himself." She groped in her pocket for a handkerchief and held it against her forehead. "It was quite a—a shock. I had done a lot of planning—or dreaming I guess you'd call it—about George and me spending our vacation together this year. Then suddenly I get the whammy, he's flying to Hawaii. Alone. Period."

"So that's what's causing your glooms?"

"Well, at least he could have *said* something, sorry you're not coming along, Willie, some little thing like that. He didn't, though. I'm afraid. I'm afraid this is the end of the line."

"You're overimagining, Willie."

"No, I don't think so. God knows I'd like to, but I can't. George acted like a different man. He wasn't *George* any more. The real George, my George, wouldn't go on a trip like that without careful planning in advance about where he'd stay and what he'd do and how long he'd be gone. He didn't tell me a single detail beyond the fact that he was leaving the next morning. So you see, I have reason to be afraid. I've got this terrible feeling he's not coming back. I keep thinking of O'Gorman."

"Why O'Gorman?"

She pushed the handkerchief across her forehead again. "Endings can happen so suddenly. I should have argued with George, begged him to take me along. Then if the plane crashed, at least we'd have died together."

"You're getting morbid, Willie. I didn't hear of any plane crash day before yesterday. Right this minute George is probably surrounded by a bevy of sun-browned maidens who are teaching him the hula."

She stared up at Quinn coldly. "If that was intended to cheer me up, I assure you it didn't. Sun-browned maidens, hell."

"With hibiscus in their hair."

"I have a hibiscus growing in my own backyard. Any time I want to put one in my hair, I can. I can also get a tan *and* do the hula, if I have to."

"I'd bet on you any day, Willie."

"Would you?"

"Try me."

"Oh, stop kidding around, Quinn," she said with a brisk shake of her head. "I'm not your type, and you're not mine. I like older, more mature men, not the kind who know where they're going, but the kind who are already there. I've been through that stardust and baked beans routine once. Never again. I want security. I don't think you even know what you want."

"I'm beginning to find out."

"Since when?"

"Since I hit rock-bottom a couple of weeks ago."

"How far down is rock-bottom for you, Quinn?"

"Far enough," he said, "so there's no direction to go but up. Have you ever heard of the Tower of Heaven?"

"I had a very religious aunt who was always using phrases like that in her conversation."

"This isn't a phrase, it's a real place in the mountains behind San Felice. I've been there twice and I've promised to go back a third time. Which reminds me, did you ever have acne?"

Her precisely plucked brows moved up her forehead. "Say, are you losing your marbles?"

"I may be. I'd like an answer to my question anyway."

"I never had acne, no," she said carefully, as though she were humoring an idiot. "My kid sister did when she was in high school. She got rid of it by washing her face six or seven times a day, using Norton's drying lotion, and not eating any sweets or oils. Is that what you want to know?"

"Yes. Thank you, Willie."

"I suppose if I asked *why* you wanted to know, you wouldn't—"

"I wouldn't."

"You're a very peculiar man," Willie said thoughtfully. "But I'm sure that's already been pointed out to you?"

"At my mother's knee. Besides, we can't all be perfect like George."

"I didn't claim he was perfect." There was a sharp note in her voice as if she had suddenly had too vivid a picture of George surrounded by the sun-browned maidens. "He's headstrong like his mother, for one thing. When he gets an idea, he goes right ahead and acts on it, without consulting anyone else or caring what I—what someone else might think."

"Like the sudden trip to Hawaii?"

"It's a good example."

"You're sure he went to Hawaii?"

"Why, I—of course. Of course I'm sure."

"Did you see him off?"

"Naturally."

"Where?"

"He came to my apartment to say good-bye," she said. "He was going to drive to San Felice, catch a plane there, and then transfer at Los Angeles to a jet liner for Honolulu."

"Leaving his car at San Felice airport?"

"Yes."

"They don't have a garage at San Felice airport."

"There must be garages nearby," she said anxiously. "Aren't there?"

"I guess so. What kind of car was he driving?"

"His own. A green Pontiac station wagon, last year's. Why are you asking me all these questions? I don't like it. It makes me nervous. You seem to be implying that George didn't go to Hawaii at all."

"No. I just want to make sure he did."

"Why, it never even occurred to me to doubt it until you started hinting around," she said in an accusing voice. "Maybe you're deliberately trying to cause trouble between George and me for reasons of your own."

"There's already been trouble between George and you, hasn't there, Willie?"

Her jaws tightened, giving her face a strong sinewy look Quinn hadn't seen before. "None that I couldn't handle. His mother has been, well, rather difficult."

"Last time you talked about her she was an old harridan. Is she improving, or are you?" When she didn't answer, Quinn went on. "I heard an interesting rumor a few days ago from what I consider a reliable source. It concerns George."

"Then I don't care to hear it. A man in George's position, especially after what happened to Alberta, becomes the target for all kinds of rumors and gossip. He's borne up under it the only way he could, by living a clean, decent, exemplary life. There's something about George you couldn't know since you haven't met him—he's an extraordinarily brave man. He could easily have left town to avoid the scandal. But he didn't. He stayed here and fought it."

"Why?"

"I told you. He's a brave man."

"Maybe he had ties in Chicote, the same kind that keep you here."

"You mean his mother? Or me?"

"Neither," Quinn said. "I mean Martha O'Gorman."

Willie's face looked ready to fall apart, but she caught it in time and held it together by sheer will power. The effort left her trembling. "That's ridiculous."

"I don't see why. She's an attractive woman and she has class."

"Class? So that's what you call it when someone acts as though she's better than the rest of us. I know all about Martha O'Gorman. My best friend works with her at the hospital lab and she says Martha throws a fit if anyone makes the least little mistake."

"The least little mistake in a hospital lab can be pretty big."

Quinn realized that Willie, not for the first time, had quite neatly turned the conversation away from George. *There are certain kinds of birds*, he thought, *that protect their nests, when they're threatened, by pretending the nest is some place else. The maneuver involves a lot of squawking and wing-beating; Willie's good at both, but she's a little too obvious, and she suffers from the current disadvantage of not being entirely sure where her nest is and what's going on inside it.*

Willie kept right on squawking, anyway. "She's a cold, hard woman. You've only to look at that frozen face of hers to figure out that much. The girls at the lab are all scared of her."

"You seem pretty scared of her yourself, Willie."

"Me? Why should I be?"

"Because of George."

She began, once again, telling Quinn how ridiculous the idea was, how absolutely absurd to think of George paying attention to a woman like that. But her words had a hollow ring, and Quinn knew she wasn't even convincing herself. He knew another thing, too: Willie King was suffering from a severe case of jealousy, and he wondered what had caused it. A week ago she had seemed a great deal more sure of herself, and the only fly in her amber was George's mother. Now the amber was polished and other flies had become visible. Martha O'Gorman and the sun-browned maidens with hibiscus in their hair, and perhaps still others Quinn hadn't yet discovered.

thirteen

It was an old white-brick three-storied house, a Victorian dowager looking down her nose and trying to ignore the oil-rich newcomers she was forced to associate with. Behind thick lace curtains and bristling turrets she brooded, pondered, disapproved, and fought a losing battle against the flat-roofed ranch-styles and stucco and redwood boxes. Quinn expected that the woman who answered the door would match the house.

Mrs. Haywood didn't. She was slim and stylish in beige-colored linen. Her hair was dyed platinum pink, and her face bore the barely visible scars of a surgical lifting. She looked as youthful as her son George, except for the ancient griefs that showed in her eyes.

Quinn said, "Mrs. Haywood?"

"Yes." No amount of surgery could disguise her voice; it was the cracked whine of an old woman. "I buy nothing from peddlers."

"My name is Joe Quinn. I'd like to discuss some business with Mr. Haywood."

"Business should be confined to the office."

"I called his office and was told he wasn't in. I took a chance on his being home."

"He's not."

"Well, I'm sorry to have bothered you, Mrs. Haywood. When your husband gets home, please tell him to get in touch with me, will you? I'm at Frisby's Motel on Main Street."

"Husband?" She pounced on the word like a starving cat. Quinn could almost feel the sting of her claws. He was both repelled and moved to pity by the desperate hunger in her eyes and the coy girlish smile that failed to hide it. "You've made a mistake, Mr. Quinn, but what a very nice one. It's too bad all the mistakes we humans make can't be so pleasant. George is my son."

Quinn was sorry he'd had to use such raw bait but it was too late now to snatch it away. "That's hard to believe."

"Quite frankly, I adore flattery, so I'm not going to argue with you."

"I'm sure the mistake's been made before, Mrs. Haywood."

"Oh yes, on a number of occasions, but it never fails to astonish and amuse me. I'm afraid poor George isn't quite so amused. Perhaps this time I won't tell him about it; it will remain our little secret, Mr. Quinn, just between you and me."

And the next hundred people she meets, Quinn thought.

Now that he had come face to face with Mrs. Haywood, he was no longer surprised by her complete rejection of her two daughters. There was no room in the house for younger females who might invite comparisons. Mrs. Haywood's maternal instinct was a good deal weaker than her instinct for self-preservation. She meant to survive, on her own terms, and she couldn't afford the luxury of sentiment. *Poor Willie, her road to security has more chuckholes and detours than she's equipped to handle. If there was no room in the house for Alberta and Ruth, there will certainly be none for Willie.*

Mrs. Haywood had assumed a picturesque, fashion-magazine

pose against the doorjamb. "Of course, I've always kept fit. I see no reason why people should let themselves go after fif—forty. I've always tried to impress upon my family my own axiom: you *are* what you *eat*."

If Mrs. Haywood subsisted on gall and wormwood, then her axiom was undoubtedly true. Quinn said, "I'm sorry to have missed Mr. Haywood. Will he be in his office later this afternoon?"

"Oh no. George is in Hawaii." She obviously didn't like either the change of subject or the idea of George being in Hawaii. "Doctor's orders. It's absurd, of course. There's nothing the matter with George that good cold showers and hard exercise won't cure. But then, doctors are all alike, aren't they? When they have no real cure to offer they recommend a change of climate and scene. Are you a friend of George's?"

"I have some business to discuss with him."

"Well, I don't know when he'll be back. The trip came as a complete surprise to me. He didn't even mention it to me until after he'd bought his ticket. Then it was too late for me to do anything about it. It seems terribly foolish and extravagant to spend all that money because some incompetent doctor suggests it. George could just as easily have gone to stay in San Felice, the climate's the same as Hawaii. I have my own share of aches and pains but *I* don't take off for exotic places. I simply increase my wheat germ and tiger's milk and do a few extra knee bends. Do you believe in vigorous exercise, Mr. Quinn?"

"Oh yes. Yes, indeed."

"I thought so. You seem very fit."

She changed her pose from fashion magazine to Olympic champion, and looked hopefully at Quinn as if she expected another compliment. Quinn couldn't think of any he could offer without gagging. He said instead, "Do you happen to know what air line Mr. Haywood took?"

"No. Should I?"

"You said he'd bought his ticket. I thought he might have showed it to you."

"He brandished an envelope under my nose but I knew he was only doing it to annoy me so I pretended complete indifference. I will not be provoked into a common quarrel, it's too hard on the heart and the arteries. I simply express my viewpoint and refuse to discuss the matter any further. George was quite aware how I felt about this trip of his. I considered it unnecessary and extravagant, and I told him point-blank that if he was really concerned about his health he'd stay home more in the evenings instead of chasing around after women."

"Mr. Haywood isn't married?"

"He was. His wife died many years ago. It was hardly unexpected. She was a poor spiritless little thing, life was too much for her. Since her death, of course, every woman in town has set her cap for George. Fortunately, he has me to point out to him some of their wiles and pretenses. He'd never see through any of them himself, he's hopelessly naïve. A very good example of this happened a few days ago. A woman called and said she had to see George about a mysterious letter she'd received—I heard her because I had picked up the extension phone, quite by accident. Mysterious letter, indeed. Why, a child could have seen through a ruse like that. But George, no. In spite of his cough, off he went before I had a chance to tell him that even if she was speaking the truth she was up to no good. The *right* people just do not receive mysterious letters. When I asked him about it later he blew up at me. I tell you, it's not easy to be a mother in this age of hard liquor and harder women." She smiled with a flash of teeth too white and perfect to have been around as long as the rest of her. "I find you restful and *simpatico,* Mr. Quinn. Do you live in Chicote?"

"No."

"What a shame. I was hoping you could come to dinner one night with George and me. We eat simple, healthful food, but it's quite tasty, nevertheless."

"Thank you for the offer," Quinn said. "You know, you've aroused my curiosity, Mrs. Haywood."

She looked flattered. "I have? How?"

"That mysterious letter. Did it really exist?"

"Well, I can't be sure because George wouldn't tell me. But I think, personally, that she invented it. It was merely an excuse to get George to go over to her house and see her in her own setting, with the two children, and a fire in the fireplace, and something bubbling on the stove, that sort of thing. Deliberate domesticity, if you follow me."

I follow you, Quinn thought, *right up to Martha O'Gorman's front door.*

There was no fire in the fireplace, and if something was bubbling on the stove, none of its aroma was escaping through the locked windows and drawn blinds. The brass lion's-head knocker on the front door looked as if it hadn't been used since Quinn's first visit a week ago. From the yard next door a girl about ten years old, wearing shorts and a T-shirt, watched Quinn curiously as he waited for someone to answer his knock.

After a time she said in a dreamy voice, "They're not home. They left about an hour ago."

"Do you happen to know where they went?"

"They didn't tell me, but I saw Richard putting the sleeping bags in the car so I guess they went camping. They do a lot of camping."

The girl chewed reflectively on her gum for a minute. Quinn said, by way of encouragement, "Have you been a neighbor of the O'Gormans very long?"

"Practically forever. Sally's my best friend. Richard I hate, he's too bossy."

"Have you ever gone camping with them?"

"Once, last year. I didn't like it."

"Why not?"

"I kept thinking of big black bears. Also, rattlesnakes, on account of that was where we were camping, on the Rattlesnake River. It was real scary."

"What's your name, young lady?"

"Miranda Knights. I hate it."

"I think it's very pretty," Quinn said. "Do you remember exactly where you camped on the Rattlesnake River, Miranda?"

"Sure. Paradise Falls, where the Rattlesnake flows into the Torcido River. It's not really a falls, though; it's just some big boulders with trickles of water falling down. Richard likes it because he hides behind the boulders and makes noises like a bear and jumps out to scare Sally and me. Richard's ghastly."

"Oh, I can see that."

"My brothers are ghastly, too, but they're smaller than I am so it's not such a terrible problem."

"I'm sure you can handle it," Quinn said. "Tell me, Miranda, do the O'Gormans usually camp at Paradise Falls?"

"I never heard Sally talk about any other place except that."

"Do you know how to get there?"

"No," Miranda said. "But it doesn't take long, less than an hour."

"Are you sure of that?"

"Naturally. Last year when I was with them and I got homesick and scared of black bears and rattlesnakes, Mrs. O'Gorman kept telling me I was less than an hour from home."

"Thank you, Miranda."

"You're welcome."

Quinn returned to his car. He thought of asking directions at a gas station and setting out immediately for Paradise Falls. But the mid-afternoon heat was so intense that it rose in waves from the streets and sidewalks, and the whole town had a blurry look as if it had grown fuzz.

He went back to his motel room, turned the air-conditioner on full, and lay down on the bed. The more he learned of Martha O'Gorman, the less he felt he knew her. Her image, like the town shimmering in the heat, had become blurred. It had been clear enough at first: she was a woman devoted to her family and still in mourning for a beloved husband, a woman of both sense and sensitivity who dreaded the thought that the inquiry into her husband's disappearance might be reopened. The dread was natural enough, she'd been through a bad time, harassed by gossip, rumors and publicity. They had all died down now and Quinn could understand why she was reluctant to start them up again. What bothered him was the fact that at the coroner's inquest Martha O'Gorman had had a chance to resolve the whole case and she had refused it. If she had not claimed that she had put the dent in the rear bumper of the car by backing into a lamppost, the coroner's jury would probably have decided that O'Gorman's car had been forced off the road. There could be only one of two reasons behind her claim: either it was the truth, or she couldn't afford to leave open that particular area of investigation: *gentlemen of the jury, I put that dent in the bumper, you needn't look any further.* Apparently they hadn't looked any further, and only a few skeptics like Frisby still believed Martha had lied, to save her own skin, or somebody else's.

A dent and a few traces of dark green paint—small things in themselves, made larger in Quinn's eyes by the contradictions in Martha's character and behavior. She was too ill to work, yet she went on a camping trip. And the spot she chose, and, according to the girl Miranda, always chose, was not just any old campground. It was the place which, if the police and John Ronda were correct, her husband's body had floated by. Quinn remembered John Ronda telling him about it: a few miles beyond the bridge where O'Gorman's car went over, the Rattlesnake River joined the Torcido, which at that time was a raging torrent fed by mountain streams and melting snow.

Why did she keep returning to the same place? Quinn wondered. Did she hope to find him, after all these years, wedged between a couple of boulders? Or was she motivated by guilt? And what did she tell the kids?—*Let's all go out and look for Daddy.*

The boy, Richard, had gathered driftwood and pine cones for the campfire and he was itching to light it. But his mother told him it wasn't cool enough yet and it would be better to wait.

His mother and sister Sally were cooking supper on the charcoal grill, beans and corn on the cob and spareribs. Sometimes the ribs caught fire and Sally would put out the flames by squirting them with a plastic water pistol. She didn't handle the pistol the way a boy would have, pretending to shoot something or someone. She was very solemn about it, using the child's toy like an adult, for practical reasons.

Richard wandered off by himself. Some day he wanted to come to this place all alone, without two females around to spoil the illusion that he was a man and that this was a very dangerous spot and he was not in the least afraid of it. Yet he was afraid, and it was not of the place itself but of the change that came over his mother as soon as they arrived. It was a change he didn't understand and couldn't put his finger on. She talked and acted the same as she did at home and she smiled a lot, but her eyes often looked sad and strange, especially when she thought no one was watching her. Richard was always watching. He was too alert and intelligent to miss anything, but still too much of a child to evaluate what he noticed.

He had been seven when his father disappeared. He still remembered his father, though he wasn't sure which were real memories and which were things his mother often talked about: *Do you remember the funny little car you and Daddy made with the wheels from your old scooter?* Yes, he remembered the car, and the scooter wheels, but he couldn't remember his father working with him to build anything; and Martha's continued references, intended to create in him a strong father-picture, confused the boy and made him feel guilty about his memory lapses.

He crawled to the top of a boulder and lay down on his stomach, as still and silent as a lizard in the sun. From here he could see the road that led into the campgrounds. Pretty soon other people would start arriving for the week end and by dusk the campsites would all be taken and the air would be filled with the smell of woodfires and hamburgers cooking, and the shriek of children's voices. But right now he and his mother and Sally were the only ones; they had the choicest campsite, right beside the river, and the best stone barbecue pit and picnic table, and the tallest trees.

Do you remember the first time Daddy brought us here, Richard? You were halfway up a pine tree before we missed you. Daddy had to climb up and bring you down. He could remember climbing the pine tree but not being brought down by anyone. He'd always been a good climber—why hadn't he come down by himself? As he lay on the boulder, it occurred to him for the first time in his life that his mother's memories might be as tenuous as his own and that she was only pretending they were vivid and real.

He heard a car in the distance and raised his head to listen and to watch for it. A couple of minutes later it was visible on the road into camp, a blue and cream Ford Victoria with a man at the wheel. There was no one else in the car and no camping equipment strapped to the roof or piled in the back seat. Richard noticed these details automatically, without being especially curious. It was a few moments before he realized he had seen the car before. About a week ago it had been pulling away from the curb in front of his own house when he had returned home from the Y. When he went inside, he found his mother in the kitchen, white-faced and silent.

fourteen

She saw Quinn getting out of the car and she said to Sally in a carefully casual voice, "Why don't you go and find Richard? Supper won't be ready for another half-hour. You could collect more pine cones so we'll have some to gild for Christmas."

"Are you trying to get rid of me?" The girl glanced thoughtfully at Quinn approaching from the road. "So you can talk to him?"

"Yes."

"Is it about money?"

"Perhaps. I don't know."

Money, or lack of it, was a key word in the O'Gorman household, and the children had learned to respect it. Sally walked briskly away in search of her brother and pine cones.

Martha turned to face Quinn. She stood at rigid attention like a soldier confronted with a surprise inspection. "How did you find me? What do you want?"

"Let's call this a friendly visit."

"Let's not. I can put up with your hounding me personally, but why do you have to bring my children into it?"

"I'm sorry, that's the way things worked out. May I sit down, Mrs. O'Gorman?"

"If you feel you must."

He sat on one of the benches attached to the redwood picnic table, and after a moment's hesitation she walked over to the other bench and sat down, too, as if she were agreeing to a kind of truce. It reminded Quinn of the last time they had met, in the hospital cafeteria. Then, too, there had been a table between them, and that table, like this one, had been invisibly loaded with questions, doubts, suspicions, accusations. Quinn would have liked to brush them all off with his hand and start over again. He knew, from the hostility on her face, that she did not share this feeling.

He said quietly, "You're not obliged to answer any of my questions, Mrs. O'Gorman. I have no official authority to ask them."

"I'm aware of that."

"You can, in fact, order me off the premises."

"The premises belong to the county," she said with a vague

gesture. "You're as welcome as anyone else on public camping grounds."

"You like this place?"

"We've been coming here for many years, since Sally was born."

The statement caught Quinn by surprise. He had assumed that Martha O'Gorman had begun coming to the campsite after her husband's disappearance. As it was, she had merely continued a practice started years before. It fitted in with what he already knew about her character: she was still trying to carry on her life, as much as possible, in the same way as she had before O'Gorman disappeared or died, as if, by repeating the pattern, she could magically invoke O'Gorman's spirit.

Quinn said, "Then your husband was familiar with the surrounding area, the river and so forth?"

"He'd explored every inch of the river—both rivers—a dozen times, as I have."

She looked as though she was daring him to make something of it. Quinn didn't have to, the point was already made. If O'Gorman had planned his own disappearance, his plans had been based on knowledge of, and perhaps experiments on, both rivers involved.

"I know what you're thinking," she said. "You're wrong."

"Am I?"

"My husband was murdered."

"A week ago you were claiming he died in an accident, you were very sure of it, in fact."

"I've had reason to change my mind."

"What reason, Mrs. O'Gorman?"

"I can't tell you that."

"Why not?"

"I don't trust you," she said bluntly, "any more than you trust me. That's not very much, is it?"

Quinn was silent for a minute. "I don't know exactly how much it is, Mrs. O'Gorman. I only know I wish it were more. On both sides."

"Well, it's not."

She got up and went over to the grill and removed the ribs from the heat. They were almost as black as the charcoal they had been cooked over.

"I'm sorry if I've ruined your dinner, Mrs. O'Gorman."

"You haven't," she said crisply. "Richard's like his father, he has to have all meat burned so it's less likely to remind him of—well, the source of it. He loves animals, as Patrick did."

"You're sure now that your husband's dead?"

"I was always sure of that. It was how he died that I couldn't make up my mind about."

"But you have recently, in fact just this week, decided he was murdered?"

"Yes."

"Have you told the authorities?"

"No." There was a brief flash of temper in her eyes. "And I'm not going to. My children and I have suffered enough. The O'Gorman case is closed and it will remain closed."

"Even though you have evidence to reopen it?"

"What gave you that idea?"

"A conversation I had this afternoon with George Haywood's mother," Quinn said. "Mrs. Haywood can't resist an extension phone when other people are on the line."

"Well."

"Is that all you have to say, well?"

"That's all."

"Mrs. O'Gorman, it's not good enough. If you've received concrete evidence of the murder of your husband, it's your duty to hand it over to the police."

"Is it really?" she said with an indifferent shrug. "I guess I should have thought of that before I burned it."

"You burned the letter?"

"I did."

"Why?"

"Both Mr. Haywood and I thought it was the most practical course to take."

"Mr. Haywood and you," Quinn repeated. "How long have you been asking for, and following, George's advice?"

"Is that any of your business, Mr. Quinn?"

"In a way, yes."

"What way?"

"I want to find out what the competition is because I think I've fallen for you."

Her laugh was brief and brittle. "Think again, Mr. Quinn."

"Well, I'm glad I amuse you, anyway."

"You don't. I'm not amused, I'm amazed that you'd consider me naïve enough to swallow such an obvious line of flattery. Did you expect me to believe you? Did you imagine I'd be so swept off my feet that—"

"Stop it," he said sharply.

She stopped, more from surprise than because he had ordered her to.

"I made a statement, Mrs. O'Gorman. Be amused, amazed, or anything else, but I'm sticking by it. Now you can forget it, if you like."

"I think we'd both better forget it."

"All right."

"You—well, you confuse me. You're so unpredictable."

"Nobody's unpredictable," Quinn said, "if someone takes the time and trouble to predict him."

"I wish you'd—we'd stop talking personally like this. It upsets me. I don't know what to think any more."

"Well, don't ask George. His advice hasn't been too good up to now. Was it his idea to burn the letter?"

"No, my own. He agreed with me, because he thought the letter was merely a hoax or a bad joke. He didn't take it seriously the way I did."

"Who wrote it, Mrs. O'Gorman?"

She stared up at the sky. The sun was beginning to set and its golden-red rays were reflected in her face. "There was no signature and I didn't recognize the handwriting. But it was from a man who said he'd murdered my husband five years ago last February."

She looked as though she would burst into tears at the least sign or word of sympathy, so Quinn offered none. "Was it a local letter?"

"No. The postmark was Evanston, Illinois."

"And the contents?"

"He said he'd just been informed that he had cancer of the lung and before he died he wanted to make peace with God and his conscience by confessing all his sins."

"Did he give the actual details of the murder?"

"Yes."

"And his motive?"

"Yes."

"What was it?"

She shook her head slowly, wincing as if the movement pained her. "I simply can't tell you. I'm—ashamed."

"You weren't too ashamed to call George Haywood and invite him over to see the letter."

"I needed his advice, the advice of a man of experience."

"John Ronda's a man of experience. He's also a good friend of yours."

"He's also," she said grimly, "the editor of a newspaper and an incurable talker. Mr. Haywood isn't. I was sure I could trust his discretion. I had another reason, too. Mr. Haywood knew my husband. I thought he could evaluate the charge made against him in the letter."

"The charge against your husband, you mean?"

"Yes. It was a—a terrible thing. I couldn't believe it, of course. No wife could, about her husband. And yet—" Her voice, which had been barely more than a whisper, now faded out entirely.

"And yet you did, Mrs. O'Gorman?"

"I didn't want to, God knows. But for some time before my husband's death I'd been aware of a darkness in our lives. I kept trying to act as though it didn't exist. I couldn't force myself to turn on the lights and find out what the darkness was hiding. Then this letter came and the lights were on, whether I wanted them to be or not." She rubbed her eyes, as if to rub away the memory. "I panicked and called George Haywood. I realize now that it was a mistake, but I was desperate. I had to talk to someone who'd known Patrick and worked with him. A man. It had to be a man."

"Why?"

Her mouth moved in a bitter little smile. "Women are easily fooled, even the smart ones, perhaps especially the smart ones. Mr. Haywood came over to the house right away. I guess I was hysterical by that time. He acted very calm, though I had the impression he was quite excited underneath."

"What was his opinion of the letter?"

"He said it was a lot of hogwash, that every murder attracts false confessions from emotionally disturbed people. I knew that was true, of course, but there was something so real and poignant about the letter, and every detail of the murder was correct. If the person who sent it was disturbed, then the disturbance certainly hadn't affected his memory or his ability to express himself."

"It often doesn't."

"I even considered the possibility that Patrick was alive and had written it himself. But there were too many discrepancies. First of all, it wasn't his style. The envelope was addressed to Mrs. Patrick O'Gorman, Chicote, California. Patrick would surely have remembered his own street and house number. Then, too, the writing wasn't Patrick's. He was left-handed and wrote with an extreme slant towards the left. The handwriting in the letter slanted in the opposite direction and it was very awkward and childish, more like a third-grader's than a grown man's. But the overwhelming reason Patrick couldn't have written the letter was the accusation against him. No man would admit such a thing about himself."

"Did the writer claim to have known your husband well?"

"No. He'd never seen him until that night. He was a hobo who'd been camping out by the river. When the weather got too bad he decided to move on to Bakersfield. He was standing on the side of the road waiting to hitch a ride. Patrick stopped and picked him up. Then Patrick—oh, my God, I can't believe it, I won't!"

Quinn knew she did, though, and no amount of tears would wash away the belief. She was weeping, almost without sound, her hands covering her face, the tears slithering out between her fingers, down her wrists, into the sleeves of her denim jacket.

"Mrs. O'Gorman," he said. "Martha. Listen to me, Martha. Perhaps Haywood was right and the letter was a sadistic joke."

She raised her head and stared at him, looking like a forlorn child. "How could anyone hate me that much?"

"I don't know. But a twisted person can hate anyone, with or without reason. What was the general tone of the letter?"

"Sorrow and regret. Fear, too, fear of dying. And hatred, but not directed against me. He seemed to loathe himself for what he'd done, and Patrick for making him do it."

"Your husband made an improper advance, is that what you've been trying to say, Martha?"

"Yes." It was hardly more than a sigh of admission.

"That's why you burned the letter instead of showing it to the authorities?"

"I had to destroy it, for the sake of my children, myself—yes, and for Patrick's sake, too. Don't you see that?"

"Yes, of course I do."

"There was nothing to be gained by going to the police, and everything to be lost. A great deal's been lost already, but it's my own private personal loss, and I can stand that as long as my children are protected and Patrick's good name is kept intact. As it will be. Even if you went to the police and told them everything I've said this afternoon, they couldn't do a thing. I would deny every word of it, and so would Mr. Haywood. I have his promise. The letter never existed."

"I suppose you realize that suppressing evidence about a murder is very serious?"

"Legally, I guess it is, but that doesn't concern me right now. It's funny, I've always been a law-abiding citizen but at the moment I couldn't care less about the legal technicalities. If a murderer goes unpunished because of me, I won't regret it. Too many innocent people would be punished along with him. Justice and the law don't always amount to the same thing—or are you still too young and starry-eyed to have found this out?"

"Not young," Quinn said. "Definitely not starry-eyed."

She was studying him intently, her face grave and a little sad. "I think you're both."

"That's your privilege."

"You'd like me to go running to the police, wouldn't you?"

"No. I just—"

"Yes, you would. You really believe that when the law demands an eye for an eye, that's what it gets. Well, you're wrong. The mathematics involved becomes amazingly intricate and somehow the law ends up with a dozen eyes. Six of them are *not* going to belong to me and my children. If necessary, I would swear on a stack of Bibles in front of the Supreme Court that no letter concerning my husband's death was ever delivered to me."

"Would George be willing to do the same?"

"Yes."

"Because he's in love with you?"

"You seem to have romance on your mind," she said coldly. "I hope it's just a phase. No, Mr. Haywood is not in love with me. He happens to view the situation in the same light as I do. Whether the letter was a hoax, as he believes, or the truth, as I do, we both agreed that it would be disastrous to publicize it. And that's exactly what handing it over to the police would have meant, so I burned it. Do you want to know where I burned it? In the incinerator in the backyard, so that every single ash of it would be blown away by the wind. It exists now only in the mind of the man who wrote it, and Mr. Haywood's, and my own."

"And mine."

"Not yours, Mr. Quinn. You never saw it. You can't be sure there ever was such a thing. I could have invented it, couldn't I?"

162

"I don't think so."

"I wish I had invented it. I wish—"

Whatever wishes she had were blown away by the wind like the ashes of the letter. Even though she was looking at Quinn he had the feeling he was invisible to her, that her eyes were focused on some point in the past, some happier and more innocent place than this.

"Martha—"

"Please, I don't want you to call me Martha."

"It's your name."

She raised her head. "I am Mrs. Patrick O'Gorman."

"That was a long time ago, Martha. Wake up. The dream's over, the lights are on."

"I don't want them to be on."

"But they are. You said so yourself."

"I can't bear it," she whispered. "I thought we were so happy, such a happy family. . . . And then the letter came and suddenly everything turned to garbage. And it was too late to clean it up, get rid of it, so I had to pretend, I must go on pretending—"

"Pretend yourself right into a butterfly net. I can't stop you. I can warn you, though, that you're making too much of everything. Your life didn't change from moonlight and roses to garbage just because O'Gorman made a pass at another man. It was always some moonlight, some roses, some garbage, like anyone else's life. You're not a tragic heroine picked out for special glory and special disaster, and O'Gorman wasn't a hero or a villain, just an unfortunate man. You told me the last time we talked that you were very realistic. Do you still believe that?"

"I don't know. I—I thought I was. I managed things so that they worked out."

"Including O'Gorman."

"Yes."

"You knocked yourself out covering up O'Gorman's mistakes and weaknesses. Now that you've come to realize you knocked yourself out for nothing, you can't face it. One minute you stick your chin in the air and announce proudly that you're Mrs. Patrick O'Gorman, and the next minute you're squawking about garbage. When are you going to reach a compromise?"

"That's no concern of yours."

"I'm making it my concern, as of now."

She looked a little frightened. "What are you going to do?"

"Do? What can I do?" he said wearily. "Except wait around for you to get tired running from one extreme to another. Maybe eventually you'll settle for something worse than paradise but better than hell. Do you think it's possible?"

"I don't know. And I can't talk about it here, now."

"Why not?"

"It's getting dark. I must call the children." She stood up. The movement seemed uncertain and so did her voice. "I— will you stay for supper?"

"I'd like to, very much. But I'm afraid the timing's wrong. I don't want to be presented to your children as a surprise intruder on their camp-out. This place belongs to you and them and O'Gorman. I'll wait until I can offer a place the three of you can share with me."

"Please don't talk like that. We barely know each other."

"When we last met, you told me something I believed at the time. You said I was too old to learn about love. I no longer believe that, Martha. What I think is that, until now, I've been too young and scared to learn about it."

She had turned away, bowing her head, so that he could see the white nape of her neck that contrasted with the deep tan on her face. "We have nothing in common. Nothing."

"How do you know?"

"John Ronda told me something about you, how you lived, where you worked. I could never adjust to such a life, and I'm not foolish enough to think I could change you."

"The change has already started."

"Has it?" Her mouth smiled but her voice remained sad. "I said before that you were starry-eyed. You are. People don't change just because they want to."

"You've had too much trouble, Martha. You're disillusioned."

"And how does one go about getting re-illusioned?"

"I can't answer that for anyone else. I only know it happened to me."

"When?"

"Not long ago."

"How?"

"I'm not sure how." He could remember the exact moment, though, the pungent smell of pine, the moon growing in the trees like a golden melon, the stars bursting out all over the sky like popping seeds. And Sister Blessing's voice, tinged with impatience: *"Haven't you ever seen a sky before?" "Not this one." "It's the same as always." "It looks different to me." "Do you suppose you're having a religious experience?" "I am admiring the universe."*

Martha was watching him with a mixture of interest and anxiety. "What happened to you, Joe?"

"I guess I fell back in love with life, I became a part of the world again after a long exile. The funny thing is that it happened in the most unworldly place in the world."

"The Tower?"

"Yes." He stared at the last faint glow in the sky. "After I left you last week, I went back to the Tower."

"Did you see Sister Blessing? Did you ask her why she hired you to find Patrick?"

"I asked her. She didn't answer, though. I doubt if she even heard me."

"Why? Was she sick?"

"In a sense, yes. She was sick with fear."

"Of what?"

"Not getting into heaven. By hiring me, by having anything to do with me in fact, she'd committed a grave sin. Also she'd withheld money from the communal fund and the word 'money' to the Master is both sacred and dirty. He's a queer man, compelling, forceful, and quite insane. He has a strangle hold on his flock, and the smaller the flock becomes, the more desperate the strangle hold gets and the more extreme his proclamations and edicts and punishments. Even his old followers, like his own wife and Sister Blessing, show signs of restlessness. As for the younger ones, it's only a matter of time until they escape from the Tower."

He thought of the tortured face of Sister Contrition as she led her three docile, rebellious-eyed children into the living room, and of the querulous voice of Mother Pureza who had already escaped from the Tower and was living in the brighter rooms of her childhood with her beloved servant, Capirote.

Martha said, "Are you going back there?"

"Yes, I made a promise to go back. I must also tell Sister Blessing that the man she hired me to find is dead."

"You won't mention the letter?"

"No."

"To anyone?"

"To anyone." Quinn stood up. "Well, I'd better be going."

"Yes."

"When will I see you again, Martha?"

"I don't know. I'm very confused right now because of the letter and—and the things you've said."

"Did you come here today to run away from me?"

"Yes."

"Are you sorry I found you?"

"I can't answer that. Please don't ask me."

"All right."

He walked over to his car and got in. When he glanced back Martha was lighting the campfire and the mounting flames made her quiet face seem vivacious and warm, the way it had looked in the hospital cafeteria when she had first talked about her marriage to O'Gorman.

"We came back as soon as we heard the car leave," Richard said. He had smelled some mystery in the air as distinctly as he had smelled the first puffs of smoke from the campfire. "Who was the man?"

"A friend of mine," Martha said.

"You don't have many boy friends."

"No, I don't. Would you like me to?"

"I guess it'd be O.K."

"No, it *wouldn't*," Sally said earnestly. "*Mothers* don't have boy friends."

Martha put her hand on the girl's shoulder. "Sometimes they do, when they no longer have a husband of their own."

"Why?"

"Men and women are meant to become interested in each other and get married."

"And have children?"

"Sometimes, yes."

"How many children do you think you'll have?"

"Of all the stupid questions I ever heard in my life," Richard said with contempt. "You don't have children when you're old and gray."

Martha's tone was sharper than she intended. "That's not very complimentary, is it, Richard?"

"Gosh, no. But you're my mother. Mothers don't expect compliments."

"It would be nice to be surprised for a change. My hair, by the way, is brown, not gray."

"Gee whiz, old and gray is just an expression."

"Well, it's an expression I don't care to hear until it's literally true. Perhaps not even then, is that clear?"

"Boy, are you touchy tonight! A guy can't say anything around here without getting ranked. When do we eat?"

"You may serve yourselves," Martha said coldly. "I'm feeling far too decrepit to lift anything."

Richard stared at her, wide-eyed and open-mouthed. "Well, boy oh boy, you're not even acting like a *mother* any more."

After the children were settled for the night in their sleeping bags, Martha took the mirror out of her handbag and sat down to study her face by the light of the fire. It seemed a very long time since she had looked at herself with any real interest, and she was depressed by what she saw. It was an ordinary, healthy, competent face, the kind that might appeal to a widower with children, seeking someone to run his house, but would have no attraction for an unattached young man like Quinn.

I acted like an idiot, she thought. *I almost believed him for a while. I should have believed Richard instead.*

fifteen

On his way back to the motel Quinn passed the stucco building occupied by the staff of the *Beacon*. The lights were still on.

He wasn't anxious to meet Ronda again since there were too many things he couldn't afford to tell him. But he was pretty sure Ronda would find out he was in town and be suspicious if no contact was made. He parked the car and went into the building.

Ronda was alone in his office, reading a San Francisco *Chronicle* and drinking a can of beer. "Hello, Quinn. Sit down, make yourself at home. Want a beer?"

"No thanks."

"I heard you were back in our fair city. What have you been doing all week, sleuthing?"

"No," Quinn said. "Mostly acting as nursemaid to an ersatz admiral in San Felice."

"Any news?"

"News like what?"

"You know damned well like what. Did you come across anything more about the O'Gorman case?"

"Nothing you could print. A lot of rumors and opinions, but no concrete evidence. I'm beginning to go along with your theory about the hitchhiking stranger."

Ronda looked half-skeptical, half-pleased. "Oh, you are, eh? Why?"

"It seems to fit the facts better than any other."

"Is that your only reason?"

"Yes. Why?"

"Just checking. I thought you might have latched onto something you prefer to keep secret." Ronda tossed the empty can into a wastebasket. "Since you got most of your information from me in the first place, it wouldn't be sporting of you to withhold anything now, would it?"

"Definitely not," Quinn said virtuously. "I'd take a dim view of such unsportsmanlike conduct."

"I'm quite serious, Quinn."

"So am I."

"Then *sound* it."

"All right."

"Now we'll start over again. What have you been doing all week?"

"I answered that before. I had a job in San Felice." Quinn knew he'd have to tell Ronda something of his activities in order to allay suspicion. "While I was there I talked to Alberta Haywood's sister, Ruth. I didn't learn anything about O'Gorman, but I found out a few things about Alberta Haywood. I found out more when I went to see her in Tecolote prison."

"You *saw* her? Personally?"

"Yes."

"Well, I'll be damned. How did you manage that? I've been trying to get an interview for years."

"I have a private detective's license issued in Nevada. Law enforcement officials are usually glad to coöperate."

"Well, how is she?" Ronda said, leaning excitedly across the desk. "Did she tell you anything? What did she talk about?"

"O'Gorman."

"O'Gorman. Well, I'll be damned. This is just what—"

"Before you go off the deep end I might as well tell you that her references to O'Gorman weren't very rational."

"What do you mean?"

"She's under the delusion that the uproar over O'Gorman's disappearance caused her to lose her powers of concentration and make the mistake that sent her to jail. She even tried to convince me that O'Gorman planned it deliberately to get back at her for snubbing him or for being fired by her brother, George."

"She blames O'Gorman for everything?"

"Yes."

"That's nutty," Ronda said. "It would mean, among other things, that O'Gorman knew about her embezzlements a month before the bank examiners, and that he calculated both the uproar over his disappearance and its effect on her. Doesn't she realize how impossible that is?"

"She's dealing with her own guilt, not the laws of possibility. She completely rejects the idea that O'Gorman's dead, because, in her words, if he was murdered, she has no one to blame for her predicament. She's got to cling to the delusion that O'Gorman planned his disappearance in order to avenge himself on her. Without O'Gorman to blame, she'd have to blame herself, and she can't face that yet. Perhaps she never will."

"How far gone is she?"

"I don't know. Too far to follow, anyway."

"What made her crack up like that?"

"Five years in a cell would do it for me," Quinn said. "Maybe they did it for Alberta."

The memory of the scene in the penitentiary filled him with contempt and disgust, not at Alberta's sickness but at the sickness of a society which cut off parts of itself to appease the whole and then wondered why it was not feeling well.

Ronda was pacing up and down the office as if he himself were confined in a cell. "I can't print what you've just told me. A lot of people would disapprove."

"Naturally."

"Does George Haywood know all this?"

"He should. He visits her once a month."

"How did you find that out?"

"Several people told me, including Alberta. George's visits are painful to her, and presumably to George, too, yet he keeps on making them."

"Then his split with her was just a phony to fool the old lady?"

"The old lady, and perhaps other people."

"George is an oddball," Ronda said, frowning up at the ceiling. "I can't understand him. One minute he's so secretive he wouldn't give you the time of day, and the next he's in here pumping my hand like a long-lost brother and telling me about his trip to Hawaii. Why?"

"So you'd print it in the *Beacon*. That's my guess."

"But he's never given us any society-page material before. He even squawks like hell if his name is included in a guest list at a party. Why the sudden change of policy?"

"Obviously he wants everyone to know he's gone to Hawaii."

"Social butterfly stuff, and the like? Nonsense. That doesn't fit George."

"A lot of things don't fit George," Quinn said. "But he's wearing them anyway, and probably for the same reason I wore my brother's cast-off clothes when I was a kid—because he has to. Well, I'd better shove off. I've taken enough of your time."

Ronda was opening another can of beer. "There's no hurry. I had a little argument with my wife and I'm staying away from the house for a while until she cools off. Sure you won't join me in a beer?"

"Reasonably sure."

"By the way, have you seen Martha O'Gorman since you got back?"

"Why?"

"Just wondering. My wife called her at the hospital this afternoon to invite her over for Sunday dinner. They said she'd taken the day off because of illness, but when my wife went over to the house to offer to help her, Martha wasn't there and the car was gone. I thought you might know something about it."

"You give me too much credit. See you later, Ronda."

"Wait just a minute." Ronda was hunched over the can of beer, staring into it. "I have a funny feeling about you, Quinn."

"A lot of people have. Don't worry about it."

"Oh, but I *am* worried. This funny feeling tells me you're holding something back, maybe something very important. Now that wouldn't be nice, would it? I'm your friend, your pal, your buddy. I gave you the low-down on the O'Gorman case, I lent you my personal file."

"You've been true-blue," Quinn said. "Good night, friend, pal, buddy. Sorry about that funny feeling of yours. Take a couple of aspirin, maybe it'll go away."

"You think so, eh?"

"I could be wrong, of course."

"You could be and you are, dammit. You can't fool an old newspaperman like me. I'm intuitive."

When Ronda got up to open the door he stumbled against the corner of the desk. Quinn wondered how long he'd been drinking and how much the beer had to do with his powers of intuition.

He was glad to get back out to the street. A fresh breeze was blowing, bringing with it half the population of Chicote. The town, deserted at noon, had come to life as soon as the sun went down. All the stores on Main Street were open and there were line-ups in front of the movie theaters and at the malt and hamburger stands. Cars full of teen-agers cruised up and down the street, horns blasting, radios blaring, tires squeaking. The noise eased their restlessness and covered up their lack of any real activity.

At the motel Quinn parked his car in the garage for the night and was closing the door when a voice spoke from the shrubbery: "Mr. Quinn. Joe."

He turned and saw Willie King leaning against the side of the garage as if she had been, or was going to be, sick. Her face was as white as the jasmine blossoms behind her and her eyes looked glassy and not quite in focus.

"I've been waiting," she said. "Hours. It seems hours. I didn't—I don't know what to do."

"Is this another of your dramatic performances, Willie?"

"No. *No!* This is *me.*"

"The real you, eh?"

"Oh, stop it. Can't you tell when someone's acting and when she isn't?"

"In your case, no."

"Very well," she said with an attempt at dignity. "I won't—I shan't bother you any further."

"Shan't you."

She started to walk away and Quinn noticed for the first time that she was wearing a pair of old canvas sneakers. It seemed unlikely that she would put on sneakers before giving a performance. He called her name, and after a second's hesitation she turned back to face him.

"What's the matter, Willie?"

"Everything. My whole life, everything's ruined."

"Do you want to come in my room and talk about it?"

"No."

"You don't want to talk about it?"

"I don't want to come in your room. I mean, it wouldn't be proper."

"Perhaps not," Quinn said, smiling. "There's a little court-yard where we can sit, if you prefer."

The courtyard consisted of a few square yards of grass around a brightly lit bathtub-sized swimming pool. No one was in the pool, but the wet footprints of a child were visible on the concrete and one tiny blue swim fin floated on the surface of the water. Hiding the courtyard from the street and from the motel units was a hedge of pink and white oleanders, heavy with blossoms.

The furniture had all been put under cover for the night, so they sat on the grass which was still warm from the sun. Willie looked embarrassed, and sorry that she had come. She said lamely, "The grass is very nice. It's very hard to keep it that way in this climate. You have to keep the hose running practically all the time and even then the soil gets too alkaline—"

"So that's what's on your mind, grass?"

"No."

"What is it then?"

"George," she said. "George is gone."

"You've known that for some time."

"No. I mean, he's really *gone*. And nobody knows where, nobody."

"Are you sure?"

"I'm sure of one thing, he didn't take any trip to Hawaii." Her voice broke and she pressed one hand against her throat as if she were trying to mend the break. "He lied to me. He could have told me anything about himself, anything in this world, and I would still love him. But he deliberately lied, he made a fool of me."

"How do you figure that, Willie?"

"This afternoon after you left the office, I began to get suspicious—I don't know why, it just sort of came over me that maybe I'd been a patsy. I phoned all the airlines in Los Angeles long distance. I told them a story about an emergency in the family and how I had to contact George Haywood and wasn't sure whether he'd gone to Hawaii or not. Well, they checked their passenger lists for Tuesday and Wednesday and there was no George Haywood on any of them."

"They could have made a mistake," Quinn said. "Or George might be traveling under another name. It's possible."

She wanted to believe it, but couldn't. "No. He's run away, I'm sure of it. From me and from his mother and the two of us fighting over him. Oh, not fighting physically or even outwardly, but fighting all the same. I guess he couldn't stand it any more, he couldn't make a decision either in her favor or mine so he had to escape from both of us."

"That would be a coward's decision, and from everything I've heard about George, he's no coward."

"Maybe I've made him into one without realizing what I was doing. Well at least I have one satisfaction—he didn't tell *her* the truth either. I wish now I had gone to her house instead of telephoning her. I'd like to have seen the expression on the old biddy's face when she found out her darling Georgie hadn't taken the trip to Hawaii after all."

"You called her?"

"Yes."

"Why?"

"I *wanted* to," she said harshly. "I wanted her to suffer the way I was suffering—to wonder, as I'm wondering, whether George will ever come back."

"Aren't you being a little dramatic? What makes you think he won't come back?"

She shook her head helplessly.

"Do you know more than you're telling me, Willie?"

"Only that he's had something on his mind lately that he wouldn't talk about."

"By 'lately' do you mean since I arrived in Chicote?"

"Even before that, though it's been worse since you started prying around and asking questions."

"Perhaps he was afraid of my questions," Quinn said. "And the reason he left town is to get away from me, not you and his mother."

She was silent for a minute. Then, "Why should he be afraid of you? George has nothing to hide except—well, except that business the first night when I picked you up in the café."

"That was George's idea?"

"Yes."

"What was the reason behind it?"

"He said"—her emphasis on the word seemed involuntary— "He *said* you might be a cheap crook planning an extortion racket. He wanted me to keep you occupied while he searched your room."

"How did he know where my room was, or even that I existed?"

"I told him. I overheard you talking to Ronda in the office that first afternoon. I heard you mention Alberta Haywood and I thought I'd better call George right away. I did, and he asked me to follow you and find out who you were and where you were staying."

"Then it wasn't the name O'Gorman that caught your attention, it was Alberta's?"

"Her actual name wasn't mentioned, but Ronda referred to a local embezzlement and a nice little lady and I knew it had to be Alberta."

"Do you run to the phone and call George every time someone mentions Alberta?"

"No. But I was suspicious of you. You had a look about you, a what's-in-it-for-me look that I didn't trust. Also, I guess I used the occasion to seem important in George's eyes. I don't," she added somberly, "very often get the chance. I'm just an ordinary woman. It's hard to compete with all that wheat germ and tiger's milk and the other stuff Mrs. Haywood goes in for to attract attention and make other women seem dull by comparison."

"You're developing a real complex about the old lady, Willie."

"I can't help it. She bugs me. Sometimes I almost think that the reason I fell in love with George was because she was so dead set against it. Maybe that's a terrible thing to say, but she's a monster, Joe, I mean it. More and more every year I can understand why Alberta committed those crimes. She was defying her mother. Alberta knew she'd be caught someday. Perhaps she deliberately arranged to be caught to punish and disgrace the old lady. Mrs. Haywood's not stupid—this is as close to a compliment as she'll ever get from me—and I think she understands Alberta's underlying motive, and that's why she cast her off completely and insisted George do the same."

But Quinn couldn't bring himself to believe it. "There were a hundred other ways Alberta could have punished her mother without going to jail herself and without dragging George into it."

Willie was plucking blades of grass one by one, like a young girl playing he-loves-me, he-loves-me-not, with daisy petals. "Where do you think he's gone, Joe?"

"I don't know. It would help if I could find out why he left."

"To get away from me and his mother."

"He could have done that some time ago."

It was the timing that interested Quinn. Martha O'Gorman had shown George the letter from her husband's murderer, and, although George professed to consider the letter a hoax, it had excited him, according to Martha. Immediately afterward he had arranged to have it known all over town that he was taking a trip to Hawaii for his health. He had even made a point of having the news published in the local paper.

Quinn said, "Wasn't it unusual on George's part to make his plans public?"

"A little. It surprised me."

"Why do you think he did it?"

"I have no idea."

"I have. But you're not going to like it, Willie."

"I don't like things the way they are now, either. Could they be worse?"

"A lot worse," Quinn said. "All the noise George made about the trip might mean that he was trying to establish an alibi in advance for something that has happened, or is going to happen, right here in Chicote."

She kept plucking away at the grass with a grim determination intended to conceal her fear. "Nothing's happened so far."

"That's right. But I want you to be careful, Willie."

"Me? Why me?"

"You were George's confidante. He might have told you things he now regrets telling you."

"He told me nothing," she said roughly. "George never had a confidante in his life. He's a loner, like Alberta. The way those two can clam up, it's not—not human."

"Maybe clams have a way of communicating with each

other. Or do you still refuse to believe he went to visit Alberta every month?"

"I believe it now."

"Think back, Willie. Was there ever a time when you were with George that he was off guard?—say he was in a state of extreme anxiety, or he'd had too much to drink, or he was heavily sedated."

"George didn't discuss his worries with me, and he very seldom drinks. Once in a while he has to take a lot of stuff for his asthma."

"Did you ever see him on those occasions?"

"Sometimes. But he never seemed to act any different. Oh, maybe a little dopey, you know, not quite with it." She hesitated, her hands quiet now, as if she was chaneling all her energies into the task of remembering. "Then there was the time he had his appendix out, about three years ago. I went up to the hospital to be with him because Mrs. Haywood refused. She was at home throwing fits about how George's appendix would have been perfectly all right if he'd eaten his wheat germ and molasses. I was in the room when he was coming out of the anesthetic.

"He was a scream. Afterwards he wouldn't believe he'd said some of the things he did. The nurses were practically hysterical because he kept telling them to put on their clothes, that it was no proper way to run a hospital, with naked nurses."

"Was he aware of your presence?"

"Sort of."

"What do you mean, sort of?"

"He thought I was Alberta," she said. "He called me by her name and told me I was a silly old spinster who should know better."

"Know better than to do what?"

"He didn't explain. He was mad at her, though, boiling mad."

"Why?"

"Because she'd given away some of his clothes to a transient who'd come to the house. He called her a gullible, soft-hearted fool. Which made about as much sense as the naked nurses. Alberta might be a fool but she's neither gullible nor soft-hearted. If there really was a transient, and if she gave him some of George's clothes, she must have had a reason besides simple generosity. I mean, the Haywoods aren't the kind who give handouts at the door. They might contribute to various organized charities but they're not impulsive off-the-cuff givers. So I don't believe it really happened, any more than the nurses had done a striptease."

"Did you ask George about it later?"

"Well, I told him some of the things he said."

"What was his reaction?"

"He laughed, not very comfortably. George is terribly dignified, he hated the idea that he'd made a fool of himself. Yet he has a sense of humor, too, and he couldn't help laughing about the naked nurses."

"Was he equally amused by his references to Alberta?"

"No, I think he felt guilty over calling her those names even when he wasn't responsible for his words."

Willie had lost interest in the grass and the little game of he-loves-me, he-loves-me-not. She had transferred her attention to a hole in the toe of her left sneaker and was picking at the frayed canvas like a bird gathering lint for its nest. Beyond the oleander hedge the city noise seemed remote and meaningless.

"What's George's financial status, Willie?"

She looked surprised that anyone should question it. "He's no millionaire, he works for his money. And though business isn't as good as it was a few years ago, it's good enough. He doesn't spend much except on his mother. She's pretty extravagant. The last face job she had done in Los Angeles cost a thousand dollars and naturally she had to buy a new wardrobe to match the quote new unquote face."

"Does George do much gambling, like his sister?"

"No."

"Sure of that?"

"How can I be sure of anything at this point?" she said in a tired voice. "All I know is that he never talked about it and he hasn't the temperament of a gambler. George plans things, he doesn't like to take chances. He nearly blew a fuse when I bought a ticket on the Irish Sweepstakes last year. He said I was a sucker. Well, I didn't win, so maybe he was right."

George and Alberta, Quinn thought. *The two planners, the two clams who could communicate with each other through closed shells. What had they communicated, a new plan? Alberta's parole hearing is coming up soon, it seems a funny time for George to disappear. Unless that's part of the new plan.*

Willie's elaborate beehive coiffure had come undone and was sagging to one side like a real hive deserted by its bees and exposed to the weather. It gave her a slightly tipsy look that suited her; Willie's judgments weren't entirely sober.

"Joe."

"Yes."

"Where do you think George is?"

"Perhaps right here in Chicote."

"You mean living under an assumed name in a hotel or boarding house or something? He couldn't get away with that. Everyone in town knows him. Besides, why would he have to hide out?"

"He might be waiting."

"For what?"

"God knows. I don't."

"If he'd only confided in me, if he'd only asked my advice—" Her voice started to break again but she caught it in time. "But that's silly, isn't it? George doesn't ask, he tells."

"You think you're going to change him after you're married?"

"I don't want to change him. I *like* to be told." Her mouth was set in a thin, obstinate line. "I really do."

"All right, all right, you like to be told, so I'll tell you. Go home and get a good night's rest."

"That isn't the kind of thing I meant."

"Let's face it, Willie. You don't like to be told one darned thing."

"I do so. By the right person."

"Well, the right person's not here. You'll have to accept a substitute."

"You're a lousy substitute," she said softly. "You're not sure enough of yourself to give orders. You couldn't fool a dog."

"Oh, I don't know. A few lady dogs have taken me quite seriously."

She turned away, flushing. "I'll go home, but not because you told me to. And don't worry about George and me. I can handle him—after we're married."

"Those are famous last words, Willie."

"I guess they are, but I've got to believe them."

He went with her to her car. They walked apart and in silence, like strangers who happened to be going in the same direction, absorbed by their own problems. When she got into the car he touched her shoulder lightly and she gave him a brief, anxious smile.

"Drive carefully, Willie."

"Oh, sure."

"Everything's going to be all right."

"Want to give me a written guarantee of that?"

"Nobody gets a written guarantee in this world," Quinn said, "so don't sit around waiting for one."

"I won't."

"Good night, Willie."

He passed the motel office on his way back to his room. The entire Frisby clan was gathered around the desk, Grandpa, Frisby and his wife, the daughter and her husband, and several people Quinn hadn't seen before. They were all talking at once and the radio was going full blast. It was as noisy as a revival meeting. The hand-clapping, foot-stamping music from the radio suited the occasion perfectly.

Frisby saw Quinn through the window and came sprinting

out of the door, his bathrobe flapping around his legs, his face glistening with sweat and excitement.

"Mr. Quinn! Wait a minute, Mr. Quinn!"

Quinn waited. A sense of foreboding shook his body, and he wasn't quite sure whether it was imagination or whether he'd experienced the shock waves of an actual earthquake. He said, "I have my key, thanks, Mr. Frisby."

"I know that. But I figured, being as the radio in your room is on the blink, you maybe missed the big news." The words tumbled moistly around Frisby's mouth like clothes in a washing machine. "You'll never believe it."

"Try me."

"Such a nice quiet little woman, the last person in the world you'd expect to pull a stunt like that."

It's Martha, Quinn thought, *something's happened to Martha.* He wanted to reach out and put his hand over Frisby's mouth to prevent him from saying any more, but he forced himself to stand still, to listen.

"You could have knocked me over with a feather when I heard about it. I yelled to the wife and she came running in, thinking I was having a fit. Bessie, I told her, Bessie, you'll never guess what's happened. 'The Martians have landed,' said she. 'No,' I said, 'Alberta Haywood has escaped from prison.'"

"God." The word was not an expression of surprise but of gratitude and relief. For a minute he couldn't even think about the news of Alberta Haywood, his mind refused to go beyond Martha. She was safe. She was sitting, as he had last seen her, in front of the campfire, and she was safe.

"Yes, sir, Miss Haywood escaped clean as a whistle in a supply truck that was servicing the candy machines in the canteen."

"When?"

"This afternoon some time. The prison authorities didn't release the details, but she's gone all right. Or all wrong, as the case may be, ha ha." Frisby's laugh was more like a nervous little hiccough. "Anyway, the police haven't been able to find her yet because the supply truck stopped at three or four other places and she could have gotten off at any one of them with nobody the wiser. Maybe it was all planned ahead of time and she had a friend waiting for her in a car. That's my story. What do you think of it, eh?"

"It sounds reasonable," Quinn said. *Except for two possible errors. Instead of a friend in a car, it might have been a brother in a green Pontiac station wagon.*

The clams had communicated, the planners were at work.

"Maybe," Frisby said, "she's coming back here."

"Why?"

"'On television, when someone escapes from prison, they always return to the scene of the crime to straighten out a miscarriage of justice. It could be she's innocent and she's going to try and prove it."

"Whatever she's trying to prove, Mr. Frisby, she's not innocent. Good night."

For a long time after he went to bed Quinn lay awake listening to the whine of the air-conditioner and the loud angry voices of the couple in the next room quarreling over money.

Money, Quinn thought suddenly. Sister Blessing's money had come from her son in Chicago, and the letter Martha O'Gorman had destroyed had been postmarked Evanston, Illinois. A son in Chicago, a letter from Evanston. If there was a connection, the only person to ask about it was Sister Blessing.

sixteen

Even while the new day was still no more than a barely perceptible lightening of the sky, Sister Blessing knew it was going to be a good one. Her bare feet sped down the dark path to the shower room, and she sang as she washed herself, unmindful of the coldness of the water and the grittiness of the gray homemade soap: "There's a good day coming, yes, Lord, there's a good day coming, yes, Lord."

"Peace be with you," she called out when Sister Contrition came in, carrying a kerosene lantern. "A fine morning, is it not?"

Sister Contrition put the lantern down with a clank of disapproval. "And pray, what's the matter with you all of a sudden?"

"Nothing, Sister. I am well, I am happy."

"You'd think a person would have more to do in this world than going around being happy."

"You can be happy and do things, too, can't you?"

"I don't know, I've never tried."

"Poor Sister, is your head bothering you again?"

"You attend to your head, I'll attend to mine." Sister Contrition poured a little water into a basin, rinsed her face and dried it on a scrap of wool salvaged from a worn-out robe. "You'd think a person would take a more sober viewpoint, especially after the Punishment."

"The Punishment's over." But she became a little less cheerful at the memory of it. It had been a black time for her, in spite of her satisfaction in knowing that things had not been easy in the colony while she was gone. The Master was finally forced to cut her isolation to three days instead of five because he couldn't manage Mother Pureza without her and because Brother Crown had sprained his ankle falling off the tractor. *They need me*, she thought, and her spirits soared again, beyond the dark grimy room and above the disgruntled face of Sister Contrition, still oily after its brief bath. *They need me and I am here.* She hung on to the words like a child to the string of a kite riding a high wind.

She began singing again. "There's a good day coming, yes, Lord."

"Well, it's about time," Sister Contrition said irritably. "I've had enough of the other kind lately, what with Karma acting up. I hear there's a new convert."

"It's too early to tell but I have hopes, very high hopes. It may be a whole new beginning for the colony. Perhaps it's a sign from Heaven that we are to prosper again like in the old days."

"Is it a man?"

"Yes. His soul is very troubled, I hear."

"Is he young? I mean, is he young enough so I'll have to keep an eye on Karma every minute she's awake?"

"I haven't seen him."

"God grant he's old and feeble," Sister Contrition said, sighing. "And poor eyesight wouldn't hurt, either."

"Haven't we enough old and feeble ones as it is? The Tower needs youth, strength, vitality."

"That's all very well, in theory. In practice, I have Karma to consider. Oh, what a terrible problem it is to be a mother."

Sister Blessing nodded soberly. "Yes. Yes, it is."

"At least it's over for you. My worries are just beginning."

"About Karma, Sister. Perhaps she should go away for a while."

"Where?"

"You have a sister in Los Angeles. Karma could live with her—"

"She'd never come back here once she got away. Worldly pleasures look good to her because she's never known them, how trivial they are, how treacherous. To send her to my sister's would be consigning her to hell. How could you even suggest such a thing? Has the Punishment caused you to lose your senses?"

"I don't think so," Sister Blessing said. She wasn't sure, though. It was certainly very odd to feel so good after so much suffering, but then the punishment had ended nearly a week ago and it was becoming blurred in her mind like an image in a cracked and dirty mirror.

Outside she began to sing again, pausing only to call out a greeting to the people she passed on her way to the kitchen.

"Good morning, Brother Heart. . . . Peace be with you, Brother Light. How is the new wee goat?"

"She's a frisky one, fat as butter."

"Is she now."

A new dawn, a new goat, a new convert. *Yes, Lord, there's a good day coming.* Good morning, Brother Tongue of Prophets. How are you feeling?"

Brother Tongue smiled and nodded.

"And your little bird is all better?"

Another nod, another smile. She knew he could talk if he wanted to, but perhaps it was just as well that he didn't. *"Yes, Lord . . ."*

She made a fire in the kitchen stove with the wood Brother Tongue brought in from the shed. Then she helped Sister Contrition fry ham and eggs, hoping that the Master would appear for breakfast and announce the admission of the new convert. So far only the Master and Mother Pureza had seen him: he spent his time in the Tower, observing the colony at work, talking to the Master, asking questions and answering them. It was a difficult period of testing for both of them. Sister Blessing knew it was no easy matter to qualify for entrance and she hoped the Master would be a little lenient with the man and not scare him off. The colony needed new blood, new strength. There had been too much sickness lately among the Brothers and Sisters because they were overworked. How welcome an extra pair of hands would be to help with the milking and the gardening and the wood-chopping, an extra pair of good strong legs to herd the cattle—

"You are dreaming again, Sister," Brother Crown said in an accusing voice. "I've asked you three times to slice a little more bread. My ankle will not heal on an empty stomach."

"It's practically healed already."

"No, it's not. You're just saying that because you're holding a grudge against me for reporting your sins to the Master."

"Nonsense. I don't have time for grudges. Your ankle doesn't show the faintest trace of swelling. Let's look at it."

Brother Tongue had been listening to the exchange, jealous

of the attention Sister Blessing was giving someone else. He put his hand on his chest and coughed loud and hard, but the Sister was onto his tricks and pretended not to hear.

"It's as good as new," she said, touching Brother Crown's ankle lightly.

New ankle, new dawn, new goat, new convert. *"Yes, Lord—"*

But the Master didn't appear and Sister Contrition took breakfast for three over to the Tower while Sister Blessing helped Karma clear the table and wash the dishes.

To the banging of tin plates and cups Sister Blessing resumed her singing. *"There's a good day coming, yes, Lord."* It was music strange to the Tower, whose only songs were old somber hymns with new words written by the Master. They all sounded alike and cheered and comforted no one.

"Why are you making so much noise?" Karma said, clearing the crumbs from the table with a disdainful air, as if each and every one of them was personally offensive to her.

"Because I feel full of life and hope."

"Well, I don't. All the days are the same around here. Nothing changes except we get older."

"Hush now, and stop copying your mother. Crankiness is a habit hard to break."

"I don't care. What reason have I got for not being cranky?"

"You mustn't let the rest of them hear you speak such words," Sister Blessing said, trying to sound very severe. "It would hurt me deeply to see you punished again."

"I'm being punished twenty-four hours a day just by having to stay here. I hate it. When I get another chance I'm going to run away."

"No, Karma, no. It's hard to think of eternity when you're young, but you must try. Having trod the rough earth, your feet uncovered, you will walk the smooth and golden streets of heaven. Remember that, child."

"How do I know it's true?"

"It is. It *is* true." But her own voice echoed falsely in her ears: *Isn't it?* "You must fill your mind with visions of glory, Karma." *Mustn't you?*

"I can't. I keep thinking of the boys and girls at school, and their pretty clothes, and the way they laughed a lot, and all the books they had to read. Hundreds of books about things I never heard of before. Just touching them and knowing they were there—oh, it was such a wonderful feeling." Karma's face was pale under the bright red pimples that spotted it like a clown's make-up. "Why can't we have books here, Sister?"

"How could the colony survive with everyone's noses buried in books? There's work to be—"

"That's not the real reason."

Sister Blessing looked uneasy. "Now, now, this isn't a safe subject. The rules clearly state—"

"No one's listening. I know the real reason. If we find out from books how other people live, we might not want to stay here and there wouldn't be any colony."

"The Master is the best judge of our welfare, you must understand that."

"Well, I don't."

"Oh, Karma, my child, what are we to do with you?"

"Let me go."

"The outside world is a cruel place."

"Crueler than this?"

There was no answer. Sister Blessing had turned away and was scrubbing a tin plate she had already scrubbed twice in the past minute. *It is time*, she thought, *time for Karma to leave and for me to help her. I would give the breath in my body to help her but I don't know how. Oh Lord, give me guidance.*

"Mr. Quinn doesn't think the world's such a cruel place," Karma said.

The name caught Sister Blessing by surprise. She had been deliberately suppressing it for days now. When it popped up in her mind like a jack-in-the-box, she forced it down again, pressed the lid over it and held it tight. But the lid was slippery and her hand not always strong and quick enough, and out he would come, the young man she wished she had never seen. She said sharply, "What Mr. Quinn thinks is of no importance. He has gone out of our lives completely and forever."

"No, he hasn't."

"What do you know about it?"

"I'm not telling if I don't want to."

Sister Blessing turned away from the tubful of dishes and, her hands still wet, grasped Karma by the shoulders. "You saw him? You talked to him?"

"Yes."

"When?"

"When you were in isolation," Karma said. "I told him about my acne and he promised to come back and bring me some lotion for it. And he will."

"No, he won't."

"He promised."

"He is not coming back," Sister Blessing said, pressing the lid down, holding it tight. "He must let us alone. He is our enemy."

Malice spread over Karma's face like a blush she couldn't prevent. "The Master says we don't have any enemies, only friends who have not yet seen the light. What if Mr. Quinn comes back to be shown the light?"

"Mr. Quinn has returned to the gambling tables of Reno where he belongs. If he gave you any promise he was foolish, and you're even more foolish to believe him. Listen, Karma, I made a bad mistake which involved Mr. Quinn and I have been punished for it severely. Now that must be the end of it. We won't see him again and there'll be no more talk about him, is that clear?" She paused, then added in a quieter, more reasonable voice, "Mr. Quinn's intentions were all right but he has caused trouble."

"Trouble over Patrick O'Gorman?"

"Where did you get that name?"

"I—I just sort of heard it," Karma said, frightened by the

Sister's intensity which she couldn't understand. "It just—floated through the air, I guess, into my ears."

"That's a lie. You heard it from Mr. Quinn."

"No. I swear, it just sort of floated through the air into my ears."

Sister Blessing's hand dropped from Karma's shoulders in a gesture of futility. "I despair of you, Karma."

"I wish everybody did," Karma said in a soft, stubborn voice. "Then they'd banish me and I could go away with Mr. Quinn when he comes with the lotion."

"He is not coming. He performed the service I paid him for in my moment of weakness and indiscretion, and there is no good reason for him to return. A promise to a child means nothing to a man like Mr. Quinn. You were very naïve to take him seriously."

"You must take him seriously, too, or you wouldn't act so scared."

"Scared?" The word fell into the middle of the room like a stone thrown through the skylight. Sister Blessing attempted to hide the stone by surrounding it with camouflage: "You are a dear girl, Karma, but what a flighty imagination you have. And I strongly suspect you developed a bit of a crush on Mr. Quinn."

"I don't know what that means, a crush."

"It means you're indulging in a silly dream about his coming back here to rescue you, to make you beautiful with a magic lotion. That's all it is, Karma, a dream."

The Sister returned to the tub of dishes. The water was cold by this time, grease floated on top of it and the harsh soap would not lather. As she forced her hands into the dirty water she tried to resume her song but she couldn't remember the music, the words no longer seemed prophetic, only wistful: *Isn't there, surely, a good day coming, Lord?*

At noon the official announcement was made in the shrine in the inner court. A tall, thin, bespectacled man, already shaved and robed, was introduced briefly by the Master: "It is with humble rejoicing that I acquaint you with Brother Faith of Angels who has come to share our lives in this world and our salvation in the next. Amen."

"Amen," said Brother Faith, and the others echoed, "Amen."

There was an undercurrent of excitement among the brethren but they dispersed quickly and quietly and returned to their jobs. Brother Light trudged back to the barn, thinking, with satisfaction, of the new convert's soft white hands and how soon they would be changed; and Sister Contrition ran toward the kitchen, her face contorted by anxiety and lack of breath: *He is not old but he is certainly not young, either, and perhaps his eyesight is failing and he will not notice Karma. How cruelly fast she has developed into a woman.*

Brother Crown headed for the tractor, whistling jubilantly through the gap between his two front teeth. He had seen the new convert's car, and oh, what a beauty it was, and how the engine's purr grew into a deep, powerful roar. He pictured himself behind the wheel, foot hard on the accelerator, taking the curves of the mountain road with a shrieking of tires. *Zoom, zoom, here I come. Zoom, zoom, zoom.*

Brother Steady Heart and Brother Tongue resumed hoeing weeds in the vegetable garden.

"Does he have a strong back, that's the important thing," Brother Heart said. "Arms, legs, hands, these you can strengthen by work and exercise, but a strong back is a gift of God. Isn't that so?"

Brother Tongue nodded agreeably, wishing that Brother Heart would shut up, he was becoming a terrible old bore.

"Yes sir, a strong back in a man, and fine, delicate limbs in a woman, these are the gifts of God, eh, Brother Tongue? Oh, the ladies, I miss them. Shall I tell you a secret? I was never much to look at, but I used to be a great hit with the ladies, would you believe it?"

Brother Tongue nodded again. *Somebody shut this bastard up before I kill him.*

"You appear a mite peaked today, Brother Tongue. Are

you feeling all right? Your pleurisy may be acting up again, maybe you'd better take a rest. Sister Blessing says you must not overdo. Go on now and have yourself a nice little nap."

The Master climbed the stairs to the top of the Tower and looked down at the blue lake in the green valley, and up at the green mountains in the blue sky. Ordinarily, the view inspired him, but now he felt old and tired. It had been a difficult period, testing Brother Faith of Angels and being tested in return, and at the same time trying to handle Mother Pureza, to keep her quiet and contented. Her flights into the past were becoming wilder as her body grew feebler. She gave orders to her servant, Capirote, who had been dead for thirty years, and became violent when her orders were not obeyed. She called out to her parents and her sisters and wept bitterly when they did not answer. Sometimes she fingered the rosary no one had ever been able to take from her, and in spite of the Master's efforts to stop her she said the Hail Marys she had learned as a child. She had disliked the new Brother on sight, cursed him in Spanish, accused him of trying to rob her and threatened him with a flogging. The Master knew the time was approaching when he would have to send her away. He hoped she would die before it became necessary.

He had left her resting in her room when he went down to make the announcement. Now he knocked softly on her door, and, pressing his lips against the crack, whispered, "Dear love, are you asleep?"

There was no answer.

"Pureza?"

When there was still no answer, he thought, *She is asleep. God be merciful and grant she dies before she wakes.*

He bolted her door so she couldn't get out, and went back to his own room to pray.

Mother Pureza, hiding behind the stone shrine in the inner court below, watched the futile bolting of her door and giggled until she was out of breath and her eyes watered.

She stayed there a long time. It was cool and quiet. Her chin tipped forward on her scrawny breast and her eyelids drooped, and with a great rush of air Capirote flew down at her from the sky.

seventeen

Quinn found her wandering up the dirt lane. She was walking stiffly, holding her hands straight out from her sides, like a little girl who had disobeyed orders and got herself dirty. Even from a distance Quinn could see that the dirt was blood. Her robe was covered with it.

He stopped the car and got out and ran over to her. "Mother Pureza, what are you doing?"

Although she didn't recognize him, she seemed neither frightened nor curious. "I am looking for the washroom. My hands are soiled. They feel sticky, it's quite unpleasant."

"Where did they get sticky?"

"Oh, back there. Away back there."

"The washroom's in the opposite direction."

"Fancy that. I'm turned around again." She peered up at him, her head on one side like an inquisitive bird. "How do you know where the washroom is?"

"I've been here before. You and I talked, you promised you'd send me an engraved invitation through Capirote."

"I shall have to cancel that. Capirote is no longer in my employ. He's carried his play-acting too far this time. I have ordered him off the premises by nightfall. . . . I suppose *you* think this is real blood?"

"Yes," Quinn said gravely. "Yes, I think it is."

"Nonsense. It's juice. It's some kind of juice Capirote thickened with cornstarch to play a trick on me. I wasn't fooled for a minute, of course. But it was a cruel joke, wasn't it?"

"Where is he now?"

"Oh, back there."

"Where?"

"If you shout at me, young man, I shall have you flogged."

"This is very important, Mother Pureza," Quinn said, trying to keep his voice under control. "It's not a joke. The blood's real."

"I'm onto him and his tricks—real?" She looked down at the stains on her robe, already darkening and stiffening. "Real blood? Are you sure?"

"Yes."

"Well, dear me, I didn't think he'd go so far as to collect real blood and pour it all over himself. One must really admire such thoroughness. Where do you suppose he got it, from a goat or a chicken? Ah, now I have it, he's pretending that he sacrificed himself in front of the shrine—young man, where are you going? Don't run away. You promised to show me where the washroom is."

She stood and watched him until he disappeared among the trees. The sun beat down on her withered face. She closed her eyes and thought of the vast old house of her youth, with its thick adobe walls and heavy tiled roof to keep out the sun and the noises of the street. How orderly everything had been, how quiet and clean, there had been no need to think of dirt or blood. She had never even seen blood until Capirote —*"You must prepare yourself for a shock, Isabella. Capirote has been thrown from his horse and he is dead."*

She opened her eyes and cried out in despair, "Capirote? Capirote, you are dead?"

She saw the Master coming toward her, and the fat, cranky little woman who brought her meals, and Brother Crown with his cruel eyes. They were calling out to her, "Pureza!" which wasn't her name. She had many names, Pureza was not one of them.

"I am Dona Isabella Constancia Querida Felicia de la Guerra. I wish to be correctly addressed."

"Isabella," the Master said, "you must come with me."

"*You* are giving *me* orders, Harry? Aren't you forgetting you were nothing but a grocery clerk? Where did you get all your fine visions, Harry, from hauling around cans of soup and baked beans?"

"Please be quiet, Pur—Isabella."

"I have nothing further to say." She drew herself up, glanced haughtily around. "Now if you will kindly direct me to the washroom? I have somebody's blood on my hands. I wish to be rid of it."

"Did you see it happen, Isabella?"

"See what happen?"

"Brother Faith of Angels has killed himself."

"Of course he killed himself. Did the silly idiot think he could fly by flapping his arms?"

The body lay where Mother Pureza had indicated, in front of the shrine like a sacrifice. The man's face had struck one of the protruding stones of the shrine, and it was crushed and bloodied beyond recognition. But Quinn had seen the car parked beside the barn, a green Pontiac station wagon, and he knew he was looking at the body of George Haywood. His throat thickened with grief, both for Haywood and for the two women who had fought over him and lost, and would never forgive each other either the fight or the loss.

Although the blood had stopped flowing, the body was still warm and Quinn guessed that death had occurred no more than half an hour before. The shaved head, the bare feet and the robe made it clear that Haywood had come to the Tower as a convert. But how long had he been here? Had he come directly after saying good-bye to Willie King in Chicote? If that was the case, who had engineered Alberta Haywood's escape? Was it possible that the two of them had planned to meet at the Tower and hide out there?

Quinn shook his head, as if responding to a question spoken aloud by someone else. *No, George would never have chosen the Tower as a hiding-place. He must have heard, from Willie, from John Ronda or from Martha O'Gorman, that this was the place where the investigation into O'Gorman's death started all over again. He wouldn't pick a hide-out I knew about and visited. In fact, why hide out at all?*

The death, the strangeness of its setting, and the sight and smell of the fresh blood were making him sick. He went outside, gulping in air like a swimmer exhausted from fighting a heavy surf.

Mother Pureza was coming up the path supported by Sister Contrition and Brother Crown, and chattering in Spanish. Behind the trio the Master walked, his head down, his face gray and gaunt.

He said, "Take her up to her room and see that she is cleansed. Be gentle. Her bones are brittle. Where is Sister Blessing? You'd better fetch her."

"She is ill," Sister Contrition said. "A touch of indigestion."

"All right, do the best you can by yourselves." When they had gone, he turned to Quinn. "You have arrived at an inopportune time, Mr. Quinn. Our new Brother is dead."

"How did it happen?"

"I was in my quarters meditating, I was not a witness to the event. But surely it's obvious?—Brother Faith was a troubled man with many problems. He chose a way to solve them that I cannot condone, though I must accept it with pity and understanding."

"He jumped from the top of the Tower?"

"Yes. Perhaps it is my fault for underestimating the degree of his spiritual despair." His deep sigh was almost a groan. "If this be true, God forgive me and grant our Brother eternal salvation."

"If you didn't see him jump, what brought you to the scene so fast?"

"I heard Mother Pureza scream. I came rushing out and saw her bending over the body, shouting at it to get up and stop play-acting. When I called to her, she ran away. I stopped long enough to see if there was anything I could do to help our Brother, then I went after her. I met Sister Contrition and

Brother Crown on the way and asked them for their assistance."

"Then the others don't know yet about Haywood?"

"No." He paused to wipe the sweat off his face with the sleeve of his robe. "You—you called him Haywood?"

"It's his name."

"He was a—friend of yours?"

"I know his family."

"He told me he no longer had a family, that he was alone in the world. Are you saying he lied to me?"

"I'm saying he has a mother, two sisters and a fiancée."

The Master looked shocked, not by the existence of Haywood's family but by the fact that he'd been deceived. It was a blow to his pride. After a minute's thought he said, "I am sure it was not a deliberate lie. He *felt* alone in this world, and so he claimed to be. That is the explanation."

"You believe he came here as a true convert?"

"Of course. Of course he did. What other reason would he have that he should want to share our humble life? It is not easy, to live as we do."

"What are you going to do now?"

"Do?"

"About his death."

"We look after our own dead," the Master said, "as we look after our own living. We shall give him a decent burial."

"Without notifying the authorities?"

"I am the authority here."

"Sheriff, coroner, judge, jury, doctor, mortician, dog-catcher, soul saver?"

"All of those, yes. And please spare me your petty irony, Mr. Quinn."

"You have a big job, Master."

"God has granted me the strength to do it," he said quietly, "and the ability to see how it must be done."

"The sheriff might be a little hard to convince of that."

"The sheriff can take care of his own, I will take care of mine."

"There are laws, and you're living within their jurisdiction. Haywood's death must be reported. If you don't do it, I'll have to."

"Why?" the Master said. "We are a peace-loving community. We harm no one, we ask no favors from the outside world beyond the favor of being allowed to live as we see fit."

"All right, let's put it this way: a member of the outside world wandered in here and got himself killed. That's the sheriff's business."

"Brother Faith of Angels was one of *us*, Mr. Quinn."

"He was George Haywood," Quinn said. "A real estate man from Chicote. And whatever his reasons for coming here, I know saving his soul wasn't one of them."

"God forgive you for your blasphemy, and your lies. Brother Faith was a True Believer."

"You were the believer, not Haywood."

"His name was not Haywood. It was Martin. He was a banker in San Diego, a widower alone in the world, a troubled man."

For a moment Quinn was almost convinced he'd made a mistake, and that the green Pontiac station wagon was merely a coincidence. Then he saw the uncertainty growing in the Master's eyes and heard the doubt in his voice even while he was denying it.

"Hubert Martin. His wife died two months ago—"

"Ten years ago."

"He was desolate and lonely without her."

"He had a red-headed girl friend named Willie King."

The Master leaned heavily against the archway as if the sudden burden of the truth was too great for him. "He was—he was not seeking salvation?"

"No."

"Why, then, did he come here? To rob us, to cheat us? We have nothing to be robbed or cheated of, only the car that he himself gave to our common fund. We possess no money."

"Maybe he thought you did."

"How could he? I explained in detail how the colony operates on a self-sufficient basis. I even showed him our account books to prove how little use we have for money here, when there is nothing we must buy except gasoline and a few spare parts for the tractor and the odd pair of spectacles for one of our Brothers whose sight is failing."

"Did Haywood seem interested?"

"Oh yes, very. You see, being a banker, I suppose he—"

"A real estate agent."

"Yes. I keep forgetting. I—it's been a very confusing day. You must excuse me now, Mr. Quinn. I have to inform the others of the sad news and arrange with Sister Blessing to take care of the body."

Quinn said, "You'd better leave everything as it is until the sheriff gets here."

"The sheriff, yes. You're going to tell him, I suppose."

"I have no choice."

"Please do me a favor and refrain from mentioning Mother Pureza. It would frighten her to be questioned. She is like a child."

"Children can be violent, too."

"There is violence in her, but only in her talk. She is too frail to have pushed him over the handrail. God forgive me the very thought of it."

He reached inside the folds of his robe and brought out a set of keys. Quinn recognized them, with a shock, as the keys to the ignition of his car. He said, "You intended to keep me here?"

"No. I merely wished to be able to control the time of your departure. I didn't realize then that Haywood had a family and friends, and that his death would have to be investigated by someone from the outside. You're free to leave now, Mr. Quinn. But before you do, I want you to realize that you are doing us an incalculable amount of damage, and we, on our part, have offered you nothing but kindness, food and drink when you were hungry and thirsty, shelter when you were homeless, and prayers though you were an infidel."

"I'm not entirely responsible for the course of events. I didn't intend to make trouble for anyone."

"That's a matter you will have to settle with your own conscience. Your lack of intention changes nothing. A flooding river does not intend to overflow its banks, nor an iceberg to ram a ship, yet the farmlands are ruined by flood and the ship sinks. Yes, the ship sinks. . . . And the people on it, they all die. Yes, yes, I see it quite clearly in my mind."

"I'd better leave now."

"They are screaming for me to help them. The ship is broken in two, the sea is boiling with anger. . . . Don't be afraid, my children. I am coming. I will open the gates of heaven for you."

"Good-bye, Master."

Quinn walked away, his heart pounding against his rib cage as if it were trying to escape. His throat felt swollen and there was a taste of old vomit in his mouth, shreds and pieces of the past too fibrous to be swallowed.

He saw Karma running toward him between the trees awkwardly, as if she had not yet become accustomed to her new body.

She shouted at him, "Where's Master?"

"I left him at the Tower."

"Sister Blessing's sick. Oh, she's terrible sick. And Brother Tongue is crying and I can't find my mother and I don't know what to do. I don't know what to *do*."

"Take it easy. Where's the Sister?"

"In the kitchen. She fell on the floor. Oh, she looks bad, she looks dying. Please don't let her die. She promised to help me get away, she promised just this morning. Please, please don't let her die."

Quinn found Sister Blessing on the floor, doubled up with pain. Her mouth was drawn back from her teeth, and a thick colorless fluid flowed from both corners, too much of it to be ordinary saliva. Brother Tongue was trying to hold a wet cloth against her forehead but she kept twitching her head away and moaning.

Quinn said, "How long has she been like this, Karma?"

"I don't know."

"Was it before lunch, after lunch?"

"After. Maybe half an hour after."

"What did she complain of?"

"Cramps. Very bad cramps, and a burning in her throat. She went outside and vomited and then she came back and fell on the floor, and I screamed for help and Brother Tongue was in the washroom and he heard me."

"We'd better get her to a hospital."

Brother Tongue shook his head, and Karma cried out, "No, no. We can't. The Master won't let us. He doesn't believe in—"

"Be quiet." Quinn knelt beside Sister Blessing and felt the pulse in her wrist. It was feeble, and her hands and forehead were hot and dry as if she had lost a great deal of body fluid. "Can you hear me, Sister? I am going to drive you to the hospital in San Felice. Don't be frightened. They'll take good care of you. Remember that hot bath you told me you wanted? And the fuzzy pink slippers? Well, you'll be able to have all the hot baths you like, and I'll buy you the fuzziest pink slippers in the country. Sister?"

She opened her eyes slightly but there was no recognition in them, and a moment later the lids dropped shut again.

Quinn got to his feet. "I'll bring the car as close to the door as I can."

"I'm coming with you," Karma said.

"You'd better stay here. See if you can get her to swallow a little water."

"I tried to and so did Brother Tongue, only it didn't work." She followed Quinn outside and down the path, talking nervously and glancing over her shoulder as if afraid someone was watching. "She was so happy this morning. She kept singing about how there was a good day coming. She couldn't have felt sick or she wouldn't have been singing like that. Why, she even said she—she felt full of life and hope. Only then she got mad at me because I told her you were coming back to bring the lotion for my acne. . . . Did you?"

"Yes, it's in the car. She didn't like the idea of me coming back?"

"Oh no. She acted scared, sort of, and she said you were our enemy."

"But I'm not your enemy, or hers. In fact, Sister Blessing and I got along very well together."

"*She* didn't think so. She said you were back at the gambling tables in Reno where you belonged and I wasn't to take your promise seriously."

"Why was she scared, Karma?"

"Maybe because of O'Gorman. When I mentioned his name she looked ready to throw a fit. It seemed like she didn't want to be reminded of you or O'Gorman—you know, like she thought things had been settled and didn't want to hear about them any more."

"Like things had been settled," Quinn repeated, frowning. Only one thing had been settled, the fact that O'Gorman had been murdered. "Is mail delivered to the Tower, Karma?"

"Three miles down the main road, where you turn off to the neighboring ranch, there are two mailboxes. One of them is ours, but the Master only goes to it about once a week since nothing important ever comes."

"If mail is delivered, it must also be picked up."

"We're not allowed to write a letter unless it's real important, such as to right a wrong we committed."

To right a wrong, Quinn thought. *To confess a murder and make peace with God and conscience.* He said, "Did Sister Blessing ever talk about her son?"

"Not to me. I know she has one, though."

"What's his name?"

"I guess the same as hers used to be, Featherstone. Maybe Charley Featherstone."

"Why maybe?"

"Well, when Brother Tongue came in after she'd fallen on the floor she looked at him and said 'Charley,' like she meant him to tell Charley she was sick. That's how it sounded to me."

"Could she have been addressing Brother Tongue as Charley?"

"That wouldn't make sense. She knows as well as I do that his name's Michael. Michael Robertson."

"You have a good memory, Karma."

She blushed and made an awkward attempt to hide the blush with her hands. "I don't have much to remember. The only reading I do is the Master's record book when I'm looking after Mother Pureza. I read it aloud to her sometimes like I would a story. It keeps her quiet except when she interrupts to ask if the people lived happily ever after. I always tell her yes."

It was to Quinn a strange and touching picture, the girl earnestly reading a list of names and the deranged old woman listening, hearing a fairy tale: *"Once upon a time there was a woman called Mary Alice Featherstone and a man called Michael Robertson—"* *"And did they live happily ever after?"* *"Oh yes, happily ever after."*

He said, "Is Charles the real name of any of the Brothers who are here now?"

"No. I'm sure of that."

They had almost reached the car. The girl ran ahead of Quinn and opened the door. With a cry of triumph she picked up the bottle of lotion that was lying on the front seat and held it against her face as if it could work its magic even through glass.

She whispered, half to herself, half to Quinn, "Now I will look like other girls. And I'll go to Los Angeles and live with my aunt, Mrs. Harley Baxter Wood. Isn't that a beautiful name? And I'll go back to school, and I'll—"

"Live happily ever after?"

"Yes, I will. *I will.*"

Although Quinn was able to maneuver the car between the trees right up to the kitchen door, it took all three of them, Karma and Brother Tongue and himself, to get Sister Blessing into the back seat. Brother Tongue put a folded blanket under

her head and a moist cloth across her forehead. This time she
didn't twitch away or moan in protest. She had lost consciousness.

Both men realized it was a bad sign but Karma didn't. "She's
gone to sleep. That means the pain must be better and she's
going to be all right, doesn't it? She'll live happily ever after,
won't she?"

Quinn was too busy to answer, and Brother Tongue said,
"Shut up," in a voice that had a squawk in it, like a door hinge
long unused, unoiled.

The unexpected sound, and the fury behind it, shocked
Karma into silence.

Quinn said to Brother Tongue, who was wiping his eyes
with the sleeve of his robe, "Do you think there's any danger
of her falling off the seat?"

"Not if you drive slowly."

"I can't afford to drive slowly."

"The gates of heaven are opening for her? Is that what
you're saying?"

"She's very ill."

"Oh God. Please God, grant an easy end to her suffering."

Quinn got into the car and started down the slope to the
dirt lane. In the rear-view mirror he could see Brother Tongue
down on his knees praying, his hands lifted toward the sky in
supplication. A moment later the Brother was swallowed up
by trees, and nothing of the Tower or its outbuildings was
visible to Quinn.

He came to the end of the irrigated land, and the trees became gradually more stunted and misshapen. The bleak brown
countryside, that could support so little life, seemed a fitting
place to die.

"Sister? Can you hear me, Sister? If someone did this to
you, it's my fault. I disobeyed your orders. You told me not
to try and contact O'Gorman, that it might do a lot of harm.
Just find out where he is, you said, and report to you. I should
have listened to you. I'm sorry. Please hear me, Sister. I'm
sorry."

Sorry. The word echoed from the sheer walls of rock that lined parts of the road, *I'm sorry*, and the gray inert mass on the back seat stirred slightly. Quinn's eye caught the movement in the mirror.

"Why did you hire me to find a dead man, Sister?"

There was no response.

"When you ordered me not to contact him, you couldn't have known he was dead. Yet you must have guessed there was something peculiar going on that involved O'Gorman. Who could have told you except the murderer? And why after all these years did he decide to confess the crime in a letter? Was it because I asked you last week to give Martha O'Gorman a break, put an end to her uncertainty? . . . Was the letter of confession forced on the murderer by you? And why have you been trying to protect him?"

She let out a sudden cry of pain or protest.

"Did you believe he was penitent, Sister, and would never kill again?"

Another cry, more vehement than the first, like a child's wail of rage at an injustice. The rage was unmistakable, but Quinn wasn't sure whether it was directed at him for his questions, or at the killer for his betrayal, or at still a third person.

"Who killed O'Gorman, Sister?"

eighteen

Through the emergency entrance of the San Felice hospital, Sister Blessing was carried on a stretcher. A young interne led Quinn into a waiting room hardly larger than a piano crate, and the questions began.

What was the name of the sick woman? Who was her closest relative? How old was she? Was she under treatment for any chronic disease or infection? What were the initial signs of her present illness? When had she last eaten, and what? Did she vomit? Was the vomitus discolored? Did it have an odor? Did she have difficulty speaking? Breathing? Had she passed any bloody urine or bloody stools? Was there rigidity of the muscles? Twitching? Face livid or flushed? Hands cold or warm? Was she delirious? Drowsy? Were the pupils of her eyes expanded or contracted? Were there burn marks around her mouth and chin?

"I'm sorry, I can't answer all those questions," Quinn said. "I'm not a trained medical observer."

"You did all right. Wait here, please."

For almost half an hour he was left alone in the room. It was stifling hot and smelled of antiseptic and something sour, the sweat and fear of all the people who had waited in this room before him, and watched the door and prayed. The smell seemed to become stronger until he could taste it in the back of his throat.

He got up to open the door and almost collided on the threshold with a tall, thickset man. He looked like a rancher. He wore a broad-brimmed Stetson hat, a rumpled Western-style suit and, in place of a tie, a leather thong fastened with a large turquoise and silver clip. He had an air of wary cynicism about him, as if he'd spent too much time in places like emergency wards and no good had come out of any of them.

"Your name's Quinn?"

"Yes."

"May I see your identification, please?"

Quinn took the papers out of his wallet. The man glanced at them briefly and without much interest, as though obeying a rule he had little use for.

"I'm Sheriff Lassiter." He returned the papers. "You brought a woman in here about an hour ago?"

"Yes."

"Friend of yours?"

"I met her ten or eleven days ago."

"Where?"

"At the Tower of Heaven. It's a religious cult located in the mountains about fifty miles east of here."

Lassiter's expression suggested that he had had dealings at the Tower, and not very pleasant ones. "How come you got mixed up with an outfit like that?"

"By mistake."

"You haven't been living there?"

"No."

"This is going to take all night if you just stand there saying yes and no. Can't you volunteer some information?"

"I don't know where to begin."

"Begin somewhere, that's all I ask."

"I drove to the Tower this morning from Chicote." He went on to explain his meeting Mother Pureza on the road, and his subsequent discovery of the dead man. He described the construction of the inner court, the position of the body in relation to it and the circumstances of the death.

The sheriff listened, his only sign of interest a slight narrowing of the eyes. "Who was the man?"

"George Haywood. He owned a real estate business in Chicote."

"He fell or was pushed from the top level, no way of knowing which?"

"None that I could see."

"This is a bad day for your friends, Mr. Quinn."

"I saw Haywood only once before in my life, you could hardly call him a friend."

"You saw him only once," Lassiter repeated, "and yet you identified the body immediately, even though the face was battered in and covered with blood? You must have more highly developed eyesight than the rest of us."

"I recognized his car."

"By the license plates?"

"No."

"The registration on the steering wheel?"

"No. By the make and model."

"That's all?"

"Yes."

"Now wait a minute, Mr. Quinn. You saw a car in the vicinity the same make and model as Haywood's and you immediately assumed it was his?"

"Yes."

"Why? There are hundreds of identical cars on the roads."

"Haywood left Chicote a few days ago under peculiar circumstances," Quinn said. "He told his mother and friends he was flying to Hawaii, but one of his associates checked the air lines and discovered his name wasn't on any of the flight lists."

"That's still a pretty thin reason for jumping to the conclusion that the dead man is Haywood. Unless, of course, you *expected* to find him at the Tower?"

"I didn't."

"You didn't go there looking for him?"

"No."

"His presence was a complete surprise to you?"

"It was a surprise."

"Even in these parts very few people have ever heard of the Tower, let alone know its location. What would a real estate agent from Chicote be doing there?"

"He was dressed as a convert. He wore the regulation robe and his head was shaved."

Lassiter assumed an expression of exaggerated concern. "You found this body in a strange place, wearing strange clothes, head shaved and face battered to a pulp, and you identified it positively as belonging to a man you'd seen only once?"

"Not positively. But if you're a betting man, Sheriff, I'll give you odds."

"Officially, I'm not a betting man. Unofficially, what odds?"

"Ten to one."

"Those are very good odds," Lassiter said, nodding gravely. "Very good indeed. Makes me kind of wonder what you base them on. Is it possible you haven't been entirely frank with me, Mr. Quinn?"

"I can't be entirely frank about Haywood. I know very little about him."

Someone knocked on the door and Lassiter went out into the corridor for a minute. When he came back his face was flushed and beaded heavily with sweat.

He said, "There was an item in this afternoon's newspaper about a woman named Haywood. Did you see it?"

"No."

"She escaped from Tecolote prison yesterday in a supply truck. Early this morning she was picked up wandering around the hills about fifteen miles north of Tecolote. She was suffering from shock and exposure and could give no explanation of her actions. Are the two Haywoods related, by any chance?"

"They're brother and sister."

"Now isn't that interesting. Maybe Miss Haywood was also a friend of yours?"

"I saw her once," Quinn said wearily. "Which happens to be the same number of times I saw her brother, which doesn't make either of them exactly a pal of mine."

"Have you any reason for believing the two Haywoods planned a rendezvous at the Tower?"

"No."

"It seems a funny coincidence, though, doesn't it? Haywood disappears, and a couple of days later his sister tries to. Were they pretty chummy?"

"Yes, I think so."

"You're a great disappointment to me, Mr. Quinn. I assumed that since you're a licensed detective you'd be brimming with information which you would naturally pass on to me. But I expect it's easier to get a license in Nevada than in California?"

"I wouldn't know."

"Well, maybe you'll find out if you try to get one here," Lassiter said. "Now about this woman you brought in, what's her connection with Haywood?"

"I have no idea."

"I presume she has a name other than Sister Blessing of the Salvation?"

"Mrs. Featherstone. Mary Alice Featherstone."

"Any close relatives that you know of?"

"A son living in or near Chicago. His name may be Charlie."

"Is that another of your hunches, Mr. Quinn?"

"Not one I'd care to lay odds on."

Lassiter went back to the door and addressed someone standing in the corridor outside: "Send Sam over here with the lab car, will you, Bill? And get in touch with the Chicago police, see if they can locate a man called Featherstone, first name possibly Charlie, and tell him his mother's dead. Somebody fed her enough arsenic to kill a horse."

In spite of the heat in the room, Quinn had begun to shiver and his throat felt as though a hand had seized it. *She was a nurse*, he thought. *Perhaps she knew right away that she'd been poisoned and who had done it, yet she made no attempt to accuse anyone, or to save her own life by taking an antidote.*

He remembered the first night he had talked to her. She had stood in front of the stove rubbing her hands together as if she felt the chill of death in the air: "*I am getting old . . . Some of the days are hard to face. My soul is at peace but my body rebels. It longs for some softness, some warmth, some sweetness. Mornings when I get out of bed my spirit feels a touch of heaven, but my feet—oh, the coldness of them, and the aches in my legs. Once in a Sears catalogue I saw a picture of a pair of slippers. . . . They were the most beautiful slippers I ever did see, but of course an indulgence of the flesh. . . .*"

"Come on, Quinn," Lassiter said. "You're about to take another trip to the Tower."

"Why?"

"You seem to know your way around the place. You can act as our guide and interpreter."

"I prefer not to."

"I'm not offering you a preference. What's the matter, feeling a little nervous? Something on your mind?"

"A pair of fuzzy pink slippers."

"Sorry, we're fresh out of fuzzy pink slippers. How about a nice cuddly Teddy bear instead?"

Quinn took a long deep breath. " 'Having trod the rough earth, my feet uncovered, I will walk the smooth and golden streets of heaven.' . . . I'd like to see Sister Blessing, if I may."

"You'll have plenty of time to see her later. She's not going anywhere." Lassiter's mouth stretched in a mirthless smile. "You don't like that kind of talk, eh, Quinn? Well, here's my advice, learn to like it. In this business, if you start thinking too seriously about death, you end up cutting out paper dolls at the funny farm."

"I'll take that chance, Sheriff."

Quinn rode in the back seat with Lassiter while a deputy in uniform drove the car. A second car followed, containing two more deputies and portable lab equipment.

It was four o'clock and still very warm. As soon as they were outside the city limits Lassiter took off his hat and coat and unbuttoned his shirt collar.

"How well did you know this Sister Blessing, Quinn?"

"I talked to her a couple of times."

"Then how come you got all choked up at her death?"

"I liked her very much. She was a fine, intelligent woman."

"Somebody evidently didn't share your high opinion of her. Any idea who?"

Quinn looked out of the window, wishing there was a way he could tell the sheriff about O'Gorman's murder without bringing in the letter to Martha O'Gorman. He had promised Martha never to mention it to anyone, but he was beginning to realize that his promise might be impossible to keep.

"I have reason to believe," he said carefully, "that Sister Blessing was acting as the friend and confidante of a murderer."

"Someone inside the colony?"

"Yes."

"A stupid and reckless position for a woman you describe as intelligent."

"In order to understand the situation, you have to understand more about the colony itself. It operates as a unit almost entirely separated from the rest of the country. The True Believers, as they call themselves, do not feel bound to obey our laws or follow our customs. When a man enters the Tower he sheds his other life completely, his name, his family, his worldly goods, and, last but not least, his sins. Under our system it's illegal to harbor a murderer. But look at it from the viewpoint of the sect: the victim belonged to a world they no longer recognized, the crime is punishable under laws they don't believe in or consider valid. In her own eyes Sister Blessing was not acting as an accessory after the fact of murder. Neither were the others, *if* they knew about the murder, and that's a big if."

"You're making a lot of excuses for her, Quinn."

"She doesn't need my excuses," Quinn said. "I'm only trying to help you realize that in a short time you'll be dealing with people whose attitudes are vastly different from your own. You're not going to change them, so you might as well understand them."

"You sound like a member of the Peace Corps making a report on Cuckooland."

"Cuckooland may not be quite as cuckoo as you think."

"All right, all right, I get the message." Lassiter yanked irritably at his collar as if he were being choked by new ideas. "So how do you fit into the picture?"

"I'd lost my shirt in Reno and was hitchhiking a ride to San Felice to collect a debt. The driver, a man named Newhouser, works on a ranch near the Tower. He was in a hurry to get home and couldn't take me all the way to San Felice. I went to the Tower for food and water. During the course of my overnight stay there, Sister Blessing asked me to find a man called Patrick O'Gorman. Just find him, that's all. I have the impression now that at the time she hired me she wasn't even sure O'Gorman had ever existed. It's possible that, when the murderer confessed killing O'Gorman, Sister Blessing didn't quite believe it, she thought the whole business might have been a delusion. Naturally she wanted to find out the truth, although it meant breaking the rules of the colony and subsequent punishment. As it turned out, no delusion was involved. O'Gorman had existed all right. He was murdered near Chicote five and a half years ago."

"You told the Sister this?"

"Yes, a week ago."

"Did it frighten her?"

"No."

"She wasn't afraid that the murderer might regret confessing his crime and make sure she didn't inform anyone else?"

"Apparently not. According to Karma, the girl who was with her this morning, Sister Blessing was in high spirits, singing about a good day coming."

"Well, it didn't get here," Lassiter said grimly. "Not for her, anyway. What made her imagine there was a good day coming?"

"I don't know. Perhaps she was thinking not of herself but of the colony as a whole. It's been going downhill for a number of years and the appearance of a new convert must have been encouraging."

"Meaning George Haywood, or the man you think is George Haywood?"

"Yes. She had no reason that I know of to suspect Haywood wasn't a genuine convert."

"Someone else obviously had," Lassiter said. "Now that's a funny thing, isn't it?—Sister Blessing knew a week ago that the murder was no delusion, it had happened, and yet it wasn't until Haywood appeared on the scene that the murderer made sure she wouldn't talk. How do you figure it, Quinn?"

"I don't."

"What's the present size of the colony?"

"There are twenty-seven people, including two children and the sixteen-year-old girl, Karma."

"Can you eliminate any of them as suspects?"

"The children, certainly, and Karma. Sister Blessing was

Karma's only hope of getting away from the colony and going to live with her aunt in Los Angeles. The Master himself would probably have to be eliminated—at the time of O'Gorman's murder he was in charge of the colony when it was still located in the San Gabriel Mountains. His wife, Mother Pureza, is both frail and senile, which makes her an unlikely prospect."

'Poisoning doesn't require brawn or brains."

"I don't believe any female members of the colony are involved in the murder."

"Why?"

Quinn knew the answer but he couldn't say it aloud: *the letter to Martha O'Gorman was written by a man.* "It seems improbable to me. Sister Blessing's role in the community was almost as vital as the Master's. She was the nurse, the manager, the housekeeper. The mother figure, I guess the psychologists would call her. Pureza's title of mother is purely nominal. She doesn't, and probably never did, function in that capacity."

"Tell me about some of the men in the group."

"Brother Crown of Thorns is the mechanic, a bad-tempered semiliterate, and probably the most fanatic believer of them all. Since he reported Sister Blessing's infringement of the rules and caused her punishment, she had reason to dislike him and quite probably he didn't like her, either. But I can't see him committing a murder unless he received his instructions in a vision. Brother Tongue of Prophets is a timid neurotic suffering from partial aphasia."

"What the hell's aphasia?"

"Inability to talk. He is, or was, as dependent on Sister Blessing as a little boy, and for that reason an unlikely suspect. Brother of the Steady Heart, the barber, poses as a jolly fat man, but I'm not sure he is. Brother Light of the Infinite, who looks after the livestock, is humorless and hard-working. Perhaps he works to the point of exhaustion in order to purge himself of guilt. At any rate he had access to poison in the form of sheep dip. Brother Behold the Vision is the butcher and the cheesemaker. I saw him only briefly, at a distance. I don't know any of the others by name."

"It seems to me you know quite a lot for a man who allegedly spent only a short time at the Tower."

"Sister Blessing was a good talker, I'm a good listener."

"Are you now," Lassiter said dryly. "Well, listen to this: I don't believe a word you've told me."

"You're not trying, Sheriff."

The car had started to climb and the altitude was already having an effect on Lassiter. Even the slight exertion of talking made him breathe faster and more heavily, and, although he was not tired or bored, he yawned frequently.

"Slow down on the curves, Bill. These bloody mountains give me the heaves."

"Think about something else, Sheriff," the deputy said earnestly. "You know, nice things. Trees. Music. Food."

"Food, eh?"

"Roast prime ribs, medium rare, baked potatoes—"

"Forget the whole thing, will you?"

"Yes, sir."

Lassiter leaned his head against the back seat and closed his eyes. "Do they know I'm coming, Quinn?"

"I told the Master I intended to report Haywood's death."

"What kind of reception do you think I'll get?"

"Don't expect a brass band."

"Damn it, I don't like these cases involving a bunch of nuts. Sane people are bad enough, but at least you can predict how they're about to act. Like you said, this is practically going into a foreign country where they don't speak our language, observe our laws—"

"Welcome to the Peace Corps," Quinn said.

"Thanks, but I'm not joining."

"You've been drafted, Sheriff."

In the front seat the deputy's shoulders shook in silent laughter. The sheriff leaned forward and spoke softly into his ear: "What's so funny, Bill?"

"Nothing, sir."

"That's how I figure it. Nothing's funny. So I'm not laughing."

"Neither am I, sir. It's just the altitude, it gives me hiccups."

Lassiter turned his attention back to Quinn. "Think they'll try and keep us out? I'd like to be forewarned if there's going to be any violence."

"Theoretically they don't believe in violence."

"Theoretically neither do I. But I sometimes have to use it."

"They have no weapons that I know of. Unless you count sheer force of numbers."

"Oh, I count it all right."

Lassiter's right hand moved instinctively toward the gun in his holster. Quinn noticed the gesture and felt a protest rising inside him. He thought of Mother Pureza the way he had first seen her, looking up at the sky as if she expected it to open for her, and the Master, torn between pity and duty, trying to guide her back from her wanderings through the halls of her childhood. . . . Brother Tongue with the little bird on his shoulder to speak for him . . . Brother of the Steady Heart plying his razor, and like any barber anywhere, talking about anything: "In my day, the ladies were fragile, and had small, delicate feet." . . .

He remembered the harassed voice of Brother Light as he brought the can of sheep dip into the storage shed: "I have a hundred things to do, but Sister says I must fix the mattress or the stranger will be eaten alive by fleas." . . . And Brother Crown, the prophet of doom: "We all carry a devil around inside us, gnawing our innards."

Quinn said, in a voice that sounded ragged, gnawed by his own devil, "There must be no violence."

"Tell them that."

"I'm telling you first. By your own aggression, you might scare them into acts of destruction."

"More Peace Corps stuff, Quinn?"

"Call it that if you like."

"You suddenly bucking for sergeant in the army of the Lord? Maybe you're hearing voices, too, eh?"

"That's right," Quinn said. "I'm hearing voices."

One, in particular: *"I have renounced the world and its evils. I have renounced the flesh and its weakness. I seek the solace of the spirit, the salvation of the soul. Having done without comfort, I will be comforted by the Lord. Having hungered, I will feast. Having trod the rough earth, my feet uncovered, I will walk the smooth and golden streets of heaven. Having here forsaken the pride of ornament, I will be of infinite beauty. Having humbled myself in the fields, I will walk tall and straight in the hereafter, which does belong to the True Believers."*

Quinn looked out at the desolate landscape. *I hope you've made it, Sister. I hope to God you've made it.*

nineteen

Nothing seemed to have changed since Quinn's first visit. The cattle grazed in the pasture, tails to the wind; the goats were still tethered to the manzanita tree, and the sheep in their log pen stared incuriously at the car as it passed. Even the spot on the path where Quinn had met Mother Pureza earlier in the day bore no traces of the encounter, no drops of blood, no footprints. Oak leaves and pine needles had drifted over it, and the dark orange flakes of madrone bark that looked like cinnamon. The forest had hidden its records as effectively as the sea.

Sheriff Lassiter got out of the car, glancing around uneasily as though he half expected to be ambushed from behind a tree. He gave orders for the deputies in the second car to stay where they were until he had a chance to inspect the place, then he and Bill, the driver, followed Quinn up the sharp ascent of the path.

There was no sound. No wind moved the quiet trees, the birds had not yet started to forage for their evening meal, and if the three men were observed as they approached the dining building, the observer gave no audible alarm. Now and then a tired little wisp of smoke climbed out of the chimney and disappeared.

"Damn it, where is everybody?" Lassiter said. His voice sounded so loud in the thin air that he flushed with embarrassment and looked ready to apologize if anyone had appeared to accept the apology.

No one did.

He knocked on the kitchen door, waited, knocked again. "Hello in there!"

"They may all be at prayer in the Tower," Quinn said. "Try the door."

It wasn't locked. When he opened it, a draft of hot dry air struck Lassiter's face, and the sun pouring in through the enormous skylight almost blinded him.

The long wooden table was set for the next meal, tin plates and cups and stainless steel utensils. The kerosene lamps were filled, ready to be lit; the fire in the wood stove was going and more logs lay piled neatly on the floor beside it, to be added later when Sister Contrition arrived to start supper.

The place on the stone floor where Sister Blessing had fallen had been scrubbed clean, and there was an acrid smell in the air like burning wool. Lassiter went over to the stove and lifted the lid with the handle. The charred remnants of the cloths used to clean the floor were still smoking.

"They've burned the evidence," Lassiter said in helpless fury. "Well, by God, they're not going to get away with this if I have to lock every one of them behind bars. Put *that* in your peace pipe, Quinn."

He made several futile attempts to retrieve some of the remnants of cloth with a poker, but they fell apart at a touch.

He threw the poker down. It barely missed his foot and he glowered at Quinn as if Quinn had been the one who had thrown it. "All right, where's the Tower? I want to ask these buddies of yours a few questions."

Bill was watching his boss anxiously. "Take it easy, Sheriff. Like Mr. Quinn says, this is foreign territory. Maybe we sort of need an interpreter, somebody can talk their language. What I mean is, sure, you have a viewpoint, but maybe they have a viewpoint, too, and if we kind of go easy at first—"

"What's happened to you?" Lassister said. "You getting soft in the head like Quinn here?"

"No. But—"

"O.K., then. No buts, Billy-boy."

The only sounds as they walked were the occasional crunch of an oak leaf underfoot and the squawk of a scrub jay sensing danger and giving the alarm. In silence, the three men passed under the entrance arch of the Tower into the inner court-yard. The dead man lay where he had fallen, in front of the shrine.

The body had been covered with a blanket, and on a bench nearby sat Mother Pureza, clutching a rosary and watching the intruders with unblinking eyes. She had been washed and wore a clean white robe.

Quinn spoke to her softly. "Mother Pureza?"

"Dona Isabella, if you please."

"Of course. Where are the others, Dona Isabella?"

"Gone."

"Where?"

"Away."

"They left you here all alone?"

"I'm not alone. There's Capirote—" She pointed a bony forefinger at the dead man, then at Quinn. "And you. And you. And you. That's four, and I make five. I'm not nearly as alone as I was when I had to sit up in my room with no one to talk to. Five is a good little conversational group. What shall we choose as an opening topic?"

"Your friends. The Master, Sister Contrition, Karma—"

"They are all gone. I told you that."

"Are they coming back?"

"I don't think so," she said with an indifferent shrug. "Why should they?"

"To take care of you."

"Capirote will take care of me when he wakes up."

Lassiter had removed the blanket from the dead man and was bending down, examining the head wounds. Quinn said to him, "I can't believe her husband would have left her like this to fend for herself."

Lassiter straightened up, his face grim. "Can't you?"

"He seemed very fond of her."

"This is another country, remember? Maybe fondness isn't a word in their language."

"I think it is."

"All right, what do you suggest? That they haven't really gone away, they're out there playing hide-and-seek in the trees?"

"No."

"What then?"

"Either the Master plans to return, or else he left his wife here deliberately, realizing the time had arrived when he could no longer care for her properly. He knew we'd be coming, that she wouldn't be alone for any length of time."

"You mean he felt the old lady would be a hindrance while he and the rest of them were on the run?"

"No. I think he intended her to be found and to be put in an institution. She needs custodial care."

"Your interpretation of the Master's motives are pretty charitable," Lassiter said. "It doesn't change the facts: a murder has been committed, perhaps two, and an old lady sick in the head has been abandoned."

"He would never have abandoned her for purely selfish reasons."

"You're having another peace-pipe dream, Quinn, and the smoke's gotten in your eyes."

"I can't hear you," Mother Pureza interrupted sharply.

"Are you saying anything interesting? Speak up, speak up. What's the good of conversation that can't be heard?"

"For Pete's sake, keep her quiet," Lassiter said. "She gives me the creeps. I can't think."

Bill, who had gone on a brief inspection of the upper levels of the Tower, returned with the news that the place was empty. He glanced sympathetically at Mother Pureza. "I have a grandmother like that."

"So what do you do to keep her quiet?" Lassiter said.

"Well, she likes to suck Life Savers."

"Then for Pete's sake give her a Life Saver, will you?"

"Sure. Come on, Grandma. Let's go sit outside. I've got something nice for you."

"Are you a good conversationalist?" Mother Pureza said, frowning. "Can you quote poetry?"

"You bet." Bill helped her to her feet and led her slowly toward the archway. "How's this? 'Open your mouth and close your eyes, and I'll give you something to make you wise.' "

"I've never heard that before. Who wrote it?"

"Shakespeare."

"Fancy that. It must have been during one of his lighter moments."

"It was."

"Do you know any stories?"

"Some."

"Will you tell me the one about how they all lived happily ever after?"

"Sure."

Mother Pureza's eyes brightened and she clapped her hands in delight. "Start right now. 'Once upon a time there was a woman—' Go on, say it."

" 'Once upon a time there was a woman.' " Bill repeated.

" 'Named Mary Alice Featherstone.' "

" 'Named Mary Alice Featherstone.' "

" 'And she lived happily ever after.' "

Lassiter watched them leave, wiping the sweat off his face

with his shirt sleeve. "We'll have to take her back to San Felice with us, County General Hospital, I guess. A hell of a thing, leaving an old lady alone like that."

The immediate problem of Mother Pureza had overshadowed the fact of Haywood's death. His body seemed hardly more than a prop of scenery against which real, live people were acting out their personal dramas.

"Are there any other buildings?" Lassiter said.

"A barn, a couple of washrooms, a storage shed."

"Take a look around, will you? I'll radio headquarters to send an ambulance and put out an A.P.B."

Quinn went to the barn first. The lone occupant was a mother goat suckling her new kid. The truck and the green station wagon were gone. The washrooms were empty, too; the only sign of recent occupancy was a bar of gray gritty soap lying in a couple of inches of water in a tin basin. The pieces of wool used for towels were all dry, an indication to Quinn that the colonists had abandoned the place shortly after his departure. They had stayed long enough to clean up the kitchen, burn the evidence, cover Haywood's body, then they had taken off.

The big question was, where could they have gone? Whatever their destination, they could hardly hope to escape notice, all of them robed and barefooted and the Brothers with their heads shaved. To avoid attracting immediate attention they must have changed to ordinary clothes, perhaps the very clothes they had worn when they first came to the Tower. It wasn't like the Brothers to throw anything away.

Quinn walked quickly along the path to the storage shed. The small room where he had spent the night at the Tower seemed to be in the same condition as he had left it. The two blankets were still on the iron cot, and underneath them was Karma's old school book which Sister Blessing had given him to read. The window was still open, the padlocks on the doors leading to the other compartments still in place. But on closer examination he saw that he was mistaken. One of the padlocks had been too carelessly or too hastily closed and had failed to snap shut. Quinn removed it and opened the door.

It was a small, square, windowless room that smelled of must and mildew. When his eyes adjusted to the dimness he could see that the place was filled with cardboard cartons of all sizes, some with lids, some without, some empty, some stuffed with clothing, books, handbags, hats, bundles of letters, hand mirrors, wallets, hair brushes, bottles of medicine, boxes of pills. There was a fan made of peacock feathers, an old-fashioned hand-crank phonograph, a miniature outrigger canoe constructed of matchsticks, a red velvet pillow pitted with holes, an abalone shell, a pair of hockey skates, a lamp with a tattered silk shade, a framed reproduction of Custer's last stand, a headless doll and an oversized coffee mug with DAD on it. Each of the cartons was labeled with the name of a member of the colony, printed in crayon.

One of the cartons looked new and bore the brand name of a detergent that had only recently been put on the market. It was labeled Brother Faith of Angels. Quinn carried it out, put it on the iron cot and opened the lid.

The dark gray fedora on top was identical to the hat he had seen George Haywood wearing when he had met Willie King at the empty house in Chicote. Both the hat and the dark gray suit underneath it came from Hadley & Son, Chicote, California. The white shirt, undershirt, shorts and two handkerchiefs carried the same laundry mark, HA 1389X. The black oxfords and striped blue tie were made by nationally known manufacturers and could have been bought anywhere. There was no wallet or personal papers of any kind.

He was in the act of replacing the clothes in the carton when Sheriff Lassiter appeared in the doorway.

"Find anything?" Lassiter said.

"George Haywood's clothes, I think."

"Let's have a look." He examined the items carefully, holding each one up to the light, squinting against the slanting rays of the sun. "Are there any more of these cartons?"

"Dozens."

"O.K., we'd better get going on them."

Sister Blessing's was brought out first. A thick layer of dust on the lid indicated that it had not been opened for some time. It contained a black wool coat, some white uniforms, a flowered crepe dress, underclothes, two pairs of white nurses' shoes, a calfskin handbag, a few pieces of costume jewelry, a man's gold watch and chain, and a sheaf of letters, some very old, signed your loving husband, Frank, and a few more recent, signed Charlie. The last one was dated the previous December:

> Dear Mother:
>
> Once again I am writing to wish you a Merry Christmas from Florence and the two boys and myself. I only wish it *could* be a Merry Christmas for you. When are you going to come to your *senses* and leave that place? Surely there's enough misery in the world without the extra you're deliberately inflicting on yourself, for no *sane* reason. There's plenty of room for you here, if you choose to reconsider.
>
> Flo and the boys had the flu last month but we are all well now. I enclose twenty dollars. Spend it, save it, tear it up, but for the love of heaven don't hand it over to that doom-spouting *madman* who seems to have you mesmerized.
>
> > Merry Christmas,
> > *Charlie*

Not even by reading between the lines could Quinn detect any sign of love or affection in the letter. Charles had written it in anger, and if he intended it as a real invitation for his mother to come and share his house, it was poorly expressed. Four words would have done the trick: *We need you here.*

"There's no time to read letters now," Lassiter said sharply.

"You'd better glance at it. It's from her son, Charlie."

"So?"

"You'll probably have to phone him and break the news."

"That will be pleasant. 'Hello, Charlie, your old lady's just been done in!' " He took the letter Quinn handed him and put it in his pocket. "O.K., let's bring out the rest of the junk. I don't want to be stuck in this joint all night."

The hockey skates belonged to Brother Light of the Infinite, the abalone shell to Brother Behold the Vision, the lamp and coffee mug to Sister Contrition. It was Brother of the Steady Heart who had cranked the phonograph, Brother Tongue of Prophets who had glued together the outrigger, and Karma who had cherished the headless doll and the velvet pillow.

Underneath the pillow Quinn found several sheets of paper filled on both sides with single-spaced typing. It had obviously been done by someone just learning to type, on a machine whose ribbon was runing out of ink. There were sentences, half-sentences, numbers, letters of the alphabet in order and in reverse order, lines of semicolons and punctuation marks, and, interspersed here and there, the name Karma.

Some of the sentences were factual, others adolescent fantasy:

> My name is name is Karma; which I hate.
> Because of my of my great beuaty beauty they are hold-ing me prisoner in the tower in the forest. It is asad fate for a princess.
> Quin said ge he would bring me a magic presnt presant for my face but I don't think ge he will.
> Today I said hell hell hell 3 times out loud.
> The princess made a brade of her long hair and strangled all her enemies and got loose and re turned to the kingdom.

"What's that?" Lassiter said.

"Some of Karma's doodling on the typewriter."

"There's no typewriter here."

"Whoever it belonged to must have taken it along."

It seemed a logical conclusion and the subject was dropped.

The carton labeled Brother Crown of Thorns contained no sentimental mementos of the past, only a few pieces of cloth-ing: a tweed suit and a sweater, both riddled by moths; a broadcloth shirt, a pair of shoes, and some woolen socks so full of holes they were barely recognizable. All of the articles had been lying undisturbed in the carton for a long time.

Quinn said suddenly, "Wait a minute."

"What's the matter?"

"Hold one of those shirts up against your chest as if you were measuring it for size."

Lassiter held the shirt up. "Pretty good fit."

"What size do you take?"

"Sixteen and a half."

"Try the suit coat on, will you?"

"Just what are you getting at, Quinn? I don't like messing around other people's clothes." But he tried the coat on anyway. It was too tight around the shoulders and the sleeves were too long.

"Now the sweater, I suppose?"

"If you don't mind."

The sweater was a fairly good fit except that once again the sleeves were too long.

"All right, Quinn." Lassiter tossed the sweater back into the carton. "What's the pitch?"

"A real sinker," Quinn said. "Those clothes don't belong to Brother Crown. He's a man of medium build, a little on the short side even."

"Maybe he's lost weight since he arrived here—"

"His legs and arms didn't shrink."

"—Or the carton was mislabeled. There could be a dozen explanations."

"There could be, yes. But I want the right one."

Quinn carried the sweater, the coat and one of the shirts over to the doorway and examined them in sunlight. Neither the sweater nor the coat bore a manufacturer's label. Inside the collar of the shirt there was a label, Arrow, 16½, 100% pure cotton, Peabody & Peabody, and the barely distinguishable remains of a laundry mark.

"Have you got a magnifying glass, sheriff?"

"No, but I have twenty-twenty vision."

"Try it on this laundry mark."

"Looks like an H to begin with," Lassiter said, blinking. "HR. Or maybe HA. That's it, HAI or HAT."

"How about HA one?"

"You may be right. HA one. The next looks like a 3 or a 2. Then an 8."

"HA 1389X," Quinn said.

Lassiter sneezed, partly from annoyance, partly from the dust hanging in the air like fog. "If you knew it already, why did you ask me?"

"I wanted to be sure."

"You think it's important?"

"That's George Haywood's laundry mark."

"Well, I'll be damned." Lassiter sneezed again. "Judging from the amount of moth damage and dust, I'd say these things had been in here for years. What's it add up to?"

"When Brother Crown first came to the Tower he was apparently wearing George Haywood's clothes."

"Why? And how did he get hold of them?"

Quinn wasn't quite ready to answer the question though he was pretty sure he knew the answer. Willie King had given it to him the previous night in the courtyard motel. Of George, coming out of the anesthetic, she had said. "He was a scream. . . . He thought I was Alberta . . . and told me I was a silly old spinster who should know better. . . . He was mad at her . . . because she'd given away some of his clothes to a transient who'd come to the house. He called her a gullible, soft-hearted fool. . . . Alberta might be a fool but she's neither gullible nor soft-hearted. If there really was a transient, and if she gave him some of George's clothes, she must have had a reason besides simple generosity."

Quinn felt a painful triumph rising inside him. The connection he'd been searching for, between Alberta Haywood and the murder of Patrick O'Gorman, was gradually becoming clear. The transient to whom she had given George's clothes, the hitchhiker O'Gorman had picked up in his car, the writer of the confession letter to Martha O'Gorman, had all been the same man, Brother Crown of Thorns.

Questions still unanswered raced around in Quinn's mind. Where was Brother Crown now? How had he managed to persuade the entire colony to disperse in order to save him from arrest? Was it George Haywood's sudden appearance at the Tower that made Sister Blessing's death necessary? And what reason besides simple generosity had prompted Alberta Haywood to hand over her brother's clothes to a stranger? Suppose, though, that he was not a stranger, or didn't remain one very long. Suppose Alberta, on opening the door to him, had sensed in him a desperation that matched her own and had offered him money to kill O'Gorman.

Quinn had been considering for some time the idea that O'Gorman had had a connection with, or at least knowledge of, Alberta's embezzlements. It was impossible to believe O'Gorman had used his knowledge to blackmail her but he might have tried to talk to her, to reason with her: *Now see here, Miss Haywood, you really shouldn't be taking money from the bank, it's not a nice thing to do. I think you ought to stop. You're putting me in an awkward position. If I keep quiet about it, I'm condoning your crime—*

Alberta was such a timid little creature it probably didn't occur to O'Gorman that she might be capable of hiring a man to kill him.

Yes, it all fitted together, Quinn thought. Even now, back in her jail cell, Alberta was blaming O'Gorman for her plight. Her irrational claims that he was not dead might be caused by her inability to face her guilt, a refusal to admit that she had been responsible for his death. Then where did George fit into the picture? How long had he suspected his sister of planning O'Gorman's murder? And were his regular visits to her intended to get at the truth or to conceal it?

"Give me a hand with these cartons," Lassiter said. "We'd better take them along in case any of the Brothers gets the notion of coming back for them."

"I don't think they'll be back."

"Nor do I. But there are always buts. Where do you suppose they're headed?"

"South, probably. The original colony was in the San Gabriel Mountains."

Lassiter lit a cigarette, put out the match and broke it in two before tossing it out the door. "Now if I were the Master, which God forbid, that's the last thing I'd do, unless I wanted to be caught. Even though they've all put on ordinary clothes, twenty-five people in a truck and a station wagon are pretty likely to attract attention."

"So what would you do?"

"Disperse. Drive to the nearest big city, L.A., and separate completely. They don't stand a chance in the mountains."

"They don't stand much of a chance in the city, either," Quinn said. "They have no money."

In the back seat, lulled by the motion of the car, Mother Pureza went to sleep sucking a Life Saver. With her legs drawn up and her chin dropped on her chest, she looked like a very old foetus.

Lassiter rode in the front. When they reached the main road he turned around to frown at Quinn. "You said there was a ranch near here?"

"Yes. The turn-off's a couple of miles down the road."

"We'll have to stop by and get some help."

"What kind of help?"

"Only a city boy would ask that," Lassiter said with a grunt. "The livestock has to be looked after. Cows can't milk themselves. It's a funny darn thing, the Brothers walking off and leaving behind a valuable herd like that."

"With only a truck and a station wagon, they had no alternative."

"I wonder if there's any possibility that they're hiding out in the hills near here and intend to come back for the cattle, perhaps during the night. Being a city boy, you wouldn't understand how much a colony like the Tower depends on its livestock. The herd looked healthy and well-tended."

"It was," Quinn said, remembering the intensity of Brother Light's voice as he had spoken of the cattle, the sheep, the goats. Wherever Brother Light was now, in the hills nearby, in the San Gabriel Mountains, or in the city, Quinn knew what he would be thinking of as the sun set.

The turn-off to the ranch was marked by a wooden sign, Rancho Arido, decorated with horseshoes. Half a mile up the road they were met by a man driving a jeep with a couple of collies in the back seat, barking and wagging their tails furiously.

At the approach of the sheriff's car the man stopped the jeep and climbed out.

":What's up, Sheriff?"

"Hello, Newhouser," Quinn said.

Newhouser leaned over and peered through the window. "Well, I'll be a monkey's uncle, it's you again, Quinn."

"Yes."

"Thought you'd be back in Reno by this time."

"I hit a detour."

"You know, Quinn, it's been kind of on my conscience, my leaving you on the road like I did. I'm glad you're O.K. You never can tell what'll happen."

Quinn's sudden deep breath was like the gasp of a man drowning in a flash flood of memories. Riding the crest of the flood was Sister Blessing, smiling a greeting to him: *"Welcome, stranger. . . . We never turn away the poor, being poor ourselves."*

"No," he said quietly, "you never can tell what will happen."

twenty

At nine o'clock Quinn was still in the sheriff's office waiting for the operator to put through a call to Charlie Featherstone on the sheriff's private phone. When the phone finally rang, Lassitter glanced first at it, then at Quinn:

"I'm no good at this kind of thing. You answer it."

"It's not my duty."

"You knew his mother, I didn't. Answer it."

"All right," Quinn said. "But I prefer speaking to him alone."

"This is my office."

"It's also your phone."

"Oh, for Pete's sake," Lassiter said and went out, slamming the door behind him.

Quinn picked up the phone. "Hello."

"Yes."

"Mr. Featherstone?"

"Yes. Who's this?"

"My name is Quinn. I'm calling from San Felice, California. I've been trying to reach you for some time."

"I was out."

"I'm afraid I have some bad news for you."

"I'm not surprised." Featherstone's voice had the whine of a chronic complainer. "I never get any *good* news from that part of the country."

"Your mother died this afternoon."

For a long time there was no response. Then, "I warned her, I told her she was a fool to stay there, neglecting her health, never looking after herself properly."

"She didn't die of neglect, Mr. Featherstone. She was poisoned."

"Good God, what are you saying? Poisoned? My mother poisoned? How? Who did it?"

"I'm not sure of the details yet."

"If that hell-ranting maniac is responsible, I'll tear that holy carcass of his apart."

"It was not his fault."

"Everything's his fault." Featherstone was shouting now, translating his grief into anger. "If it weren't for him and that line of bull he shoots, she'd have been here, leading a decent life."

"Her life was decent, Mr. Featherstone. She did what she wanted to do, serve others."

"And these *others* were so full of gratitude that they poisoned her? Well, it figures, from what I know of the place, it really figures. I should have suspected something funny was going on when I had a letter from her last week. I should have—should have acted."

He must have broken down at this point: Quinn could hear muffled sobs and a woman's voice pleading, "Charlie, please don't take it so hard. You did everything you could to reason with her. Please, Charlie."

After a time Quinn said, "Mr. Featherstone? Are you still there?"

"Yes. Yes, I— Go on."

"Before she died, she spoke your name. I thought you'd want to know that."

"I don't. I *don't* want to know it."

"Sorry."

"She was my mother. It was my duty to look after her, and I couldn't do a thing once that madman got to her with a line that wouldn't fool a two-year-old child. Other women lose their husbands, it doesn't mean they have to stop wearing shoes."

"About that letter she wrote you—"

"There were two letters," Featherstone said. "One was a short note telling me she felt well and happy and not to worry about her. The other letter was in a sealed envelope which I was to post here in Evanston as a favor to her."

"Did she explain why?"

"Only that the letter would clear up a situation that was making someone unhappy. I thought it was just some more of her religious nonsense so I posted it. It was an air-mail letter addressed to a woman named Mrs. O'Gorman, in Chicote, California."

"What about the handwriting?"

"It wasn't my mother's. It looked more like a kid's, third- or fourth-grade level, or perhaps it was other-handed writing."

"Other-handed?"

"Written left-handed by a right-handed person, or vice versa. Or else whoever wrote it was semiliterate."

He was, Quinn thought. It must have been a chore for Brother Crown to have written the letter at all. Why had he done it? Fear of dying before receiving absolution? It hardly seemed possible. He appeared to be in excellent health, much better than any of the rest of them. If fear hadn't motivated his confession, what had? Or who had?

Quinn recalled his second visit to the Tower when he had gone to see Sister Blessing, in isolation for her sins. He had told her about Martha O'Gorman and her uncertainty over her husband's death: *"She deserves a break. Give it to her if you can, Sister. You're a generous woman."* He had thought Sister Blessing wasn't listening to him, but she must have heard, must have considered Martha O'Gorman's plight and then gone to Brother Crown, demanding that he write the letter and set the record straight. She was a persuasive, strong-minded woman, and Brother Crown had agreed to her demand.

That's how it must have happened, yet the situation did not seem to Quinn either real or plausible. He could believe Sister Blessing's part of it, but not Brother Crown's. Brother Crown had made no secret of his antipathy toward the Sister, he was not dependent on her, like some of the others; he was stubborn and he was self-righteous. Such a man would be unlikely to write a letter confessing a murder, at the request of one woman, on behalf of another. *No,* Quinn thought, *it's not the situation that's unreal, it's the cast of characters. I can see Sister Blessing giving Crown an order, but I can't see Crown obeying her. In their relationship the balance of power was in his hands, not hers.*

Featherstone had returned to his favorite subject: his mother had been duped by a maniac, the man should be arrested, the whole colony taken to a booby hatch, and the buildings burned to the ground.

Quinn finally interrupted him. "I can understand your feelings, Mr. Featherstone, but—"

"You can't. She wasn't your mother. You don't know what it's like to watch a member of your own family being hynotized by a madman into leading a life not fit for a dog."

"I'm sorry you didn't have a chance to see your mother before she died. Her life was a lot happier than you seem to realize. If she made sacrifices, she also had compensations. She told me that she had at last found her place in the world and that she would never leave it."

"That wasn't *her* talking, it was *him*."

"It was your mother, telling me quite seriously what she really believed."

"The poor, crazy fool. *A fool,* that's what she was."

"At least she was a fool in her own way."

"Are you sticking up for him?"

"No, for her, Mr. Featherstone."

There was a groan on the other end of the line, then a woman's voice: "I'm sorry, my husband can't talk about this any more, he's too upset. I'll have to make the arrangements about the—the body. There'll be an autopsy?"

"Yes."

"When it's over, when she can be shipped here for burial, will you let me know?"

"Of course."

"Then I guess there's nothing more to say right now except —well, please excuse Charlie."

"Yes. Good-bye, Mrs. Featherstone."

Quinn replaced the phone. His hands were shaking, and though the room was cold, sweat slithered down behind his ears into his collar. He wiped it off and went out into the corridor.

Lassiter was standing just outside the door, talking to a severe-looking young man in a policeman's uniform.

He said to Quinn, "O.K. for Charlie?"

"O.K. for Charlie."

"Thanks. This is Sergeant Castillo. He's been working on those cartons we found in the storage shed. Tell him, Sergeant."

Castillo nodded. "Yes, sir. Well, the clothes contained in the first one, labeled Brother Faith of Angels, have not been in there more than a week, perhaps much less."

"We know that," Lassiter said impatiently. "They belonged to George Haywood. Go on, Sergeant."

"Yes, sir. The contents of the carton labeled Brother Crown of Thorns haven't been touched for several years. My estimate would be six years, based mainly on the amount of moth damage. Entomology is one of my hobbies. If you'd like me to go into detail about the life cycle of this particular kind of moth and how each generation—"

"That won't be necessary. We'll take your word for it. Six years it is."

"Another interesting point concerns Brother Crown's name on the carton. I'd say it was pasted on quite recently. When I removed it, there was evidence underneath that another label had been there previously and torn off. Only a trace of it remained."

"Any letters visible?"

"No."

"All right. Thanks." Lassiter waited for the sergeant to get out of earshot. "Six years. What does it prove, Quinn?"

"That the clothes didn't belong to Brother Crown. He joined the colony only three years ago."

"How do you know that?"

"Karma told me. She's the young daughter of the cook, Sister Contrition."

"So we've tabbed the wrong man," Lassiter said harshly. "Not that it makes any difference. No one's seen hide or hair of any of them. The whole damn caboodle has disappeared, leaving me with a herd of cattle, a flock of sheep, five goats and some chickens. How do you like that?"

Quinn liked it quite well, in a way, though all he said was, "Am I free to go now?"

"Go where?"

"To a restaurant for some dinner and a motel for some sleep."

"And after that?"

"After that I don't know. I have to find a job. Maybe I'll head for L.A."

"Then again, maybe you won't," Lassiter said. "Why not stick around here for a while?"

"Is that an order?"

"It's a nice little city, San Felice. Mountains, ocean, parks, beaches, harbor."

"And no jobs."

"You have to look for them, I'll admit that. But the place is gradually opening up to a few smokeless industries. Try applying."

"Is that an order?" Quinn repeated. "I hope not, Sheriff. I can't stay here. I have to go back to Chicote, for one thing. . . . Has anyone broken the news to George Haywood's mother?"

"I called the Chief of Police there. He'll have done it by this time."

"Somebody had better tell Alberta, too," Quinn said. "She might have something to tell in return."

"For example?"

"Why she hired one of the Brothers to kill O'Gorman, and how Haywood found out about it."

twenty-one

Alberta Haywood lay staring up through black thoughts at the white ceiling. It was no ordinary ceiling, though. Sometimes it receded until it seemed as far away as the sky, and sometimes it closed in on her, its soft satin whiteness touching her face until she thought she was in a coffin. But even in her coffin she had no more privacy than she had had in prison. People moved around her, poked her in the chest and back, stuck tubes in her nose and needles in her arm, talked. If what they said was interesting, she responded; if not, she pretended to have heard nothing.

Occasionally she asked a question of her own, "Where is George?"

"Now, Miss Haywood, we told you that several days ago."

"I don't remember."

"Your brother George is dead."

"Really? Well, he'll have to find his own coffin. There certainly isn't any room in this one. I'm quite cramped as it is."

A medley of voices: "She's still delirious." . . . "But the pneumonia's clearing up, her white count's practically back to normal." . . . "It's been nearly a week now." . . . "Continue the glucose." . . . "Wish we could get a decent x-ray." . . . "She keeps trying to take the tube out of her nose." . . . "Apathy." . . . "Hysteria." . . . "Delirium." . . .

The voices came and went. She took out the tube and it was replaced. She pulled off the blankets and they were put back. She fought and was beaten.

"Miss Haywood, there's a man here to ask you some questions."

"Tell him to go away."

But the man did not go away. He stood beside the bed, looking down at her with strange, sad eyes. "Did you hire anyone to kill O'Gorman, Miss Haywood?"

"No."

"Did you give your brother's clothes to a transient?"

"No."

It was absolutely true. She'd done neither of those things. The man who asked such absurd questions must be an idiot. "Who are you?"

"Joe Quinn."

"Well, you're an idiot, Joe Quinn."

"Yes, I guess I am."

"I don't answer the door to transients, let alone arrange murders. Ask George."

"I can't ask George. He was killed six days ago."

"Of course."

"Why do you say, 'Of course,' Miss Haywood?"

"George interfered with people's lives. Quite natural someone should kill him."

"Did he interfere with yours?"

"Every time he came here he tormented me with questions. He shouldn't have done that." Tears, some for George, some for herself, squeezed out from under her closed eyelids. "He shouldn't have done it. Why couldn't he let people alone?"

"What people, Miss Haywood?"

"Us."

"Who is 'us'?"

"Us people. All us people of the world."

She could sense, from the sudden quietness in the room, that she had made a bad mistake. To distract attention from it, she reached up and wrenched the feeding tube out of her nose. It was replaced. She threw off the blankets from the bed, and they were put back. She fought, even in her sleep, and even in her sleep she was beaten. There were no fresh sweet dreams left for her.

It was the first time Willie King had appeared at the office since George's funeral. Nothing in it had changed. On the floor, desks and chairs and wastebaskets were in the same position, and on the walls, Washington was still crossing the Delaware, and young Lincoln was still smiling inscrutably.

She stared around her, filled with resentment that nothing had changed. She wanted to take a crowbar and vandalize the place, smash the windows and ash trays and telephone, demolish the chairs and desks, then everything would look the way she felt inside.

Earl Perkins, hanging up his coat on the rack, gave her a small tentative smile. "Hello, Willie. You all right?"

"Fine. Just fine, thanks."

"Gosh, Willie, I'm sorry. I mean, gosh, what can I say?"

"Try shutting up." She glanced at the pile of mail on Earl's desk, some of it already opened. "Business as usual, eh?"

"Mrs. Haywood's orders were to keep going just as if George hadn't died."

"That's a laugh. She's a very funny woman. I get hysterics when I think about her."

"Now don't start that again, Willie."

"Why not?"

"It won't do any good. And after all, maybe in her own way she's not as bad as you think."

"She's worse."

"So all right, she's worse," Earl said in a resigned voice. "There's nothing you can do about it."

"Yes, there is." She went over to her desk and picked up the telephone. "I can call her, tell her a few of the things I couldn't tell her when George was alive."

"You don't want to do that, Willie."

"Oh, but I do. I've been planning it for days. Listen, you old harridan, I'll say. Listen, you selfish, conniving old woman. You want to know who killed George? You did. Not last week, or last month, but years ago, years and years. You choked the life out of him with those scrawny claws of yours—"

"Give me that phone," Earl said.

"Why should I?"

"Stop arguing and give it to me."

She shook her head stubbornly and began to dial. George was dead. She didn't care what happened now, there was no future for her. "Hello?"

"Hello."

"Mrs. Haywood?"

"Yes, this is Mrs. Haywood speaking."

How old she sounds, Willie thought with surprise. *How very old and sick and defeated.*

"This is Willie, Mrs. Haywood. I'm sorry I haven't called sooner. How are you getting along?"

"Adequately, thank you."

"Perhaps you'd like me to come over one of these nights. We could keep each other company. I'm lonely, too."

"Indeed? Well, you cope with your loneliness, I'll cope with mine."

"If you change your mind, let me know."

Willie put the receiver back on the hook and turned to face Earl. She had not particularly noticed him before except as a kid who shared the same office and had trouble with his digestion. He was a little young, perhaps, but he had a nice appearance and he worked hard. And if she could keep him on his ulcer diet—

She said, "Thanks, Earl. I'm really grateful to you."

"What for? I didn't do anything except stand here."

"Maybe that's enough. You just keep standing there, will you?"

"Well, sure. Only I don't know what in heck you're talking about."

"You will."

From the telephone in the hall, Mrs. Haywood went back to the kitchen and resumed her preparation of breakfast. Celery stalks, spinach, carrots, a head of lettuce, wheat germ, powdered protein and two eggs went into the blender and came out the thick gray-green mixture which started Mrs. Haywood's dietary day.

So far she hadn't admitted to herself or to anyone else that George had been murdered. In her reconstruction of his death, George, standing at the top of the Tower, had suffered an attack of vertigo and fallen, due to poor eating habits and lack of proper exercise and rest. To Quinn, to Sheriff Lassiter, to the police officials of Chicote, to John Ronda, the local publisher, she had reiterated this belief without attempting to explain why George had gone to the Tower in the first place or what he had hoped to accomplish there. On the subject of Alberta, she was silent.

"Lonely, are you, Willie?" she said aloud. "Well, you deserve to be. Who kept George out at nights so he didn't get his eight hours of sleep? Who made him eat restaurant dinners high in cholesterol and low in calcium and riboflavin? Who persuaded him to sit for hours at a movie when he should have been using his muscles at the Y?"

In the past two weeks she had begun to talk to herself and to people who were not there and never would be. Much of what she said consisted of excerpts and homilies from her collection of self-help books on nutrition, positive thinking, dynamic living, health and happiness through concentration, peace of mind, and the uses and development of will power. She took all the self-styled authorities with utter seriousness, even though they frequently contradicted themselves and each other. It kept her busy and prevented her from thinking.

"The authorities are too stupid to recognize a simple truth. First, there was the exertion of climbing the stairs when his system was not prepared for it. His heart muscles were flabby, his arteries choked with cholesterol. Then, too, he should have had at least eighty-five grams of protein that day, and one full gram of calcium, and of course he didn't."

She poured the mixture from the blender into a glass and held it up to the window over the sink. In the opaque grayness she could see youth and health and vigor, will power, happiness, peace of mind, free-flowing arteries, firm abdominal muscles, a fortune in real estate and eternal life.

She took a sip of her dream cocktail.

"If George had started his day with this, he'd be alive right now. The vertigo would never have happened."

The first sip had tasted bitter and the texture was wrong. She took a second and it was the same, bitter, too thin to eat, too thick to drink.

"I must have left something out. What did I leave out?"

September came. The O'Gorman children went back to school and every night Martha helped them with their homework. Richard had written a theme on *How I Spent My Sum-*

mer Vacation and given it to her to check for spelling and grammatical errors.

"This handwriting is terrible," Martha said. "Don't they teach handwriting in school any more?"

"Sure they teach it," Richard said cheerfully. "I guess I just don't learn it."

"I don't think I'll be able to read it."

"Just keep trying, Mom."

"Oh, I'll keep trying, all right, but will the teacher?" Martha returned to the theme. According to Richard's version of the summer, he had done more work than a company of Seabees. "This *is* you you're writing about?"

"Sure. That's the title, isn't it? How *I* Spent *My* Summer. Listen, Mom. Do you know what a lot of the kids are doing this year?"

"I certainly do," Martha said dryly. "I've been told often enough. Some of them are driving their own Cadillacs. Others get fifty a week allowance, are allowed to stay out until midnight—"

"No, I'm serious, Mom. Some of the kids—one of them, anyway, does his homework on a typewriter."

"At your age?"

"Sure. Why not?"

"If you use a typewriter for everything now, by the time you're ready for college you'll have forgotten how to write by hand."

"You said I couldn't anyway."

Martha looked at him coolly. "Well, what I didn't say, but what I'm saying right now, smarty pants, is that you'd better pay stricter attention to your handwriting. Is that clear?"

Richard groaned, twitched and rolled his eyes, but he said, "Yes, ma'am."

"Beginning now. You should copy this theme over before you give it to the teacher, if you're interested in a decent grade on it."

"Didn't we have a typewriter once? A long time ago?"

"Yes."

"What happened to it?"

Martha hesitated before she answered, "I don't really know."

"Gosh, maybe it's still around some place in the storeroom or the garage. I'm going to look for it."

"No. You won't find it, Richard."

"I might. You said you didn't really know where it is."

"I *do* know where it isn't. There's no need to ransack the storeroom and the garage looking for something that doesn't exist. Now please don't start telling me what the other kids are allowed to do. Just accept the fact that you're under-privileged, abused, neglected and short-changed, and carry on from there. Will you do that?"

"Well, gee whiz."

"That just about sums it up, friend. Gee whiz."

She kept her tone light so the boy wouldn't suspect how much the sudden mention of the typewriter had shaken her. It had been Patrick's, an old portable he had bought second-hand, and which had never worked properly. The keys stuck together, the margin regulators were temperamental, and the bell rang only when it wanted to. She remembered how earnestly and patiently Patrick had hunched over it, trying to teach himself the touch system and never succeeding at that any more than he had at all the other things he had tried. *I encouraged him too much*, she thought. *I let him climb too high and when he fell I provided too soft a cushion so he never broke a bone or learned his own limitations.*

When Richard went back to his room to rewrite his theme, Martha picked up the telephone and put in a long-distance call to San Felice.

Quinn answered on the second ring. "Hello."

"This is Martha, Joe."

"I was just sitting here wondering whether I should make a nuisance of myself by calling you again. I have some news for you. One of the members of the Tower, Brother Crown, has been picked up in San Diego, working at a garage. Sheriff Lassiter and I drove down yesterday to question him but we didn't get any answers. Even when he confronted me, Crown wouldn't admit his identity, so it looks like another dead end. I thought you would like to know about it anyway."

"Thank you," Martha said. "How's the new job?"

"Fine. I haven't sold any boats yet but it's fun trying."

"Will you be up this week end?"

"I can't promise. I have to go to L.A. and make another attempt to contact Mrs. Harley Baxter Wood."

"Karma's aunt?"

"Yes."

"You said the house was all closed up."

"Yes, but I figure she'll be opening it again now that school's started. She has a couple of children, she can't afford to keep on the run."

"Why do you think she went away?"

"If I'm right, Karma's with her, and the aunt's taking no chances on any members of the colony getting to her again."

For a minute there was the kind of awkward silence that occurs between people who are talking about one thing and thinking about another.

"Joe—"

"Do you miss me, Martha?"

"You know I do. . . . Listen, Joe, I've got something to tell you. I'm not sure it's important. It didn't come out at the inquest into Patrick's death because I simply didn't remember it then, and later, when I did, it seemed too slight a matter to bring to anyone's attention. Richard mentioned it a few minutes ago."

"Mentioned what?"

"Patrick's typewriter. He'd put it in the car a week before, intending to take it into the repair shop. But he kept forgetting about it. I think it was in the back seat when he picked up the hitchhiker that night."

twenty-two

Quinn had been waiting in his car outside Mrs. Wood's house for half an hour. When he had pressed the door chime, no one had answered, but he was pretty sure there was someone inside. Drapes were pulled back, windows were open, a radio was playing.

He looked at his watch. Ten o'clock. The tree-lined street was quiet except for an occasional car and the ringing of distant church bells. After a time he became aware that someone was watching him from one of the second-floor windows. There was no breeze to account for the sudden twitching of the pink net curtain.

He went back to the front door and pressed the chime again. A cat meowed softly in reply.

"Mrs. Wood?" he called out. "Mrs Wood—"

"She's not here." It was a girl's voice, speaking through the crack in the door. "And I'm not supposed to answer the door when she's not here."

"Is that you, Karma?"

"You better go away or my aunt will call the police."

"Listen, Karma. It's Joe Quinn."

"I know. I've got eyes."

"I want to talk to you," Quinn said. "I won't hurt you. Haven't I always been on your side?"

"Sort of."

"Then come out here on the porch and talk to me. I'd like to see you again. I'll bet you've changed. Have you?"

"You'd never recognize me," she said with a sudden giggle.

"Try me."

"You won't tell my aunt?"

"Of course not."

The door opened, and Quinn saw that she'd been right: he

would never have recognized her. Her dark hair was cut short, pixie style, and a deep tan covered the remains of her acne. She wore a tight silk sheath dress, needle-heeled shoes, a pound of orange lipstick, and so much make-up on her eyes that she seemed to have difficulty keeping them open, or else she was deliberately trying to look sultry.

"Good heavens," Quinn said.

"Surprised?"

"Oh yes. Yes, very."

She came out on the porch and arranged herself carefully on the railing. "If my mother could see me now, wouldn't she have a fit?"

"A justifiable one, I think," Quinn said. "Does your aunt allow you to go to school like that?"

"Oh no. I can only use lipstick—pink at that—and those terribly juvenile sweaters and skirts, and low heels. But when she goes out, I experiment to find my right *type*."

"Are you happy here, Karma?"

After a long hesitation she nodded her head. "Everything's so different, I have so much to learn. I think my aunt likes me, but I make a lot of mistakes and my cousins laugh at me sometimes. I wish I could laugh."

"Can't you?"

"Not really. I just pretend."

A plane passed high overhead, and Karma stared up at it as if she wanted to be on it.

Quinn said, "Do you ever hear from your mother?"

"No."

"Does your aunt?"

"No, I don't think so. She doesn't tell me about it, anyway."

"What happened at the Tower that last day, Karma?"

"My aunt says I'm never to mention the Tower to anyone. I'm to act as though it never existed."

"But it did exist. You spent a quarter of your life there, with your mother, your brother and sister."

"I'm supposed to forget all that," she said in a frightened

246

voice. "And I'm trying to. You mustn't remind me, it's not fair. It's—"

"How did you get here to your aunt's house, Karma?"

"By bus."

"From where?"

"Bakersfield."

"How did you get to Bakersfield?"

"In the truck."

"Who was driving the truck?"

"Brother Crown of Thorns."

"Who else was in it?"

"I'm not supposed to—"

"Who else, Karma?"

"A lot of us. My family, and Sister Glory of the Ascension, and Brother Behold the Vision—oh, I don't remember all of them." Her eyes had gone bleak, as if the mere recital of the names made the Tower too vivid, too ominously real. "I was scared, I didn't know what was happening. At Bakersfield my mother gave me some money and told me to take a bus to Los Angeles and then a taxi to my aunt's house."

"How much money?"

"Fifty dollars."

"Where did this money come from?"

"I don't know, but I guess the Master must have given it to her before we left the Tower."

"Why did everyone leave the Tower?"

"I think it was because of Sister Blessing being sick."

"She wasn't sick," Quinn said. "She was poisoned. She died soon after we reached the hospital."

Karma pressed her fists tight against her mouth. Tears welled in her eyes and mixed with the mascara and slid blackly down her cheeks. "She can't really be dead?"

"She is."

"That last day, she promised she'd get me out of the Tower, to my aunt's, and she did, didn't she? She kept her promise, didn't she?"

"Yes, Karma."

She leaned over and wiped her cheeks with the hem of her dress. There were no more tears. Sister Blessing, though she'd been a friend to her, had also been part of a life she preferred to forget.

"What happened to the others who were in the truck?" Quinn said.

"I don't know. I was the first to get out."

"Were you given any instructions other than to come here to your aunt's house?"

"No."

"No future plans were mentioned?"

"Not what you'd call real *plans*. But I think they intended to return when they thought it would be safe."

"Return to the Tower?"

"Yes. They don't give up easily. When people believe that hard in something, they can't just stop believing in a minute."

"When did you last see Brother Tongue, Karma?"

"When he helped you put Sister Blessing in the car to go to the hospital."

"He wasn't in the truck with you?"

"No. He must have gone with the Master in the new convert's station wagon. I can't swear to it, though, because the truck left first, and everything was so rushed and confused, with people running around, and the kids crying, and all that."

"Was Brother Light of the Infinite in the truck?"

"No."

"Brother of the Steady Heart?"

"He wasn't, either."

"The decision to leave," Quinn said, "was made very suddenly?"

"Yes."

"By the Master?"

"He was the Master," Karma said simply. "No one else made decisions. How could they?"

"Think carefully now, Karma. Did you notice whether anyone else in the truck had money besides your mother?"

"Sister Glory of the Ascension did. She kept counting hers. She's very stingy, I guess she wanted to be sure she hadn't been cheated."

"Cheated of her share?"

"Yes."

"Where did the shares come from?"

"The Master, I suppose."

"As far as I know, he had no money, and Mother Pureza's had all been used up in the construction of the Tower."

"Maybe she had some left that she kept secret. She was always playing tricks on people, even on the Master."

Karma had climbed down from the railing and was staring uneasily toward the street. "You'd better go now, Mr. Quinn. My aunt will be home any minute and I have to wash my face and put my cousin's dress away. It's her second best, genuine silk."

"Thanks for the information, Karma."

"You're welcome, I guess."

"I'm giving you a card with my address and phone number on it. If you think of something else that you haven't told me, call me collect, will you?"

She looked briefly at the card he offered her, then turned away without touching it. "I don't want it."

"Keep it anyway, just in case."

"All right, but I won't ever be calling you. I won't ever be thinking of the Tower any more."

The door closed behind her.

Quinn drove back to San Felice and went directly to Sheriff Lassiter's office. Ten minutes later Lassiter arrived, short of breath and temper.

"This is supposed to be my day of rest, Quinn."

"Mine, too."

"Well? Did you find the kid?"

"Yes."

"What'd she have to say?"

"Not much. She doesn't know much. Brother Crown drove

the truck to Bakersfield, Karma was let off at the bus depot and told to go to her aunt's in L.A. Her mother gave her fifty dollars to cover the trip. Apparently all the members of the Tower were given money to help them maintain themselves until the time came to reëstablish the colony."

"I thought you said they took their poverty seriously."

"They do."

"Then where did the money come from?"

"Karma doesn't know," Quinn said. "Neither do I."

"Perhaps George Haywood was carrying a lot of cash that he turned over to the Master."

"I don't think so. His savings account was untouched, and the last sizeable check against his commercial account was written two weeks before he left Chicote. It was for two hundred dollars. Divide two hundred dollars among twenty-five people and you don't get fifty dollars or more apiece."

"Why do you say 'or more'?"

"Karma received fifty dollars, but she was a child on her way to a place of security. The others would need a great deal more, especially the women."

"But you don't actually know they all received money."

"It seems unlikely that an entire colony would agree to disperse like that without money changing hands. I realize how loyal they are to each other, but I can't see all those people uprooting themselves completely for the sake of one man, unless they were given some reimbursement or guarantee."

"I can see it," Lassiter said, "if that man happened to be the Master, the guy who issued the orders. They were used to obeying him, weren't they?"

"Yes."

"About everything?"

"About everything."

"But you don't think he gave the order to disperse?"

"Oh, I think he gave it all right," Quinn said slowly. "Only it might not have been his own idea."

"You mean he was bribed?"

"He wouldn't look at it like that."

"I would. When money changes hands and no goods or services or act of charity is involved, it's a bribe."

"All right, call it that. But put yourself in his place: the colony was going downhill, people were deserting and no new converts were showing up. Even before the death of Haywood and of Sister Blessing, he must have seen the beginning of the end. Two murders brought it perilously close."

"You're breaking my heart, Quinn."

"I'm trying to reconstruct what might have happened."

"Well, go on. The end is perilously close. And?"

"The murderer may have offered him a deal: disperse the colony for the time being, and later reconvene under better circumstances."

"Meaning with working capital?"

"Yes."

"Well, that's a mighty nice theory, Quinn," Lassiter said with an ironic smile. "However, there are a few teeny-weeny holes in it."

"I know that, but—"

"Now, according to the confession letter which Martha O'Gorman finally decided to tell me about, O'Gorman was killed by a transient in a fit of anger. O'Gorman had about two dollars on him and there was an old typewriter in the back seat of the car. Total value of the take, say ten bucks. Maybe I'm a pessimist, but if I were about to refinance a religious colony, I'd figure on a little more than ten bucks as working capital. . . . No, don't interrupt. I'm aware of your idea that Alberta Haywood paid the man to murder O'Gorman. Here you're in real trouble: first, nothing of this was mentioned in the letter. Second, Alberta Haywood had no reason for wanting O'Gorman dead. Third, she has denied, very convincingly, that she knew any transient and that she gave him any money, or any of George Haywood's clothes. Now, where are you?"

Quinn shrugged. "Where you said. In real trouble."

"Well, I'm right behind you."

Lassiter went over to the window. The bars across it had been fashioned to look like fancy iron grillwork, but they were still bars and he didn't like them. In moments of weariness and discouragement, he wondered whether the bars were there to keep his own self from escaping.

He said, without turning, "Twenty-four people give up everything they possess for the sake of a twenty-fifth—their residence, their community life, their sheep and cattle—even, to a certain extent, their beliefs—because they can't live in the outside world without accepting many things about it that they find sinful. So what made them do it? Only two reasons seem powerful enough for me to accept. Either a great deal of money was involved or the Master himself is the man we're after. Take your choice."

"I choose the money."

"And where did it come from?"

"Alberta Haywood's embezzlements."

"For Pete's sake." Lassiter whirled around impatiently. "*You* were the one who convinced me she was telling the truth about not paying anyone to murder O'Gorman, not knowing the transient, not giving him George Haywood's clothes—"

"I still think it was the truth."

"You're contradicting yourself."

"No," Quinn said. "I don't believe she gave a lot of money and George's clothes to a transient. I believe she gave them to somebody else."

twenty-three

He had become part of the forest.

Even the birds were used to him by now. The mourning doves waddling around outside their sloppy nests or paired in swift whistling flights, the towhees foraging noisily with both

252

feet in the dry leaves, the goshawks waiting in ambush to pounce on a passing quail, the chickadees clinging upside down on the pine branches, the phainopeplas, scraps of black silk basted to the gray netting of Spanish moss, the tanagers, quick flashes of yellow and black among the green leaves, none of them either challenged or acknowledged the presence of the bearded man. They ignored his attempts to lure them by imitating their calls and offering them food. They were not fooled by his coos and purrs and warbles, and there was still food enough in the forest: madrone berries and field mice, insects hiding beneath the eucalyptus bark, moths in the oaks at dusk, slugs in the underbrush, cocoons under the eaves of the Tower.

The birds were, in fact, better fed than he. What cooking he did was hurried and at night, so the smoke of his fire wouldn't be seen by rangers manning the lookout station. Even at best, the supplies at the Tower were meager and now they were also stale. He ate rice with weevils in it, he fought the cockroaches for the remains of the wheat and barley, he trapped bush bunnies and skinned them with a straight razor. What saved him was the vegetable garden. In spite of the weeds and the depredations of deer and rabbits and gophers, there were tomatoes and onions to be picked, and carrots and beets and potatoes to be dug up and cooked, or half cooked, depending on how long he felt it was safe to keep the fire going.

The fawns, the only wild creatures willing to make friends with him, were, of necessity, his enemies. When they came to the vegetable garden, at dawn and at dusk, he threw stones to chase them away, feeling sick at heart when they fled.

Sometimes he apologized to them and tried to explain: "I'm sorry. I like you, but you're stealing my food and I need it. You see, someone is coming for me but I'm not sure how much longer I have to wait. When she comes, I'll go away with her and the vegetables will all be yours. I have been through a great deal. You wouldn't want me to starve now, just at the point where our plan is working out. . . ."

He still called it "our plan," though it had been hers from the beginning. It had started with such innocence, a meeting on a street corner, an exchange of tentative smiles and good mornings: "I'm afraid it's going to be another hot day." "Yes ma'am, I'm afraid it is."

After that he ran into her unexpectedly at all sorts of places, a supermarket, the library, a parking lot, a coffee house, a movie, a laundromat. By the time he was beginning to suspect that these meetings were not entirely accidental, it no longer mattered because he was sure he was in love with her. Her quietness made him feel like talking, her gentleness made him bold, her timidity brave, her lack of criticism self-confident.

Their private meetings were, necessarily, brief and in places avoided by other people, like the dry, dusty river bed. Here, without even touching each other, they voiced their love and despair until the two seemed inseparable, one word, love-despair. Their mutual suffering became a neurotic substitute for happiness until a point of no return was reached.

"I can't go on like this," he told her. "All I can think of is chucking everything overboard and running away."

"Running away is for children, dearest."

"Then I'm childish. I want to take off and never see anyone again, not even you."

She knew the time had come when his misery was so great that he would accept any plan at all. "We must make long-term arrangements. We love each other, we have money, we can start a whole new life together in a different place."

"How, for God's sake?"

"First we must get rid of O'Gorman."

He thought she was joking. He laughed and said, "Oh, come now. Poor O'Gorman surely doesn't deserve that."

"I'm serious. It's the only way we can be sure we'll always remain together, with no one trying to separate us or interfere with us."

During the next month she worked out every detail down to the very clothes he would wear. She bought, and stocked with supplies, an old shack in the San Gabriel Mountains where he was to hide out while waiting for her. His nearest neighbors were members of an obscure religious cult. It was with the children that he first became acquainted, the oldest a girl about ten. She was fascinated by the sound of his typewriter, peering at him from behind trees and bushes as he sat on the back porch typing because there was nothing else to do.

She was a timid little creature with odd flashes of boldness. "What's that thing?"

"A typewriter."

"It sounds like a drum. If it was mine I'd hit it harder and make more noise."

"What's your name?"

"Karma."

"Don't you have another name, too?"

"No. Just Karma."

"Would you like to try the typewriter, Karma?"

"Does it belong to the devil?"

"No."

"All right."

He used Karma as an excuse for his first visit to the colony. As his loneliness grew more unbearable, there were other visits. Excuses became unnecessary. The Brothers and Sisters asked him no questions: they accepted it as perfectly natural that he, like themselves, should have turned his back on the world and sought refuge in the mountains. In turn, he appreciated their community life. There was always someone around, always some chore to be done which kept him from brooding, and their rigid rules gave him a sense of security.

He had been in the mountains for over a month when the bad news came in a letter:

Dearest, I have only a minute now to write. I've made a mistake and they're onto me. I'll be gone for a while. Please wait. This is not the end for us, it is just a postponement, dear one. We must not try and contact each other. Have faith in me as I have in you. I can endure anything knowing you'll be waiting for me. I love you, I love you. . . .

Before he burned it, he read the brief note a dozen times, whimpering like an abandoned child. Then he took the blade out of his safety razor and cut both his wrists.

When he returned to consciousness he was lying on a cot in a strange room. Both his wrists were heavily bandaged and Sister Blessing was bending over him: "You are awake now, Brother?"

He tried to speak and couldn't, so he nodded.

"The Lord spared you, Brother, because you are not yet prepared for the hereafter. You must become a True Believer." Her hand on his forehead was cool, and her voice firm and gentle. "You must renounce the world and its evils. Your pulse is steady and you have no fever. Could you swallow a bit of soup? As I was saying, you can't enter the Kingdom of Heaven without some preliminary spadework. You'd better start now, don't you think?"

He had neither the strength nor the desire to think. He renounced the world out of apathy and joined the colony because it was there and he had no other place and no other people. When the Brothers and Sisters moved north to their new quarters in the Tower, he dug up the money he had buried in an old suitcase and went along. By that time the colony had become his home, his family, and, to some extent, his religion. He reburied the suitcase and the long wait continued.

On a trip into San Felice with Brother Crown he had learned Alberta's fate from a newspaper he found lying in a gutter. He sent her a religious pamphlet with certain words lightly underlined to let her know where he was living. He made it look like the kind of thing a crank might send to someone in trouble. Whether it passed the prison censor, and whether she understood it if it had, he could only hope. Hope and fear alternated in him; they were twin heads on a single body, equally nourished.

The years passed. He never spoke her name aloud to anyone. He made no further contact with her nor she with him. Then, on a summer morning, he was in the kitchen with Sister Blessing, and, still dazed with weariness, he heard her speak the ominous words: "You were talking in your sleep last night, Brother. Who's Patrick O'Gorman?"

He tried to avoid a reply by shrugging and shaking his head, but she was insistent.

"None of that now, do you hear me? I want an answer."

"He was an old friend. I went to school with him."

Even though it was the truth she didn't believe him. "Really? You didn't sound as if he were an old friend. You were grinding your teeth and scowling."

She dropped the subject at that point, only to pick it up a few days later: "You were mumbling in your sleep again last night, Brother, all about O'Gorman and Chicote and some money. I hope your conscience isn't bothering you?"

He didn't answer.

"If it is, Brother, you'd better tell someone. A bad conscience is worse than a bad liver. I've seen plenty of both. Whatever you did in the outside world is of no importance here except to you, how it affects your spiritual health and peace of mind. When the devil gnaws your innards, cast him out, don't give him sanctuary."

Throughout the days that followed he would turn to see her watching him, her eyes sharp and curious as a crow's.

The stranger Quinn came and went, returned and left again. Sister Blessing, released from her isolation, was pale and haggard.

"You didn't tell me O'Gorman was dead, Brother."

He shook his head.

"Were you responsible, Brother?"

"Yes."

"It was an accident?"

"No."

"You meant it? Planned it?"

"Yes."

257

She looked at him with eyes no longer curious, only worried and sad. "Quinn said that O'Gorman left a wife and the poor woman is suffering from terrible uncertainty. Wrongs like this must be righted, Brother, for the salvation of your soul. You cannot bring a murdered man to life, but you can do something to help his widow. You must write a letter, Brother, confessing the truth. I'll see to it that you're not caught. The letter will be posted in Chicago and no one will ever suspect that you wrote it."

He took precautions anyway. He used his left hand to disguise his handwriting. He mixed fact and fantasy, and, in the mixing, revealed more of himself than he thought he was revealing. Composing the letter afforded him a peculiar satisfaction. It was as if he was finally laying O'Gorman to rest, inscribing on his tombstone a nasty little epitaph which he doubted a grieving widow would ever show to anyone.

At his insistence, Sister Blessing read the letter, making little clucking noises of disapproval. "You needn't have been so— well, frank."

"Why not?"

"It seems vindictive to me, against her as well as him. That isn't good, Brother. I fear for the salvation of your soul. You've not cast out the devil if you still harbor hatred for your victim. . . ."

Every morning when he woke up in the hayloft his first thought was that this might be the day; the day of liberation, of reward, of security and a new life. But the days came and went and they were all the same, and when each one was over he put another mark on the wall of the barn. The days were as alike as the marks. There weren't even any alarms. The last of the sheriff's men had departed a month ago, and even if they came back they would find no signs of him in the Tower or the community kitchen. He avoided both these places and stuck to the barn; hour by hour he concealed all traces of his presence. Before he left the hayloft in the morning he fluffed up the hay with a pitchfork to remove the imprint of his body. He buried his spoor and garbage, and at night, after putting out his small fire, he covered the ashes with pine needles and oak leaves. What had started out as a game of outwitting his enemies had become a ritual of self-effacement.

Only rarely did he think of leaving the Tower and going to a city to hide. The idea of being alone in a city terrified him. Besides, more than half the money was gone now, he had to save the rest of it for the future. He often worried about explaining the missing money to her when she came. He planned his approach: "Listen, dearest, I had to do what I did. If I'd run away from the Tower by myself, the authorities would have known immediately that I and I alone was the guilty one. As it is, by bribing the Master to disperse the colony, I confused the issue. They probably still haven't narrowed the search down. . . . Oh, the Master was bribable, all right, because he was desperate. He saw the beginning of the end for the colony and he knew the only way to save it was for the members to go out in the world to seek new converts, and then eventually return here. And the only way this could be accomplished was with the money, your money. That's why I've stayed here at the Tower, to save the rest of it."

He remembered the night she had first told him about the money and his feelings of utter incredulity and shock and pity.

"You've been *stealing?*"

"Yes."

"In the name of God, what for?"

"I don't know. I don't spend it, not much, anyway. I just —well, I want it. I just want it."

"Listen to me. You've got to put it back, make restitution."

"I won't do that."

"But you'll go to prison."

"They haven't caught me yet."

"You don't know what you're saying."

"Yes, I do. I stole some money, a lot of money."

"You must put it back, Alberta. I couldn't go on living without you."

"You won't have to. I've got a plan."

Her plan seemed crazy to him at first, but eventually he came to accept it because he had no better one to offer her; in fact, he had no plan at all, he was not used to doing his own thinking.

He insisted on one promise from her, that after O'Gorman was out of the picture, she would take no more chances at the bank. She would stop falsifying the books and wait for the time when it would be safe for her to leave Chicote without anyone connecting her with O'Gorman's disappearance. She had broken the promise and made the mistake that sent her to prison. It wasn't like Alberta to make mistakes. Had she been thinking too much of him and of their future together? Or had she acted out of an unconscious desire to be caught and punished not only for her embezzlements but for her relationship with him? Though she had never voiced her feelings of sexual guilt, he was aware that they were strong in her, and aware, too, that she had known no other man.

His own feelings of guilt were strong, too, but they were assuaged by the hardships and austerity of the life he led. Occasionally, in rare moments of insight, he wondered whether he had chosen such a life in order to make his guilt more bearable. On being awakened each morning by the scurrying rats in the hay or the sharp bite of a flea, the sting of cold or the pangs of hunger, he did not resent any of these things, he used them as excuses to an unseen, unheard accuser: *See me, how miserable I am, see the circumstances I live under, the pain, the hunger, the loneliness, the privation. I have nothing, I am nothing. Isn't this penance enough?*

His long wait for the future had become a way of life to such an extent that he was afraid to think beyond it and reluctant to repeat the past. Though desperate for companionship, he didn't want the members of the colony to come back. The only ones he had really liked would not be coming back anyway: Mother Pureza, whose wild flights of fancy amused him, and Sister Blessing, who had looked after him when he was ill. He did not miss Sister Contrition's querulous whining,

Brother Steady Heart's boasts of his success with the ladies, Brother Crown's sour self-righteousness, or the Master's harangues with the devil.

As time passed, his memory began to fail about certain events. He had only a dim recollection of the colony's last day at the Tower. His mind had been numbed by the sudden shock of seeing Haywood again and realizing that all the careful planning and the long wait had been for nothing. He had not intended to kill Haywood, only to reason with him.

But Haywood wasn't reasonable. "I'm going to stay here, I'm going to hound your footsteps every minute of every day until I discover where you've hidden the money."

He was too dazed even to attempt a denial. "How—how did you find me? Alberta told you?"

"I followed Quinn's car from Chicote. No, Alberta didn't tell me, lover-boy. I give her credit for one thing, anyway, obstinacy. Once a month for over five years I've coaxed and bullied and nagged her to tell me the truth so I could help her. I suspected something right from the first, ever since she told me she'd given some of my clothes to a transient. She gave them to you, didn't she?"

"Yes."

"You couldn't take the chance of buying a new set of clothes that might later be reported as missing from your wardrobe. Oh, you two were very careful, all right. Everything was thought out in advance, everything went into the great scheme except plain ordinary common sense. Her planning must have begun months in advance. She started going out alone every night, to the movies, lectures, concerts, so that when she went out in her car that particular night no one would think anything of it. She started to buy the Racing Form, always from the same newsstand, laying the groundwork for the gambling story in case she was ever caught embezzling and questioned about where the money went. All that planning, and for what? The poor woman sits in a prison cell, still dreaming great dreams. Only they're not going to come true."

"Yes they are. I love her, I'll wait for her forever."

"You may have to."

"What does that mean?"

"It means," Haywood said, "that when her parole hearing comes up in a few weeks, some people aren't going to believe her story of gambling away the money any more than I believe it. And if they don't believe it, if they consider her uncoöperative, she'll have to serve her full term. This is where I enter the picture. I want that money. Now."

"But—"

"All of it. When I have it, Alberta will know the game's up and she'll be forced to tell the parole board the truth and make restitution to the bank. Then she'll be a free woman, free of prison and free of you, too, I hope to God."

"You don't understand. Alberta and I—"

"Don't start prattling about love and romance. Big romance. Big deal. Hell, I don't even think you're a man. Maybe that's the reason behind the whole thing: Alberta isn't quite a woman and you're not quite a man, so you decided to play the star-crossed lovers' game. The game had a big advantage for both of you. It kept you apart for the present while allowing you to believe in a future of togetherness."

He couldn't remember pushing Haywood over the railing, but he remembered the sight and sound of him as he fell, a great gray flapping bird uttering its final cry. He didn't wait to see Haywood land. He hurried back to his room at the third level of the Tower where Brother Steady Heart had sent him to rest after hoeing in the vegetable garden. He waited until Mother Pureza ran out and the Master went after her. Then, walking like a robot that had been given orders, he went directly to the barn to get the rat poison.

He had only one vivid recollection of Sister Blessing's death, her scream as the first pain struck her. Sometimes a bird made a noise like it and the bearded man would turn numb and fall to the ground, as though he believed Sister Blessing had returned to life as a bird to haunt him. These were the worst times, when he doubted his own sanity and imagined that the creatures of the forest were human beings. The mockingbird, arrogant and loud-mouthed, was Brother Crown. The tiny green-backed finch, clowning among the tall weeds, was Mother Pureza. The crow, strong and hungry, was Brother Light. The band-tailed pigeon, haughty in a treetop, was the Master. The mourning dove, sounding the sorrows of the world, was Sister Contrition, and the scrub jay was Haywood, criticizing him, taunting him.

"Creep!" it squawked.

"Shut up."

"Cheap creep."

"I am a man."

"Cheap creep."

"I am a man! I am a man! I am a man!"

But the jay always had the last word, *creep*.

One morning he was awakened in the hayloft by the rustling of wood rats on the roof. Even before he opened his eyes he was aware that during the night a change had taken place: the colony had returned.

He lay still and listened. He heard no voices, no bustle of activity or familiar coughing of the truck engine, but there was another sound he used to know well, a quick, spasmodic drumming. It was Karma playing with the typewriter in the storage shed.

Forgetting for once his ritual of self-effacement, he climbed down the crude ladder and ran between the trees toward the storage shed. He was halfway there when the noise stopped and an acorn woodpecker flapped out of a sugar pine with a flash of black and white.

He shook his fist at it and cursed it, but his rage was for himself and the trick his mind had played on him. He realized the typewriter wasn't in the shed, the sheriff's men had taken it away along with a lot of other stuff. Well, it wouldn't do them any good, they couldn't prove it belonged to him, they still didn't know he was the one they were looking for, they still—

"Karma."

He spoke the name aloud and there was more of a curse in it than what he had screamed at the woodpecker because this time the anger was aggravated by fear.

He went numb as he remembered something he had forgotten about the last day at the Tower, Karma following him out to the shed.

"Are you taking the typewriter with you, Brother?"

"No."

"May I have it?"

"Stop bothering me."

"Please, may I have it?"

"No. Now leave me alone. I'm in a hurry."

"When I go to my aunt's house, I can get it all fixed up good as new. Please let me have it, Brother."

"All *right*, if you'll shut up about it."

"Thank you very much," she said solemnly. "I'll never forget this, never in my whole life."

I'll never forget this. They were simple words of gratitude, at the time. Now, recurring to his mind, they were enlarged and distorted. *I'll never forget this* had become *I'll tell everyone the typewriter belonged to you.*

"Karma!"

The name rang through the trees, and through the trees he followed it.

twenty-four

The long-distance call came just before noon on Saturday. Quinn was puttering around his apartment waiting for Martha to arrive from Chicote. He had arranged to spend the day on the beach with her and the two children, swimming and sunning. But a high thin fog obscured the sun as efficiently as a layer of steel, and from his window Quinn looked out on a deserted beach and a grim gray sea. He was trying to decide on an alternate plan when the phone rang.

Half expecting that Martha had changed her mind about coming, he picked up the phone. "Hello."

"I have a person-to-person call for Mr. Joe Quinn."

"Quinn speaking."

"Here's your party. Go ahead, please."

Then Karma's voice, tremulous and quick. "I said I wasn't ever going to phone you, Mr. Quinn. I even tore up your card, but I remembered the number on it and—well, I'm scared. And I can't tell my aunt because she's not here, and even if she were I couldn't tell her because I want the message from my mother and my aunt won't let me have anything to do with her any more."

"Take it easy, Karma. Now what's this about a message from your mother?"

"Brother Tongue called me a few minutes ago and said he had a very important message for me from my mother and that he wanted to deliver it in person."

"Where?"

"Here at the house."

"How did he find out where you were?"

"Oh, he knows about my aunt. I often mentioned her. Anyway, I told him he couldn't come here because my aunt was home, which was a lie, she's working on her garden-club display for the flower show. Chrysanthemums and pampas grass with a hidden electric fan to keep the grass blowing. It's going to be very pretty."

"I'm sure it is," Quinn said. "Why didn't Brother Tongue just give you the message over the telephone?"

"He said he promised my mother he'd see me personally. To report on how I am, etcetera, I guess, though he didn't say that."

"Was his call a local one?"

"Yes, he's in town. He's coming to the house this afternoon

at four o'clock, I told him my aunt would be away by that time. I thought I'd better phone you about it because you said if anything at all happened involving any member of the colony I was to let you know."

"I'm glad you did. Listen carefully now, Karma. Does it seem likely to you that your mother would choose Brother Tongue to deliver an important message to you?"

"No." After a moment she added, with a child's candor, "I always thought they hated each other. Naturally we weren't supposed to hate, but some of us did anyway."

"All right, let's assume there is no message, that Brother Tongue has an entirely different reason for wanting to see you. Can you guess what it might be?"

"No."

"Perhaps it's something quite trivial to you but not to him."

"I can't think of anything," she said slowly. "Unless he wants his silly old typewriter back. Well, he can have it. My aunt bought me a brand new portable for my birthday last month. It's a gray and pink—"

"Wait a minute. Brother Tongue gave you an old typewriter?"

"Not exactly *gave* it to me. I talked him out of it."

"It belonged to him?"

"Yes."

"And he kept it in the storage shed?"

"Yes. I used to go out there and fool around with it until the ink dried up and the ribbon broke and I didn't have any more paper anyway. I was a mere child then."

"Why are you so sure it belonged to Brother Tongue?"

"Because it was how I first met him. We were living in the San Gabriel Mountains and I was exploring around when I heard a funny noise like a drum. Brother Tongue was on the back porch of his shack, typing, only he wasn't Brother Tongue then. It's funny, if it hadn't been for me hearing his typewriter he would never have become Brother Tongue."

Quinn heard the front door of his apartment open and

Martha's quick light step as she crossed the room. He spoke hurriedly into the phone: "Listen, Karma. Stay right where you are. Lock the doors and don't open any of them until I get there. I'm driving right down."

"Why?"

"I have some questions to ask Brother Tongue."

"Do you think that maybe my mother really gave him a message for me?"

"No, I think he wants his typewriter back."

"Why should he? It's so old and broken-down, he couldn't use it for anything."

"No, but the police could. That typewriter was in the back seat of O'Gorman's car the night he was murdered. I'm telling you this because I want you to realize he's a dangerous man."

"I'm scared."

"You don't have to be scared, Karma. When he comes at four o'clock I'll be in the house with you."

"Promise?"

"Promise."

"I believe you," she said gravely. "You kept your other promise about the acne lotion."

It seemed to Quinn, as he hung up, a very long time ago, in a different world.

He went into the front room. Martha was standing at the window, looking out at the sea the way she always did when she came to the apartment, as though the sea was a miracle to her after the parched earth of Chicote.

She said, without turning, "So it's not ended yet."

"No."

"Will it go on forever, Joe?"

"Don't talk like that." He put his arms around her and pressed his mouth against her neck. "Where are the kids?"

"Staying with the neighbors."

"They didn't want to see me?"

"Yes, they did. It was a real sacrifice for them to miss a day with you on the beach."

"And just what was the sacrifice for?"

"Us," she said with a faint smile. "Richard got the idea I would like to be alone with you for a change."

"And would you?"

"Yes."

"He's a very perceptive boy, our Richard."

She turned and gazed earnestly up into his eyes. "Do you really feel that way, that he's our Richard?"

"Yes. Our Richard, our Sally."

"You make it sound as though we'll all live happily ever after—"

"We will."

"—without any problems."

"With lots of problems," he said. "But with lots of solutions, too, if we love and respect each other. And I think we do, don't you?"

"Yes." Doubt was evident in her voice, it always was, but each time they met, the doubt was becoming weaker, and he believed that eventually it would disappear entirely.

"There are times," he added, "when you'll think of O'Gorman and I won't measure up."

"That's not true."

"Yes. And other times when the children will resent any discipline or advice from me because I'm not their real father. There will be disagreements, money problems—"

"Don't go on." She pressed her finger tips against his mouth. "I've thought of all those things, Joe."

"All right then, we both have. We won't be walking into marriage with our eyes closed. Why do you hesitate?"

"I don't want to make another mistake."

"Are you telling me O'Gorman was a mistake?"

"Yes."

"Because it's true or because you think I want to hear it?"

"It's true," she said, and her shoulders beneath his hand went suddenly tense. "Hindsight's not as good as foresight but it serves a purpose. The marriage was my idea, really, not Patrick's. My nesting instinct was so strong that it smothered my rationality. I married Patrick in order to raise a family, he married me because—well, I suppose there were lots of reasons but the main one was that he didn't have the strength to oppose or displease me. Now that I know he's dead, I can be more objective, not only about him but about myself. The basic fault of our marriage was too much interdependence on each other. He was dependent on me and I was dependent on his dependence. No wonder he loved birds, he must often have felt like a caged bird himself. . . . What's the matter, Joe?"

"Nothing."

"But there is, I can feel it. Please tell me."

"I can't. Not right now, anyway."

"All right," she said lightly. "Some other time."

He wished some other time would be a long way off, but he knew it wouldn't. It was waiting around the corner and he could already see its shadow.

He said, "I just made a pot of coffee. Would you like some?"

"No thanks. If we're to be in L.A. by four o'clock, we'd better start now in case we run into a traffic tie-up."

"We?"

"Well, I didn't drive all the way down here just to see you for ten minutes."

"Listen, Martha."

"I'll be listening but I won't hear, not if you're going to try to stand me up."

"It's not a question of standing you up. Karma's phone call took me by complete surprise. I don't know what's behind it. Perhaps nothing, perhaps Brother Tongue actually has a message for her from her mother. But in case things aren't going to be that simple, I'd prefer not to have you around."

"I'm pretty good in an emergency."

"Even ones involving yourself?"

"Especially those," she said with a tinge of bitterness. "I've had a lot of experience."

"Then you've made up your mind to come with me."

"If you don't object."

"And if I do?"

"Please don't. Please."

"I have to," he said patiently. "Because I love you, I must steer you away from trouble when I can."

"I thought we were going to share trouble, going to have lots of problems but lots of solutions, too. Was that all just so much talk, Joe?"

"I'm trying to warn you, Martha, I'm trying to tell you something and you won't listen."

"Don't be afraid for me. It makes me feel like half a woman, the way my fears for Patrick must have made him feel like half a man. If you see me walking in front of a speeding bus, by all means yell a warning or pull me back. But this—this is wispy, unreal. What harm will it do me to go to Karma's house with you? The girl might need looking after, she's only a child and in a frightening situation. Don't shut me up in a closet when I could be of some use."

"All right," he said with a noise that was almost a groan, "Step out of the closet, ma'am."

"Thank you, sir. You'll never regret this decision."

"Won't I."

"You sound so funny, Joe. What's really the matter? What's on your mind?"

"I'm wishing," he said, "that it was a larger closet so there'd be room for both of us."

twenty-five

He walked along the city streets stopping every now and then to focus his eyes on the sky as if he expected to see some of his companions from the forest, the bold black and white flash of an acorn woodpecker, the blurry blue of a band tail, the rufous flapping of a flicker. But all he saw was an occasional sparrow on a telephone wire or a pigeon on a roof-top.

He had an intermittent fantasy about all the city people turning into birds. On the roads and freeways cars would stop, suddenly and forever, and birds would fly up out of the windows. From factories, office buildings, houses, hotels, apartments, from doorways, chimneys, patios, gardens, sidewalks, the birds would come soaring, gliding, fluttering, swooping, trilling, twittering, whistling, whooping, in a riot of color and movement and sound. One bird was larger, grander, louder than all the rest. It was a golden eagle, himself.

The fantasy grew in his mind like a bubble, and burst. No cars stopped on the freeway. People remained people, wing-less, hapless, and the golden eagle was grounded on the swelter-ing sidewalk, no different from the rest, at the mercy of the tyrant gravity.

For too long he had been out of contact with human beings. Even the old ones frightened him and the young ones he hurried past, expecting them to jeer at his robe and shaved head and bare feet. Then he caught sight of himself in the window of a little neighborhood grocery store and he realized they would have no reasons to jeer at him now. He looked like any ordinary man. During his weeks in the forest his hair had grown in, curly and black with touches of gray. He had had it trimmed in a barber shop and his beard shaved off, and bought the clothes he was wearing in a men's wear store, gray suit and tie, white shirt, and black leather moccasins which were beginning to pinch his toes. He was no longer Brother Tongue. He was a nameless man walking along a city street, his image unreflected in the blank eyes of strangers, his pres-ence unmarked by any show of interest or curiosity. He was nobody, noticed by nobody.

He went into the grocery store to ask how to get to Green-grove Avenue where Karma lived. The proprietress told him, without looking up from her paper.

He said, "Thank you very much, ma'am."

"Huh."

"I'm sure I'll be able to find it. Hot day, isn't it?"

"Huh."

"Do you happen to have the time?"

"Hapestry."

"I beg your pardon. I didn't quite catch—"

"You deaf? You for'n? It's hapestry."

"Thank you." *No, I am neither deaf nor foreign. I am a golden eagle in disguise, you fat-bellied pigeon.*

Half-past three. He had plenty of time. As he turned the next corner he put his right hand in his pocket and felt the warm smooth bone of the razor handle. The razor was no longer sharp enough to shave with, but a man's whiskers were tougher than a girl's throat. Which was a funny thing, so funny that, before he could swallow it or choke it back, a titter escaped his mouth. It was the sound of a little bird, not the animal bark of a golden eagle, and he wished he had not heard it. It shook his confidence, drained the strength out of his legs, so that he had to stop and lean against a lamppost for a moment to steady himself.

From the bench at the bus stop nearby, three young girls eyed him suspiciously as if they saw, sticking out from under his new suit, the tattered gray robe of Brother Tongue. Although he hated them, he felt he had to appease them in some way, make them accept him.

He said, "Hot day, isn't it?"

One of them stared at him, one giggled, one turned away.

"On a hot day like this it pays to have cool thoughts."

There was another silence. Then the tallest of the girls said primly, "We're not allowed to speak to strange men."

"But I'm not a strange man. Do I look strange? Why, no, I look quite ordinary, common. That's who I am, the common man. There are thousands of me—"

"Come on, Laura, Jessie. Member what mom said."

"—going to work every day, never having quite enough money, never sure, never safe, never free like the birds, but always hoping things will be evened up a little in heaven. Only it's a long wait, a very long wait."

He knew the girls were gone by now and he was addressing an empty bench, but he knew, too, that this must be a common procedure for the common man: when no one would listen to him he had to talk to empty benches, to silent walls and ceilings, deaf trees, blank mirrors, closed doors.

He started walking again. The neighborhood grew richer, the lawns greener, the fences higher, yet the houses were more deserted-looking, as if the wealthy had built them for show and then gone somewhere else to live. Only now and then did a door slam, a voice speak, a curtain move. *They're in there,* he thought. *They're in there, all right, but they're hiding. They're afraid of me, the common man.*

When he reached Greengrove Avenue he stopped for a minute, standing on his right foot to ease his left, then on his left to ease his right. It seemed to him that he had been walking all day and with each step his shoes had shrunk a little. He wondered how many common men had been walking all day in shrinking shoes on their way to commit a murder. Probably quite a few. Probably a lot more than people realized. He was doing nothing really unusual. Besides, Karma had taken her vows of poverty and renunciation; rich living would ruin her chances of walking the smooth and golden streets of heaven. He would be doing her a favor by saving her from her own folly.

Sometimes, when he thought of his years of listening to and obeying the Master, his mind rebelled and dismissed the Master as a fraud and the Brothers and Sisters as his dupes, but these occasions were infrequent. Constant repetition had left a deep imprint on him. He couldn't efface it as he had effaced the imprint of his body in the hayloft, he couldn't bury it as he had buried his garbage, or cover it with pine needles like the ashes of his fires. Especially here in the city, the material world looked evil to him, the gaudy men and painted women wore the brand of the devil. Rich houses contained sick souls, and unbelievers rode in big cars on wide streets to a large hell.

The Master's brand was on him, and he realized, in the back

273

of his mind, that this was what the girls on the bench had seen, not the gray robe of Brother Tongue sticking out from under the new suit. They had spotted the Master's brand, and, while not recognizing it, they had become instantly aware that he was not a common man at all but a strange one on a strange mission. Although the girls had been gone for some time, he quickened his pace as if to get away from their critical eyes.

The minutes passed, and the houses. Some bore numbers only, others had numbers and names. Number 1295 was identified by a name plate on a miniature wrought iron lamppost: Mrs. Harley Baxter Wood. Like many of the other houses it looked deserted, but he knew it was not. On the telephone Karma had sounded suspicious at first, but her suspicion had turned into curiosity, and her curiosity into eagerness. He knew she had a deep attachment to her mother, in spite of their skirmishes; she would be waiting for a message from her.

He ignored the door chime and tapped lightly on the diamond-shaped panes of glass with his knuckles. It was more like the signal of a friend than the knock of a stranger. It remained unanswered, and yet he had a strong feeling that Karma was there, on the other side of the door. He even fancied he could hear her breathing, very quickly and nervously and vulnerably, the way his little bird had breathed just before it dropped its head and closed its eyes and died in his hand. Later he had dug a grave for it under a manzanita tree and then he had taken an axe and smashed its cage into pieces. He could remember his wild excitement as the axe fell on the wire bars, as if it had been he himself who had been a prisoner inside them and the blows he struck were for freedom. When his excitement had passed he threw the remnants of the cage into a ravine, like a murderer trying to conceal the evidence of his violence.

"Karma?"

Yes, he could hear her breathing.

"It's me, Brother Tongue. You don't recognize me, is that the trouble? Don't be concerned over a few outward changes.

It's really me. Come, take a look, see for yourself, you silly girl."

He pressed his mouth against the crack of the door.

"Come on out, Karma. I have a very important message for you from your mother."

She spoke finally, in a thin, quavering voice. "You can tell it to me from there."

"No, I can't."

"I don't want to—to come out."

"Are you afraid, is that it? Bless my soul, you have nothing to fear from poor old Brother Tongue. Why, we've been friends for years, Karma. I'm like an uncle to you. Didn't I give you my most prized possession, the typewriter?"

"It wasn't yours to give," she said. "You stole it from O'Gorman's car."

"You're calling me a thief? It was *mine*, I tell you. It belonged to *me*."

"I know where it came from."

"Someone's been feeding you lies, you stupid girl, and you've been swallowing them like candy. Nobody knows the truth except me, and of course I can't tell you with a door between us. Open it, Karma."

"I can't. My aunt's here. She's upstairs in her room."

It was such a feeble story he almost laughed out loud, and even if it were true, what help would an aunt be, with her woman's throat softer than a man's whiskers?

He said softly, "What a little liar you are, and a mischief-maker. When I think of the times you teased me, tried to goad me into talking—Brother Tongueless, you called me, Tongue, Tongue, who's got your tongue?—remember that, Karma? But I didn't break down, did I? I couldn't afford to. People with secrets must learn not to talk, and I learned. I learned, and then I betrayed myself in sleep. I have always betrayed myself in some way. What irony that I should do it in sleep, when the issue was life itself."

She said nothing, and for a moment he had the sensation of being back in the forest, alone, trying to explain himself to all the living things that couldn't or didn't care to hear.

A police patrol car cruised by the house. He stood up straight, and tried to look grave and dignified like a minister paying a Sunday afternoon call on a member of the church. He had always fancied himself as a minister. How easy it would be, advising other people what to do and how to act, obeying a few simple rules of conduct for yourself and memorizing the odd text or two.

The police car worried him, though. He wondered whether the three young girls he had met at the bus stop had gone home and told their mother about him and the mother had phoned the police. Then the two men in the patrol car might be looking for him. Perhaps this time they had not noticed him, but if they came around again—No, that was nonsense. Why should they come around again? The girls' mother had no reason to report him. It was not as if he had accosted them or tried to pick them up or offered them candy. The silly girls, their silly mother, they had no reason, no reason—

"The first patrol car's spotted him," Quinn said. "Stall him a few minutes more, Karma."

"I can't." Even with Quinn beside her and Martha's supporting arm around her shoulders, the girl was afraid because she knew they were afraid, too, and she could not understand their fear. It seemed much deeper and more terrible than the fear they would have of a mere man, however dangerous. She looked at the white line around Quinn's mouth and the desperation in Martha's eyes and she repeated, "I can't. I don't know what to say."

"Encourage him to talk."

"What about?"

"Himself."

Karma raised her voice. "Where have you been hiding, Brother Tongue?"

The question annoyed him. It implied that he was a criminal, forced to hide out, instead of an intelligent man who had chosen the forest of his own free will as the best place to live.

"I can't stand here all afternoon," he said irritably. "Your mother's waiting for us."

"Where?" Karma said.

"At a friend's house. She's very ill, she may be dying. She asked me to bring you to her."

"What's the matter with her?"

"Nobody knows. She refuses to call a doctor. If you come with me, perhaps you can persuade her to seek medical attention. Will you?"

"How far are we going?"

"Practically just around the corner." *Not a street corner, though. A corner of time you pass only once. For you there will be no return.* "Your mother's illness is critical, child. You'd better hurry."

"All right. I'll be ready in a minute."

"Aren't you going to ask me to step inside to wait?"

"I can't. You might wake my aunt, and she wouldn't let me go with you because she hates the Tower people, she thinks they might try and take me away. She says they might—"

"Stop chattering, girl, and get ready."

He waited, watching the street for the return of the police car, counting off the seconds as they passed through his mind's eye like little toy soldiers, saluting, calling out their names to him: one, sir, two, sir, three, sir, four, sir, five, sir, six, sir, seven, sir.

Respectful creatures. Always called him sir, briskly but affectionately. Yes, they liked their genial general. They knew he had once been a common man, had risen from the ranks to become the commander of time and wear stars on his sleeves. But of course the stars were invisible, it was still light, still afternoon. It was only at night that the stars swooped down from the sky to perch on his sleeves.

A hundred and fourteen, sir. A hundred and fifteen, sir. A hundred and—

Suddenly an alarming change took place. The toy soldiers switched uniforms and became policemen in blue serge. They were no longer saluting him, no longer calling out their names, they were demanding his name, instead, in coarse disrespectful voices.

"What's your name?"

"Commander," he said.

"Commander what?"

"I am the commander of time."

"You are, eh?"

"It's a specialized job. I decide on the times that things are to happen to people, to animals and birds, to the trees of the forest—"

"O.K., Commander. Let's go and review some troops."

"This isn't the proper time."

"I think it is."

"But that's *my* decision."

"Let's go, Commander. We've got a real mixed-up clock down at the station. We want you to talk to it, straighten it out, see?"

It struck him suddenly then, the realization that these men were not policemen at all. They were agents of a foreign power sent to take over the country by disrupting the time schedule and kidnaping the commander.

The door of the house opened and a man he recognized as Quinn came out, and a woman who looked familiar to him although he couldn't remember her name.

He called out to Quinn, "Don't let them take me away! They're enemy agents, I tell you. They're going to overthrow the government!"

Quinn stepped back, as if the words had hit him in the stomach and knocked him off-balance, and the woman with him began to scream, "Patrick, Patrick! Oh, my God, Patrick!"

He stared at her, wondering why she looked so familiar to him and who Omigod Patrick was.

ABOUT THE AUTHOR

Margaret Millar was born in Kitchener, Ontario, Canada, and educated at the Kitchener Collegiate Institute and the University of Toronto. In 1938 she married Kenneth Millar, better known under his pen name of Ross Macdonald, and for over forty years they have enjoyed a unique relationship as a husband and wife who have successfully pursued separate writing careers.

She published her first novel, *The Invisible Worm,* in 1941. Now, over four decades later, she is busily polishing her twenty-fifth work of fiction. During that time she has established herself as one of the great practitioners in the field of mystery and psychological suspense. Her work has been translated into more than a dozen foreign languages, appeared in twenty-seven paperback editions and been selected sixteen times by book clubs. She received an Edgar Award for the Best Mystery of the Year with her classic *Beast in View;* and two of her other novels, *The Fiend* and *How Like an Angel,* were runners-up for that award. In addition, she is a past President of the Mystery Writers of America and in 1965 received the *Los Angeles Times* Woman of the Year Award. Noted critic Julian Symons has written that *How Like an Angel* shows Mrs. Millar's skill "at its finest."